THE TELE-SCREEN

An Empirical Study of the Destruction and Despiritualization of Consciousness

Jeffrey Grupp

THE TELE-SCREEN

Published by ProgressivePress.com

ISBN 1-61577-075-5

EAN 978-1-61577-075-5

Length: 77,000 words on 199 pages

Second printing April, 2014

TOPICS:

9/11, ALEX JONES, AMERICANS, ARTIFICIAL ENEMY IMAGES OF IRAQ AND IRAN, BRAINWASHING, BUSH, CONSCIOUSNESS, CONTROL OF THE WORLD, CORPORATOCRACY, CULTURE, DARWIN, DESPIRITUALIZED MODERN EXISTENCE, FAKE REALITY, GUNS VS. GUN CONTROL, HEZBOLLAH, HISTORY, INFORMATION, JEFFERSONIAN MILITIA, MADE-UP NEWS, MEDIA, MONEY, NAZIS, NEW WORLD ORDER, NON-EXISTENT WMD'S, OBAMA, ORWELL, PATRIOTS, POLICE AND MILITARY, POLLS, PROPAGANDA, SECRET GOVERNMENT, TELEVISION, TERRORISM, VACCINES.

BISAC SUBJECT AREA CODES:

TEC043000	TECHNOLOGY / TELEVISION & VIDEO
POL039000	POLITICAL SCIENCE / CENSORSHIP
EDU040000	EDUCATION / PHILOSOPHY & SOCIAL ASPECTS

TABLE OF CONTENTS

For Thomas, Henry David, Alex, Dr. Bill, Hubert, and Jordan

Acknowledgements

This book is about how your consciousness is created by the endless information flux from the media world (the endless pounding of the mass media into your psyche, which I call the "telescreen world"). I mean this quite literally too: your consciousness is created by ideas and feelings, and in our telescreen world of contemporary America, the force and power of this telescreen madness is such that it gets into our minds, overpowers all other input and in-forming factors, and composes our minds, our selves. Our ancestors had trees, sky, religions, wild animals, farm crops, children, weapons, and stillness to create their consciousness. We do not; we have endless, pounding, shallow, unsatisfying *noise*. We are an irreligious culture, as a result: we only know what the soul is because somebody has told us it exists; we don't see and feel it as our ancestors did. In the first chapters, I introduce our predicament. I get into the deep mechanics of brainwashing in chapters 4-6. I am quite confident that these later chapters offer the reader an analysis of brainwashing that they have not seen before, and which is quite disquieting in how it gets to the core of the issue. The last chapter is largely unrelated to the topics just mentioned. The last chapter is a collection of articles I published at Infowars.com during the first half of 2009. I am confident that many readers will find them the best part of this book, as they offer a particularly powerful analysis of our world.

I would like to thank Alex Jones, David Icke, Jordan Maxwell, George Orwell, Dr, William Deagle, Thomas Jefferson, Henry David Thoreau, Michael Tsarion, Dr. Paul LaViolette, Russell Blaylock, Walter Cruttenden, Hubert Benoit, and William Henry for providing me with such a powerful education that enabled me to stand on their shoulders to write this book. I would like to thank Progressive Press for being patient with me while I finished this manuscript. And I would like to thank my family for giving me the energy I need to carry on in this time of emerging tyranny and global collapse.

"When finally you surrender to us, it must be of your own free will. We do not destroy the heretic because he resists us: so long as he resists us we never destroy him. We convert him, we capture his inner mind, we reshape him… We bring him over to our side not in appearance, but genuinely, heart and soul."

— From Orwell's *1984*

1. Introduction to the Telescreen World

They could be made to accept the most flagrant violations of reality,
because they never fully grasped the enormity of what was demanded of
them, and were not sufficiently interested in public events to notice what
was happening. By lack of understanding they remained sane.
They simply swallowed everything, and what they swallowed did them no
harm, because it left no residue behind, just as a grain of corn will pass
undigested through the body of a bird.
—1984, page 156

"Could a media system, controlled by a few global corporations, have the
ability to overwhelm all competing voices, and have the ability to turn lies
into truth? These corporations are not answerable to the people."
—Robert Pappas[1]

"I imagine that Exxon would love to own the media... Or Philip Morris,
so that any debate about cigarettes has to go through them."
—Robert McChesney, Professor, University of Illinois[2]

The Contemporary World is a *Telescreen World*

The citizens of the world today continually flood their consciousness with
images and impressions from the mass media: film, television, radio,
billboards, logos, textbooks, magazines, newspapers, etc.—all of which
collectively I call the "telescreen," or the "telescreen world," which is a term
that comes from Orwell's *1984*. This book is about the destruction of
consciousness and of human society that results when humans give their
attention, consciousness, and consequently their vital spirit to the telescreen
world. We will find in a later chapter that due to their adherence to the
telescreen world, human consciousness in the telescreen world is quite
literally *constructed by* the telescreen, and the result is that such
consciousness is a consciousness that is undeveloped, despiritualized, small,
and discontented. It is a less than human, a subhuman consciousness that
results: thus a destroyed consciousness. The result is a society of zombies (if
you will) and subhumans: a world of people who no longer act like people:
they cannot turn off the television/telescreen even to have dinner and/or talk
to each other or to their children, they are people who talk mostly or only
with each other about the images or impressions they encounter from the
telescreen world ("hey, did you see what happened on 24 or Law and Order
last night?"), they are people who have their inner subjective consciousness
assembled and deformed by the telescreen—they are people who suicidally

---

[1] Pappas 2003.

[2] This quote is from Pappas 2003.

go and fight wars at the drop-of-a-dime merely if the telescreen tells them they should.

In other words, instead of having their consciousness and their deepest inner recesses freely and spontaneously shaped out of their inalienable freedom and their personhood, humans nowadays have their consciousness formed and constructed for them by ultra-wealthy corporate and government entities that control the telescreen. These are the forces behind MTV, NBC, CBS, ABC, NPR, VH1, ESPN, Universal Pictures, Fox, CNN, Thomson-Wadsworth (a textbook publisher), Rush, Hannity, Beck, Newsweek and Time, just to name a few—all of which will be discussed in detail in later chapters. I call this the *telescreen world*, which is a zombic domain, due to what Mander refers to as "the replacement of experience:"

> ...in the generation since 1945, 99 percent of the homes in the country had acquired at least one television set. On an average evening, more than 80 million people would be watching television. Thirty million of these would be watching the same program. In special instances, 100 million people would be watching the same program at the same time. The average household had the set going more than six hours a day. If there was a child, the average was more than eight hours. The average person was watching for nearly four hours daily... As these numbers sank in, I realized that there had been a strange change in the way people received information, and even more in the way they were experiencing and understanding the world... America had become the first culture to have substituted secondary mediated versions of experience for direct experience of the world. Interpretations and representations of the world were being accepted as experience, and the difference between the two was obscure to most of us.[3]

In George Orwell's book, *1984*, the citizens of that world lived lives that were in constant contact with "the telescreen:" television screens in the homes, workplaces, stores, and everywhere else, which continually fed the citizens completely fabricated information (which the citizens thought was real), and which monitored the citizens since the telescreens also "looked" at the citizens (as if the telescreens were surveillance cameras and TVs combined). In this book you will learn how this is also very similar what is going on in the modern world right now.

In Orwell's book, the information from the telescreen inundation clearly shaped the behavior of the citizens in the Orwellian world. For that reason, the telescreen information also shaped their consciousnesses. Have you ever noticed that the word "information" is two words put together: *in* +

---

[3] Mander 1978, 24.

formation. The information we gather from *out* in the world during our daily lives, has the power (if we let it) to assemble and structure our *inner* selves (our consciousnesses). Therefore, if it were the case that a select group of people created and controlled virtually all information that the citizenry of a society witnessed, then that select group *could create the selves and consciousnesses of the mass of people*: the citizenry clearly could be constructed by a ruling power. This is the power that occupies the fantasies and dreams of tyrants and fascists, and it is the reality of the telescreen world we all currently inhabit.

In this book I will show that our current telescreen world that we all inhabit is precisely what the United States is, and what the entire world is fast becoming. Information in the United States is controlled by very few people—whether it is information found in a college textbook, on a cable television channel, in a church sermon, or the information you hear from friends and neighbors, and so on. This may seem hard for you to believe at this point, but as you read on, in later chapters you will see that such assertions are surprisingly easy for me to prove. There is mind-control that is all coming from one source: the wealthiest group of people in the world, who control industry, resources, money, war, and media (information).[4]

This book is not predominantly about some of the other mind-control, brainwashing, and telescreen world issues other authors have already very widely discussed: CIA mind control and MKULTRA, mind control in Red China, mind chips and chip implants, Big Pharma's attack on the frontal lobes of humanity, and so on. I will cover those when needed and when applicable to my theses in this book, but rather than further cover these issues in significant detail that others have already so wonderfully covered, this book embarks into new territory: the telescreen world's effects on consciousness, on the construction of consciousness, and on society and your deep subjective self/personhood. This book is specifically about ideas that I have not seen discussed much anywhere else. It is about the way the corporatist secret world government of the world today carries out mind-control operations which are

1. Teaching humans to believe that an entirely false reality is the true reality,

2. Shrinking and destroying the consciousness of humans, and consequently,

3. transforming humans—who have magnificent and vast minds and brains—into animal-like subhumans who do not understand who and

---

[4] For a detailed account of this, see Grupp 2007.

what they are, and who do not think they are much more than cogs within a monopolistic, global, corporate system.

In the next chapter I will discuss an easily understandable example that shows how mass brainwashing occurs to virtually all citizens, and the rest of the book is devoted to discussing these specific details of this destruction of the self and consciousness. By brainwashing we mean mind control, control of thoughts and feelings.

Few people have any idea of the magnitude, sophistication, and cunning of the mass brainwashing going on in the United States. People are like a fish in water: the water is invisible (transparent), and even though it surrounds the fish at all times, the fish might never know that the water is there, since it could desensitized, if you will, to its existence. This brainwashing occurs in many ways, such as via:

Education systems (elementary schools and universities),

Corrupted religion,

Remote control brain/nervous system microchip implants,[5]

Fear,

Mass media,

Spontaneous social conformity of human behavior and thought,

just to name a few.

Consciousness in the United States is *controlled*, and in such a way that it results in Americans ubiquitously having weakened, distorted, pain-filled, unenlightened consciousness—what can be called semi-consciousness, or destroyed consciousness. Consider what Jim Keith writes in a particularly informative passage:

Walter Bowart in the classic expose *Operation Mind Control* characterizes the purpose of intelligence agencies as being

...to take human beings, both citizens of the United States and citizens of friendly and unfriendly nations, and transform them into unthinking, subconsciously programmed "zombies," motivated without their knowledge and against their wills to perform in a variety of ways in which they would not otherwise willingly perform. This is accomplished

---

[5] See Constantine 1995, esp. ch. 1, for copious, very well-researched and documented information on this already well-advanced technology, which will likely be implemented in the next ten years or earlier. See Horgan (2003, 101) for interesting information on the history of these implants.

through the use of various techniques called by various names, including brainwashing, thought reform, behavior modification, hypnosis, and conditioned reflex therapy.

...The advent of television in the late 1940s has provided a potent mind drug administered to the vast majority of the population. Providing a substitution for actual human life in the modulating and hypnotic flicker of the television tube, studies have been conducted showing that television actually induces a trance state that, with years of watching, becomes permanent. Television is, without a doubt, the most potent societal soporific in the mind-control arsenal.[6]

Most Americans are caught up in the telescreen dream-state, and thus they are unaware that they are dreaming, or brainwashed. They have no idea that their consciousness is fabricated and destroyed. The purpose of this book is to show that the entirety of the worldview that almost everyone on planet earth holds is carefully constructed by corporatist[7] groups, and therefore, humanity as-a-whole is completely ignorant of the actual nature of reality.

During any person's life, they gain a worldview due to their environment (information, social networks, technology, etc.) They find their self within throughout their life, from birth to death. But as not so many people understand, corporatist monopolists are responsible for deliberately controlling and creating that environment,[8] in order that a person develops a worldview that is entirely to the liking of the corporatists. For example, if the corporatists want people to possess a consciousness suitable for war, then they merely have to fill the telescreen world with information and impressions that create fear in the consciousnesses of the citizenry. As another example, if the corporatists want to develop slave-like mentalities that make people good factory workers or criminals, rather than good poets and scientists, then

a. the schools (which are controlled by the corporatists[9]) will not teach interesting topics that energize children and stimulate learning, and they will not teach critical thinking, evidential inquiry, or cutting edge or genuine science, and

---

[6] Keith 2004, 24.

[7] The corporatists are the group of very few people in the world who control the largest monopolistic corporations (Exxon, GE, News Corp., Lockheed Martin, Monsanto, etc.), and, as I showed in Grupp 2007, who control all people on planet earth. The corporatists control the governments of the world. See Grupp 2007 for copious empirical evidence for this thesis.

[8] See Grupp 2007.

[9] See Grupp 2007, ch. 4.

b. the visual telescreen media will teach forlornness, lost-ness, disoriented or counterproductive rebellion, by promoting childish and empty sitcoms, empty and pathetic films, mind-numbing video games, and music videos filled with losers and clueless dopes.

As for schools, instead of presenting farming skills, real empirical information (i.e., actual science, rather than "theory science" [the CO_2 "threat", monkey-to-man evolutionary theory, etc.]), sacred geometry,[10] meditation, critical thinking skills, and so on, they ubiquitously present boring or inaccurate subject-matter,[11] and the schools will merely become "discipline and behavior camps" (including behavior modification via semi-forced drugging: Ritalin, SSRIs, vaccines, school lunches,[12] etc.), rather than inspiring places of creative, dynamic learning.

Everything You Know is Wrong

Now here is an absolutely central issue in this book that I have found so many just cannot get their minds around:

> *Worldwide, the worldviews that people hold are entirely incorrect: the set of worldviews that the average person anywhere in the world holds do not in any way represent actual (empirical) reality (what actually exists) in any way.*[13]

---

[10] Along with fractal geometry and quantum Lie geometry, this is the geometry that reality is actually based on. See Gaunt 2000 for more information. Amazingly, schools do not teach these, and instead teach entirely outdated, non-empirical, and almost useless forms of mathematics, such as very simple aspects of Euclidean geometry, pre-calculus mathematics, or "business math," whatever that might be.

[11] Such as requiring college students to learn a foreign language that they will never use, requiring business students in college to get a degree without ever giving them "on the job" training, or requiring high school students to learn all about the civil war without ever talking about white slavery (see Hoffman 1991), or learning all about the Nazi holocaust without ever learning about how the US corporatists were instrumental in bringing it about (See Black 2001). There are many other examples that I could have given here.

[12] See Grupp 2007, the last section (Conclusion) of chapter 1, for more information on these issues. As is not so much a secret any more, the food supply in the United States and worldwide is entirely poisoned. (See Pawlick 2006.) For example, when one goes to the grocery store to buy fruit, vegetables, bread, milk, and various processed foods, they are being deliberately poisoned with MSG, aspartame, pesticides, herbicides, hormones, antibiotics, steroids, radiation, feces, and so on— all of which are the primary causes of the epidemics that are escalating worldwide (diabetes, allergies, Alzheimer's, etc.)

[13] See Grupp 2007 for copious examples.

This was certainly not always the case, and it is a relatively recent development that's gradually intensified over the past few hundred years. Again, just like the way that the fish never really notices that water, analogously, today's world citizens cannot grasp that their view of reality has been implanted in them, and more importantly, is replete with inaccuracies to such an extent that everything they know is wrong. I mean this literally, and it is astonishingly easy to prove, as I will do shortly.

This is the expected result of a telescreen world that is controlled by fascistic, underworldly corporatists. Rather, the worldviews that the people of the world are given are completely false, and for that reason, citizens of the world are thoroughly brainwashed:

> *they believe in a reality that is not real,*
> *and they are oblivious to non-imaginary*
> *(empirical, actual) reality.*

Now let's go through several examples in order to prove this point, which I am guessing most readers of this book are dubious about. Let's start off with some basic but broad-ranging examples. How many people believe that water freezes at 32 degrees Fahrenheit? Answer: billions. But if that is true, then why do we have deep ocean water that is below 32 degrees Fahrenheit and is not frozen? Answer: because water does not always freeze at 32 degrees Fahrenheit.

Let's consider another example. Scientists have found that the basic building blocks that compose physical reality are not physical at all: they do not have magnitude (size), color, shape, or materiality.[14] But everything we humans see in our physical world has shape, color, and size—that's what we believe characterizes the physical stuff we see all around us. So here's a question for you: How do sizeless, shapeless, colorless particles (basic building blocks) make-up the physical reality that we see with our eyes that has shape, size, and color? Answer: *they can't.* So, something is quite erroneous about our perceptions about our world, since all our notions and experiences of shape, size, and color are illusions.[15] They are our body's ways of "interpreting" the universe of energy all around us. Are you starting to get the idea here? Our ideas about the world we live in are not very accurate, to say the least. (You might wonder: It could be either that our senses are wrong and particle physics is right, or particle physics is wrong and our senses are right, so why did we conclude in this paragraph that our senses are wrong? Answer: because our senses are replete with error and imprecision—try to watch a bullet shoot out of a gun, you can't see it [it's

---

[14] See Grupp 2006a.

[15] Ibid.

invisible to you, which is a perceptual error] because your senses are too imprecise—and particle physics is spot-on, so we have to go with the more trustworthy, error-free of the two, which is not our senses.[16])

Ideas are *just ideas*, and they may or may not actually represent things that are real in the world. For example, you can think (have an idea about) a unicorn, but that does not mean unicorns are real. They are only ideas, existing only in our heads. You can think Iraq was a threat in 2003, but that does not mean that it *really* was. Yet interestingly, well over 200 million Americans thought the little desert nation of Iraq, which hardly even had a military, was a threat to the U.S. during the quite long time-span from 1991 to 2003: *but that was of course just an idea, based on nothing real whatsoever!* Iraq is/was a unicorn – just like the swine flu, vaccine "protection", overpopulation, the CO_2 "threat", eco-crime, fluoride being a cure for osteoporosis, monkey-to-man evolutionary theory, and the idea that the world is "Running Out of Water" (*Scientific American*[17]): unicorns all! But, returning to discussion of Iraq... Nevertheless, Americans believed in unicorn-Iraq, and off they went, smilingly marching their children into DU-laced Iraq (and Afghanistan).

Let's consider another example: *billions* of people on planet earth believed that cave-men brought down the WTC towers on 9/11. Nobody saw them do it, but they were *told* the cave-men did it, and thus *billions* believed this story. But nobody saw them do it, there is no evidence they did, and, well, what-do-you-know, it's just an idea, again! Funny how this all works, isn't it. But in this case, it was billions, not millions, that believed in the unicorns (cave-men) they were merely told about (and not *shown*).

Another example: *billions* of people on planet earth believed that a large passenger jetliner hit the Pentagon on 9/11. Question: how many saw it, or at least were in position near the Pentagon where they could have seen it? Answer: a room full of people (back to that figure of speech, again). So, um, why did *billions* believe that there was a jetliner (unicorn-jetliner, that is)? I think you know the answer. Odd how this all works, isn't it.

Are you starting to get how this works? How much of our reality that we think about each day is like this: *just ideas that are not verified?* Answer: so much of it that we can "round off" and say that all of our reality we believe to be real consists of incorrect ideas.

Suppose I walk up to the average person on the street or in my family, and tell them that there is *no evidence* that CO_2 causes global warming, and in fact there is copious evidence that it *does not* cause global warming. Most

---

[16] Ibid.

[17] This was the cover of the August 2008 issue of Scientific American.

likely, the person I utter this to will *become angry at me*, call me names, and perhaps even accuse me of having a mental disorder (such as, for example, if they said I "was *crazy* to believe that," thus insinuating that I have a mental illness: craziness).[18] Instead of questioning, thinking independently, and forming their own solid opinion, they merely will believe what they have been told by fiat, and become angry with anybody who does not agree. The point here is that the average person *believes what they are told, not what they see*. It is that basic aspect of human nature that makes the telescreen world successful for corporatists—it allows only a few thousand monopolistic corporatists to thoroughly control and rule over all the rest of the people on the planet.

Why do so many Americans believe that bottled water, soy, vaccines, genetically modified food, treated water (from a city water treatment plant), meat, and fluoride are *healthy* for them? Why do so many Americans believe that radiation "therapy" cures cancer, when it is widely known that radiation (e.g., x-rays) causes cancer? Why do so many Americans think that Republicans are interested in a closed border with Mexico, when three Republican Presidents (Reagan, Bush Sr., and Bush Jr.) failed to simply close the border, or even to send a large number of troops to secure the border? (Instead, those troops were sent to Iraq.) Why do so many Americans think that drinking salt water is harmful for you, when hospital IVs are composed of a solution that is water and salt (and this is given to people when they are *severely dehydrated*, such as babies with rotavirus)?

We can go on and on. All we need to do is start to analyze some of the commonly-held ideas that people hold, and if we merely apply some skepticism to them, we see that they fall apart, and that all of our ideas about reality fall down like a "house of cards."

Why do so many Americans think that extraterrestrials do not exist, or have never visited earth, when

---

[18] There is copious evidence that CO_2 does not cause global warming. See the following article from the most prestigious science magazine in the world: "Plants and Temperature—CO_2 Uncoupling," *Science*, September 3, 1999, vol. 285, no. 5433, by Sharon Cowling, pp. 1500-1501. Here is the abstract from that article:

In the recent geological past, temperature and atmospheric CO_2 concentrations have been coupled: Cooling generally coincides with low CO_2 and warming with high CO_2 concentrations. However, some geological records indicate that in the more distant geological past, temperature and CO_2 may have been uncoupled. Such temperature-CO_2 uncoupling, if confirmed by further studies, may influence our ideas about climate-forcing mechanisms and about functioning of paleoecosystems.

I.   Morgellons disease exists (and the best theory on Morgellons disease is that it's extraterrestrial, since no known human technology is so advanced as this nanobot),[19]

II. when it is impossible (with current known human technology) to build some of the ancient monuments that "somebody" built on earth long ago, such as the great pyramids of Egypt, Baalbek, or Tiahuanaco (this implies that a superior race of creatures built these ancient cities in the past),

III. when the network of pulsars (flashing beacons of light seen clustered mainly at the middle of our Milky Way Galaxy) through much of the galaxy are clearly not the product of anything but intelligent creatures using them for some reason, most likely to communicate across galactic distances (as if the pulsars are "lighthouses" in space),[20]

IV. when the US Capital's map (when viewed from the bird's eye view) forms an Egyptian word for the Sirius star system,[21] and

V.   when it is clear that the moon and solar system were created by an intelligent entity (presumably an alien entity or race, since humans have no known technology to do so, but also a superbeing, such as God, could be theorized to have been responsible). The solar system has too many oddities about it to have been created by random solar system evolution.[22] For example, the moon at summer solstice follows the *exact* path in the sky that the sun does at winter solstice, and the sun at summer solstice follows the *exact* path in the sky that the moon does at winter solstice.[23] The moon does not rotate, it only orbits (tidal forces *cannot* explain this). The moon's motions are described by

---

[19] See Grupp 2007, end of chapter 5. Morgellons is a nanobot infestation which represents a technology so advanced, that some experts have theorized that it can only be an entirely unknown technology, and thus likely extraterrestrial technology.

[20] See LaViolette (2006) for copious information on this subject. The information on pages 10-12 of this book alone are enough to prove this point. This is very straightforward and simple evidence for galaxy-wide extraterrestrial life, which professional astronomers have mysteriously missed or ignored.

[21] See Ovason 1999, 4-5. The symbol for the Sirius star system for the Egyptians was an arrangement of an obelisk, the inside of a pentagram (a pentagon), and an oval (like the Oval Office).

[22] For more information on all issues in this fifth point, see Knight and Butler 2005, and see Gaunt 2000, chapter 3.

[23] If you would like verification that they follow the exact same path, do some research on Newgrange, an ancient temple in Ireland devoted to this phenomenon, and the verification you want is found there.

numbers that certainly do not sound random, and which are "surprisingly neat" (such as numbers like 6800), as Knight and Butler put it. Scientists are completely baffled as to why the moon exists, and they can't explain its existence.[24] The moon is precisely the same size in the sky as the sun in appearance, as solar eclipses demonstrate, which is an incredible "coincidence". Also, the moon's center of mass is off-center, meaning that its core density is not at the center of the planet, and that is completely contrary to gravitational theories of spherical celestial body formation. In other words, if the moon is round, it has sufficient gravity to give it that shape, but then it also should have density increasing toward the center of the planet, but it does not! This is just the beginning of what could be said about incredible mysteries of the solar system.

The structures of Tiahuanaco, and the pyramids of Egypt, cannot be built according to human technology known today.

Notice that these examples are simple empirical (easily verifiable with the senses), which hardly any people are aware of. They are not taught in schools, are not discussed on the news or cable television, are not discussed on "educational television" (see chapter 2 for more information on "education television"), and are not discussed by contemporary ministers and priests. This is rather amazing: Why would academics not entertain these ideas?

The answer is perhaps found in the psychology of brainwashing that we will be discussing in this book: humans are innately conformist creatures, and *ipso facto*, they accord their behaviors with what others are doing, rather than with their own feelings, or with what their senses report to them. In other words, if the average person perceives the mass of people around them to believe that a massive jetliner hit the Pentagon on 9/11/2001, and if the big spectacle of cable television also tells her/him that a massive jetliner hit the Pentagon on 9/11/2001, *then she/he will unquestionably believe it, and will renounce (often bitterly or violently) anybody who says otherwise, even though she he has no evidence whatsoever for this belief.* She/he only bases her/his belief on what others have *told* her/him, utterly rejecting what her/his senses report to her/him (which is that she never saw the plane, so she can't empirically know it existed), and that's called *conformity*. I could have given a huge number of examples to prove this point, and this example about the Pentagon clearly shows how devastating and knife-like human conformity is. So I feel very confident in saying that human beings are innately conformist creatures to the core, and whatever created them made them to exist in this sort of way (at least when we are in a lowly cultural state such as we are now on this poverty-filled, war-riddled planet). Humans will follow what they are told (what the "authority figures" and the masses of people purport), before they follow what they see with their eyes, even if what they are told is absurd, as is illustrated well in Orwell's *1984*. So, if an astronomy professor is not informed about point V above, for example, she/he will then not be aware of it amid her/his teaching later in life and thus will pass on false information (that the solar system is a product of random evolution). If she/he were somehow to be made aware of point V above, she/he will almost certainly believe these "coincidences" are not significant, because, well, why doesn't everyone else talk about it?

An Example: Human History: Deep History

If you doubt that humans are conformist in this way, then go into a church sometime, and tell the Christians that their God is the same God as the one worshipped in Islam, and check the reaction you get. Or go into an anthropology department at a major university, and tell the professors some of the problems with the idea that humans came from chimps, and you will see what I mean. You will see people deny the truth of what they can experience with their senses, and you will see then latch onto what they have been told. They will reject what their eyes report, and they will (often bitterly) fight for the theories they hold in their thoughts (and which violently disagree with what their eyes report).

What has just been written shows two profound issues:

brainwashing is created out of the basic nature of humanity (which is conformity), and brainwashing is created out of the natural social interactions of people.

In other words, it may be almost inevitable that we humans live in an Orwellian sort of state, where we all believe in lies about reality, tell them to each other, and by that endless discussion of the lies about reality, the lies are reinforced. We are destined to be brainwashed creatures—at least in our current state. So how do we rise above this? Only by being vigilant, by closely monitoring oneself (self-analyzing and self-observing), does one overcome these natural human tendencies of irrationality, unskeptical thinking, and conformity.

Examples like these of the brainwashing of humanity are seemingly endless, and they can cause one to wonder what, if any, correct information the average human possesses. It is as if every sentence they can utter about a belief they have about reality can be shown to be exactly what is *not* verifiable with our senses: it can be shown to be exactly what is *not* true. In simpler terms: if you believe what culture tells you is true, if you have a cultural belief, call it CB, then CB is *not true*, it is a figment of non-reality, and only not-CB is true. The purpose of this chapter is to give an example of how this happens; to show the disastrous consequences for humanity when they are tricked by the underworldly secret corporatist government that controls this world and their telescreen society into forgoing skepticism, scientism, meditation, Constitutionalism, religion, freedom, positivism, and spiritualization, in order to sacrifice themselves to lives of robotized behavior, unfreedom, brainwashing, and mass enslavement.

I find that people in American society typically *demand* that these sorts of ideas that I have discussed over the past few pages are untrue, and they demand that the masses of people of the world are not brainwashed in the ways I have just described. But you will see in this book that such global mass brainwashing is easily provable, and therefore, people resist these concepts *merely because they are themselves trapped in the sleep of mass brainwashing*. They do not want to admit that their consciousness was not created by themselves, and thus is not entirely their own. Their consciousness is not free, and it is contaminated by unseen or unnoticed psychological, corporate, and economic forces that are seriously harmful. This brainwashing pervades the universities and science, the corporate (corporatist) world, the religions, politics, schools, neighborhoods, sport stadiums, media, and anything else that people are involved in. In each of these institutions, worldviews are endorsed and accepted by the masses, but in each, the worldview is entirely false, and it is astonishingly easy to prove it.

Before I proceed with what I have planned for this first chapter, let me give a quick example: *human origins*. We are told on "educational television" (e.g., the Discovery Channel, National Geographic Channel, etc.), in universities, in the museums, and so on, that humans come from bonobo chimpanzees, and gradually (and not in accord with the philosophy of punctuated equilibrium) over millions of years they changed into humans by the "force" of natural selection. Fine, but what is the evidence for this? There must be enormous evidence for this, due to the fact that, as just stated, our university experts and PhDs are confident in telling us that this monkey-to-man thesis is correct. But alas, there is no evidence, *amazingly*. Let me explain.

In order to call this monkey-to-man thesis a well-worked out scientific theory, we should expect to find fossilized bone samples to support this gradualist monkey-to-man thesis, but there are no such samples. The temporally closest bone find is *Homo erectus*, which is older than 1.7 million years old. It's quite a stretch (and not a scientific inference) to assert that those bones have something to do with contemporary humanity.

Making matters more dire for the mainstream (i.e., university associated) domain of the field of human archaeology, the field has a surprising but well-known history of fakery, forgeries, and scandals, as far as bone finds are concerned (e.g., the famous Piltdown fakery). Also, a very large number of scientists (including Richard Leakey[25]) have very strongly questioned the few genuine bone finds we do have as being either erroneous, or merely the bones of monkeys being misconstrued as proto-humans. But these scientists have been completely ignored and gradually rejected and removed from academia.[26] There have been fossil finds that, without exaggeration, completely throw apart the neat and tidy progression of fossil finds and the progression of chimps to humans.[27] There have been, in fact, all sorts of things, such as conehead skulls and hobbits[28], many of which are in our world's museums, that the professionals will not discuss since they do not fit their theory. Amazing! This is not discovery, it is rejection of discovery. The

---

[25] See "Controversial Human Ancestor Gets Major Facelift," by Ker Than, LiveScience, March 29, 2007, http://www.livescience.com/humanbiology /070329_rudolf_reconstruct.html. This article is about how many bones (in this article, specifically a cranium) have been found that do not fit into the fabricated picture of human evolution, where Australopithecus transformed into H. habilis, who in turn transformed into H. erectus. According to this article,

> So troublesome was the skull that famed paleo-anthropologist Richard Leakey, the leader of the team that discovered it, once told reporters: "Either we toss out this skull or we toss out our theories of early man. It simply fits no models of human beginnings."

[26] See Cremo 2003, chapter 2.

[27] See "Skull Of New Early Human Relative Found In Kenya — Did Humans Descend From Lucy Or From Newly Discovered Creature?", Science Daily, March 21, 2001. The abstract of this article reads as follows:

> March 21, 2001 After the partial skeleton of a 3.2-million-year-old human relative known as Lucy was found in Ethiopia in 1974, many researchers believed her species Australopithecus afarensis was the ancestor of modern humans. Now, in a stunning discovery, scientists working in Kenya have found the skull and partial jaw of a completely different genus and species, with a flattened face and small molar teeth much different than those of afarensis. The discovery of the 3.2- to 3.5-million-year-old fossils raises the question of whether modern humans descended from Lucy's species or from the newly discovered species.

Also see, "Evolution's Surprise: Fossil find uproots our early ancestors," Bruce Bower, *Science News*, July 13, 2002; Vol. 162, No. 2 , p. 19.

[28] See "Study Says 'Hobbit' Not a Modern Human", Associated Press, Sept. 22, 2007, by Randolph E. Schmid.

anomalies appear to far outnumber the accepted cases. Professional scientists in anthropology and archaeology have told us that they have found fossils that show a gradual progression of chimps to humans[29] over the past five million years. Yet when you look at the data, you find that they have, amazingly, merely thrown aside any bones that do not fit the pattern, calling them "anomalies that need further investigation since they do not fit the theory." That's a classic case of theory creating evidence, rather than evidence creating theory.

Even if these bone finds could be verified as not monkey bones, and fit into some sort of coherent *ad hoc* gradualist theory of chimp-to-Homo erectus, that still does not indicate in any way that these creatures are our ancestors. Just because a creature lived 1.7 million years ago (H. erectus), why does that automatically mean that she's our ancestor? We have scientists telling us that she is our ancestor, no doubt about it, but then we are supposed to believe that Neanderthal (who lived much more recently, and who is *much* more similar to modern humans than H. erectus, when considering things like culture and brain size) is not supposed to be of much, if any, relation to humanity. How do we know that H. erectus is not just a species that went extinct, and our real ancestors are some other primate group (if there is any such group) whose bones have not been discovered yet? The real question is: How can our best scientists be on the bandwagon of such careless and non-empirical theory-building?

Do you still doubt that there is such undisciplined theory-making in our prestigious academia? Well, then consider the perhaps the most cherished form of "evidence" that the mainstream pro-monkey-to-man academics give us: the thesis that the information in the retroviruses ("junk DNA") in both chimps and humans is correlated in such a way that it proves chimp ancestry to humans. But when I have asked for the proof of this from friends of mine who are biologists in the Purdue area where I live, they don't seem to have it. It's just a thesis they have been told about, and they went along with it,

---

[29] Actually, this "gradual progression" is a problem for the monkey-to-man assumption also, since it has been long established that punctuated (quick) changes happen in evolution, after long periods of almost no change, and there is little gradualism in the fossil record. Punctuated equilibrium, as it's called, is a further problem for evolution *overall*, since evolution is supposed to be driven by natural selection (which only works for change on a gradual time frame, at least in the case of large scale changes, such as the change of a deer in to a horse). Punctuated equilibrium then, it seems, cannot have natural selection as its engine for change. There are, in summary, all sorts of problems and contradictions that the mainstreams professional government-paid professional scientists merely will not discuss, but they are often quick to tell you that you are fiddling with "quackery" if you disagree with them.

without hard visual evidence. And the truth is that there is no proof, and in fact the opposite scenario is true: retroviruses show a lack of ancestry of chimps to humans. According to *Science Daily*,

It's been known for a long time that only 2%–3% of human DNA codes for proteins. Much of the rest of our genomes—often referred to as junk DNA—consists of retro-elements: genomic elements that are transcribed into RNA, reverse-transcribed into DNA, and then reinserted into a new spot in the genome. Human endogenous retroviruses make up one class of these retro-elements. Retroviruses can insinuate themselves into the host's DNA in either soma (non-reproductive cells) or the germline (sperm or egg). If the virus invades a non-reproductive cell, infection may spread, but viral DNA will die with the host. A retrovirus is called endogenous when it invades the germline and gets passed on to offspring. Because endogenous retroviruses can alter gene function and genome structure, they can influence the evolution of their host species. Over 8% of our genome is made of these infectious remnants—infections that scientists believe occurred before Old World and New World monkeys diverged (25–35 million years ago). In a new study, Evan Eichler and colleagues scanned finished chimpanzee genome sequences for endogenous retroviral elements, and found one (called PTERV1) that does not occur in humans. Searching the genomes of a subset of apes and monkeys revealed that the retrovirus had integrated into the germline of African great apes and Old World monkeys—but did not infect humans and Asian apes (orangutan, siamang, and gibbon). *This undermines the notion that an ancient infection invaded an ancestral primate lineage, since great apes (including humans) share a common ancestor with Old World monkeys.* Eichler and colleagues found over 100 copies of PTERV1 in each African ape (chimp and gorilla) and Old World monkey (baboon and macaque) species. The authors compared the sites of viral integration in each of these primates and found that few if any of these insertion sites were shared among the primates. It appears therefore that the sequences have not been conserved from a common ancestor, but are specific to each lineage.[30]

It appears that academia is also thoroughly along the brainwashing path that I described in the last section—indeed, they may be guiding the stride of the brainwashed citizenry. Continuing with this topic of human origins (and the academicians' account of it), humans have brains that are absolutely and spectacularly *huge* compared to that of their (supposed) nearest relatives, the

---

[30] "The Chimp Genome Reveals A Retroviral Invasion In Primate Evolution," *Science Daily*, Apr. 5, 2005. http://www.sciencedaily.com/releases/2005/03/050328174826.htm

chimpanzees. But what accounts for this increase? Humans really don't carry out much behavior that is much more complex than chimpanzees. We can learn mathematics that chimpanzees cannot, but usually that takes decades of schooling, from the elementary level to college and beyond (it takes more schooling than it takes to teach a chimpanzee sign language). Human tool use and language is sometimes slightly more complicated than chimpanzees (chimps can use sticks as weapons, and humans can build guns), but our social behavior is not much more complicated. In fact, for the average human on planet earth, daily life does not involve or require much more mental/brain processing power than the average chimpanzee day, except for some more complicated language sentences that the human might use. And chimpanzees have most of the features of modern humanity: war, religion, art, gang mentality, illiteracy, political networks and charismatic politicians, conformity, tool use, mild and usually repetitious creativity, sexual promiscuity, relaxation behavior, and so on.[31] So if human behavior is, in general, not much more complex than chimpanzees, then why do humans have such truly massive brains compared to these "ancestors" of ours? I won't speculate on the answer to that question in this book, but I can say two things in response to it: (i) scientists don't have the answer, and (ii) this question leads to the idea that citizens of the world may have *much* more potential, and much more *inside of them*, than they currently see or understand in themselves. The reason for this lack of understanding is simple: mass brainwashing. It seems that groups of scientists have taught us to *not* know who we are, and to look up the wrong tree when we are trying to find out who and what we are. This is, like the other examples I have given, an example of how people around the globe are tricked into believing what is not real is real.

Today, much of the world appears to be under the impression that the monkey-to-man thesis is the correct one, even though there is no evidence at all to support it. This is a classic example of pervasive, powerful brainwashing: billions of humans all over the world are tricked into believing a false theory that has no evidence whatsoever to support it, even though it is about what is most sacred to them (who and what they really are). This ruse extends into and pervades universities, academic journals, mass media, "educational television," freelance research, and even into some aspects of religion. What this results in is that all over the world, billions of people are tricked into *not* knowing who and what they are. They are fooled into believing they are more like "stupid animals" than they are like poets and geniuses, when in fact there is, interestingly, no evidence for such a "stupid

---

[31] See the work of Jane Goodall (esp. the book *Through A Window*) for accounts of these chimp behaviors.

animal" theory. And what amazing consequences this has on our human psychology. In his recent book, David Icke discusses how the citizens of the world are, unbeknownst to them, trapped in a telescreen-matrix life, where their behavior is programmed. Their thoughts are constructed for them, rather than by their own free will. Consider how he puts these issues about evolution and the destruction of humanity's consciousness:

> The Matrix is a system which manipulates consciousness trapped within its vibratory illusions to generate the energy that fuels the system. That energy is fear and its related emotions. To achieve this, the Matrix must... convince consciousness that it is not in control of its own destiny and instead is at the mercy of random events because life is an accident of evolution, a series of chemical reactions, and death is a ticket to oblivion, no returns available.[32]

It is as if the monkey-to-man theory, to some degree, gets people to believe that they are something different (namely, *animals*) from what we actually are, that we are not valuable entities, and that our lives are not in our control and are not important. If we all can be taught to believe that we are just stupid animals, rather than big-brained spiritual entities that can develop ultra-high math, meditative religions, and quantum physics, then it is much easier for politicians, corporatists and the New World Order to convince people that the slaughter of war, and the banality and despiritualization of modern corporatist life is "normal," and "just they way things are" — as if things could not be, and have never been, any different.

Intrusive Mind and Behavior Control

In this book I will not be so concerned with what can be called "intrusive mind and behavior control," which can be defined as the deliberate implantation of devices or machines into people in order to control their mind and behavior. A classic example of this is the now well-known micro-chipping of humans or animals. According to this technology, a person has a microchip implanted into them which can interfere with their brain and nervous system in such a way that it enables a person (the implanter of the chip, presumably) to control their behavior, for example, by remote control.[33]

This sort of technology is not new. Professor José Delgado of Yale University worked to develop this technology fifty years ago.[34] The very famous science writer John Horgan has discussed this issue:

---

[32] Icke 2005, 145-6.
[33] This technology is discussed in lucid detail in Constantine 1994, chapter 1.
[34] Ibid.

José Delgado of Yale University showed that he could induce pleasure, rage, and other emotions in psychiatric patients with implanted electrodes and could control patients' bodies. In an exhibition in a bullring in Spain in 1963, Delgado stopped a bull charging toward him by radioing a signal to an electrode implanted in its brain. He carried out similar tricks with psychiatric patients. In 1969 Delgado prophesied in *Physical Control of the Mind* that before long, implanted devices might eliminate human violence and other maladaptive behaviors.[35]

It is naïve to believe that the corporatists and the governments of the world that work for the corporatists would not have heard about this or taken serious interest. Control of humanity is perhaps the number one biggest interest of the corrupt globalist tyrants, and thus it is assured that they would have seized upon such technology. And of course companies like Verichip and Alien Technology (yes, that's really its name, look it up for yourself), which have top military-industrial complex corporatists running them, will exhibit a huge advancement over-and-above Delgado's initial technology.

In the contemporary technological world these chips are so small that they can be placed inside food, medications, vaccines, and so forth,[36] since the chips get so small that collections of them resemble a substance that is more like a powder than anything else.[37] So, in theory, all humans could be chipped with Manchurian Candidate microchip technology. What I have written in this section is not even really any sort of secret. For example, according to *Business Week* several years ago:

> The use of implantable mini-generators is more widespread than you probably think. Already, 190,000 patients are wearing electrodes in their heads to control Parkinson's disease tremors or spinal-cord stimulators to relieve pain or prevent urinary incontinence.... These numbers are likely to grow—and quickly.[38]

The School Shootings are Staged, Fabricated, Not Spontaneous and Genuine

There are very interesting consequences of what I have written about in the previous section on invasive mind control (which is not the type of mind control we will discuss in the rest of this book). For example, you may not

---

[35] Horgan 2003, 101.

[36] See Constantine 1994, chapter 1;

[37] "Hitachi Powder Chip, Japan." *Printed Electronics World*. February 14, 2008. http://www.idtechex.com/printedelectronicsworld/articles/hitachi_powder_chip_japa n_00000823.asp

[38] "Rewiring the Body." *BusinessWeek*. March 7, 2005. Thanks goes to Infowars.com for alerting me to this article.

immediately see it, but what I have just written apparently proves that the wave of shootings in America since 1999 (the Columbine high school shooting is one of the most famous ones) is covertly being orchestrated by the New World Order.[39] For example, consider this argumentation:

1. Guns give citizens power, and restrict the ability of corrupt government to oppress the people. Shootings and massacres (Virginia Tech, Rwanda, etc.) only occur in unarmed populations or groups; armed citizen groups don't get massacred.

2. 1 proves that corrupt and oppressive governments who want citizens to have limited power need to take away the empowering items (economic stability, guns, genuine education, etc.).

3. 1 and 2 show that disarming citizens is in the extreme interest of our government.

4. History and the contemporary world show us that governments are virtually always magnets for ultra-corrupt liars and murderers (this also echoes what our Founding Fathers taught us).

5. 2 - 4 show that a corrupt government will "do what it takes" (i.e., "play dirty") in replacing 1 with 3.

6. Manchurian candidate technology exists (this is the chip technology—invasive mind control—discussed in the previous section.

7. All school shootings (Columbine, etc.) involve people taking massive antidepressant doses (which, paradoxically, cause suicidal thoughts[40]), and who are in various sorts of government programs,

---

[39] Again, if you are not clear on what the New World Order is, see Grupp 2007. The New World Order is the international money and resource controllers that are not part of any nation (IMF, World Bank, WTO, etc.), but who all work together for the detriment of humankind, and who all have an infinitely shadowy nature.

[40] For more information on how antidepressants cause suicidal thoughts and behavior, there is an incredible amount of information on this, See, for example, "Antidepressants continue to be linked to suicidal thoughts," NaturalNews.com, March 2, 2005, http://www.naturalnews.com/005203.html; "Studies Raise Questions About Antidepressant-Suicide Link", FoxNews.com, February 21, 2005, by Salynn Boyles, http://www.foxnews.com/story/0,2933,148044,00.html; "Antidepressants a Suicide Risk for Young Adults: Study Says Cases Double for Those 18 to 25 Using Medicine to Control Depression," by Shankar Vedantam, Washington Post, Thursday, December 14, 2006; Page A16. The first paragraph of this last article reads as follows:

Widely used antidepressants double the risk of suicidal behavior in young adults, from around three cases per thousand to seven cases per thousand, according to a

firing on unarmed groups for massive dramatic effect for the media display.

8. **CONCLUSION**: 1-7 show that the best theory is that the school shootings are faked/staged and/or Manchurian-candidate events orchestrated by the New World Order.

Non-Intrusive Mind and Behavior Control: Food, Medicine, Telescreen, and Education all Mix to Create "Scientific Government"

The extent of the brainwashing of humanity is *totalistic*, and the public has little idea of how far it currently goes, and how much further the corporatists plan for it to go in the future. Millions were horrified by a prediction of Nobel Prize winner Bertrand Russell in Alex Jones's popular 2007 documentary, *Endgame*. In a passage where he was discussing how the future will be like Huxley's *Brave New World*, or Plato's *Republic*[41], Russell had the following prophecy to make, which has indeed come to pass:

Gradually, by selective breeding the congenital differences between rulers and ruled will increase until they become almost different species. A revolt of the plebs would become as unthinkable as an organized insurrection of sheep against the practice of eating mutton.[42]

This comes from Chapter 3 of Russell's book, which is titled "Scientific Technique in an Oligarchy." The point of this chapter was, in Russell's words, to analyze the scientific dictatorships of the "new oligarchs."[43] He writes as if it is an analytical account of the dangers of such a government,[44]

---

huge federal analysis of hundreds of clinical trials. It marks the first time regulators have acknowledged that the drugs can trigger suicidal behavior among patients older than 18.

These may, however, be conservative numbers, as future studies may confirm.

[41] This is a fascinating issue, that Russell described society to be thus, and not, for example, like Orwell's 1984, since it now appears that the Republic and the Brave New World are the true models that the corporatist New World Order is shaping up for their mutton. I have long thought that Plato's Republic very accurately represents America in the present day. You have the workers making the most money (whether this is a "blue collar" worker or a New World Order corporatist). However, they are controlled by "philosopher-kings" who are unseen, and whom very few understand nor see as being the controllers (e.g., the Pope, the Queen of England). See Maxwell (2000) for more information.

[42] Russell 1985, 63.

[43] See Russell 1985, 56-57.

[44] For example, see the very end of page 58 of Russell 1985, where he calls such an oligarchy's economic system "an abomination," and six lines down on page 60, where he calls it "a terrible system."

and speculating about what the future holds. He says: "Scientific societies are as yet in their infancy. It may be worthwhile to spend a few moments in speculating as to possible future developments of those that are oligarchies."[45] But the very peculiar thing is how he could have been so astute in his predictions. The same certainly goes for Aldous Huxley and others. In addition to the above "mutton" passage that was given in Jones's film, consider a fuller account of the future that Russell "speculates" about:

> It is to be expected that advances in physiology and psychology will give governments much more control over individual mentality than they now have even in totalitarian countries [e.g., Soviet Russia]. Fichte [a very famous European philosopher] laid it down that education should aim at destroying free will, so that, after pupils have left school, they shall be incapable, throughout the rest of their lives, of thinking or acting otherwise than as their schoolmasters would have wished. But in his day, that was an unattainable ideal... In future such failures are not likely to occur where there is dictatorship. Diet, injections, and injunctions will combine, from a very early age, to produce the sort of character and the sort of beliefs that the authorities consider desirable, and any serious criticism of the powers that be will become psychologically impossible. Even if all are miserable, all will believe themselves happy, because the government will tell them that they are so... [Government controllers] would probably... [take] to scientific breeding. Any nation which adopts this practice will, within a generation, secure great military advantages. The system, one may surmise, will be something like this: except possibly in the governing aristocracy, all but 5 per cent of males and 30 per cent of females will be sterilized. The 30 percent of females will be expected to spend the years from eighteen to forty in reproduction, in order to secure adequate cannon fodder. As a rule, artificial insemination will be preferred to the natural method... Children will, as in Plato's *Republic*, be taken from their mothers and reared by professional nurses. Gradually, by selective breeding the congenital differences between rulers and ruled will increase until they become almost different species. A revolt of the plebs would become as unthinkable as an organized insurrection of sheep against the practice of eating mutton... To those accustomed to this system, the family as we know it would seem as queer as the tribal and totem organization of Australian aborigines seem to us... The upper class, being deprived of the softer pleasures both by the abolition of the family and by the supreme duty of devotion to the State, would acquire the mentality of ascetics: they would care only for power, and in pursuit of it would not shrink from cruelty. By the practice of

---

[45] Russell 1985, 61.

cruelty men would become hardened, so that worse and worse tortures would be required to give the spectators a thrill.[46]

There are a lot of peculiarities to this passage. There are surprisingly many more question-begging comments[47] than we'd expect from a famous philosopher. For example, why do the future tyrants of the scientific world government prefer artificial insemination to "the natural method," as Russell puts it? Why would Russell make this prediction when in the past tyrants have not done this, even when the technology existed? Also, why is it that Russell is coming largely to the very same conclusions as Huxley, H.G. Wells, and others? And why doesn't Russell give argumentation for his predictions? In other words, why is it reasonable for him to conclude that that the family would cease to exist to some degree, even though it has, to my knowledge, always been *the* pillar human institution? We certainly need evidence for that most curious claim, but none is given. Even more strange, how would Russell know to predict that vaccines, food, and hi-tech propaganda (what he calls "injunctions," but which Russell makes it clear that he means the education system, for example) would all work together to give rise to total subservience? This is an amazing prediction, since it is precisely what is going on right now[48]—so amazing that it can lead one to become suspicious that Russell didn't have a tip-off from New World Order corporatist controllers of their long-term plans. In the contemporary world, hi-tech flickering and subliminal telescreen information combine with diet

---

[46] Russell 1985, 61-63. Russell gives this passage partly in commenting about how life would be if the Nazis would have won, but he intends this passage to be about a prediction of what future dictatorships are going to be like. Russell says immediately following this passage (p. 64) that democracy is the cure for this sort of situation creeping in (and earlier in chapter 3 of Russell 1985, he said "democracy" is rule by the majority, not the minority), but he fails to state that, of course, citizens in a scientific dictatorship that Russell has described may be tricked into believing that all the equality that they hold may make it appear that "the people" rule, especially since the leaders will become "ascetic," as Russell says, and thus would not be visibly leaders (just as the Pope is not visibly a leader). So this "quick fix" that Russell prescribes is very suspicious, especially since today in contemporary America, leaders tell the people that they are free and that the United States is a democracy, but as I show in Grupp 2007, contemporary America is actually a corporatist state.

[47] *Question begging* or *circular reasoning* is a logical fallacy, which any college student will study in an introductory-level critical thinking or elementary logic and reasoning class. These are comments that leave one scratching one's head, wanting some reasoning for them, since they take for granted what they are supposed to prove. The key to a question-begging comment is that no verification or evidence is provided.

[48] See Grupp 2007.

and vaccine chemicals like aspartame, MSG, fluoride, and others to sedate and dumb-down children world wide.[49]

I find most interesting about this passage the idea that diet, injections, and injunctions, will all be combined to make humans completely servile. *How would Russell be able to make this astonishing prediction when it is so different from what has ever happened in "mainstream history"?* According to this prediction, the human person is injected with supposedly helpful vaccines at birth and after, but instead of helping to fight disease, they alter the nervous system and consciousness so as to make the person "a slave that loves her servitude," to put it in a Huxleyan way. This is precisely what vaccines do,[50] but how would Russell have known this?

Let's stop beating around the bush. Russell could not have made these predictions; he only could have been informed by secret-world-government-planners. What Russell writes about is precisely what is going on worldwide today.[51] This New World Order project appears to have been a project that has been in the works for many decades or centuries, with many researchers, all around the world. Dr. José Delgado said that with knowledge of the brain, "we may transform, we may shape, direct, robotize man. I think the great danger of the future is... that we will have to robotize human beings who are not aware that they have been robotized."[52]

The Matrix, *Literally*

Few know that television has a flicker-rate which induces hypnosis in viewers. According to Jeff Rense, the TV has a flicker which you don't see when you are watching, timed to such a cadence that it takes the mind and brain *from* a beta wave state *to* theta, which is the hypnotic state.[53] This reveals that Americans are living much of their life in a matrix-like simulated state, since they are in a hypnosis-like state when watching television or playing video games, activities which comprise much of their daily life,

---

[49] See Grupp 2007, 43-44 (these issues are discussed in many other areas in Grupp 2007 also).

[50] See Grupp 2007, ch. 5.

[51] See Grupp 2007.

[52] Constantine 1995, 8. Constantine goes on to say on page 8 that "America's EM arsenal [e.g., HAARP, and other such devices [see Smith 2006 for more information and examples] owes its very existence to his [Delgado's] brain transponder experiments, which robotize humans." Dr. José Delgado had his work used by the CIA and Navy. He was the first, to my knowledge, to develop an implantable computer chip that could control behavior via a remote control (the famous Delgado bull).

[53] Rense said this while in a radio conversation with David Icke on the Rense Radio Show, www.rense.com, May 4, 2004.

which further influences the rest of their lives (work, school, family). Thus the film *The Matrix* was not entirely fictional; strictly speaking, it was about real-life Americans, to some degree.

Corporatists have plans to further advance this technology, as Paul Joseph Watson and Alex Jones (Prison Planet reporters) have shown:

> Sony is preparing to unveil a simulated reality world in which PlayStation gamers can create a new life for themselves, complete with their own apartment, friends, movies, shopping and entertainment, bringing the reality of an actual matrix a step closer. "Sony has unveiled plans for its own virtual universe for the PlayStation 3 where users will be able to socialize, shop and even go to the movies—all without setting foot outside in the real world. The service—a kind of MySpace meets Linden Lab's Second Life meets the video-sharing site YouTube—will become available for PS3 users worldwide in late 2007, Sony announced in a statement available here Thursday," reports AFP... All this paves the way for a potential Matrix-like scenario where people are literally plugged in to a falsely constructed reality. Whoever controls that Matrix thus controls the activities of its users and participation may eventually become mandatory, with babies subsequently being born directly into the matrix. Or on the other hand, the Matrix could act as a kind of subscription based escapism, where users pay extortionate fees to exist inside a mock utopia in order to flee the horror of the real world... Travel down any average suburban American street and no longer will you see people outside talking to their neighbors or children playing, these activities having been replaced by the blue glow of the television that can be seen emanating from every window... There will also be a prominent segment of the population, the Trans-Humanist movement, which will vociferously advocate the simulated reality nexus and call for those who refuse to participate to be punished and relegated to the fringes of society as some kind of caste sub-species.[54]

This is just one example of the general theme of this book: Americans are living in a *matrix reality* (a reality that is not real, but is created for them by corporate New World Order leaders). In other words, Americans don't know it, but they are brainwashed—and they do not know it *because of* this brainwashing.

---

[54] "Sony Brings Real Life Matrix A Step Closer: Sets Precedent for Future Utopias Constructed to Escape Hellhole of Real World," Prison Planet, by Paul Joseph Watson and Alex Jones, March 8, 2007.

Americans have Accepted Thought Control

It is interesting to note how mainstream it is to endorse the idea that authentic media thought control and brainwashing is occurring in America. For example, even in the mainstream mass media (which is, we will see, one of the primary vehicles of brainwashing), frequently there is light discussion of how the media controls thought. For example, on June 27, 2006, on NPR's *All Things Considered*, there was a segment that featured George Lakoff of UC Berkeley and Frank Luntz, president of Luntz Research in Virginia. They each discussed how labeling the Iraq situation a "war" or an "occupation" can significantly alter the public's perception of the Iraq situation, depending on which word is espoused. It is as if they were admitting that media dictate the thoughts of citizens, which is to say that the media *control* cultural thought and therefore control minds (mind control).

The point here is that it is odd that these sorts of admissions go on frequently in the mass media, while at the same time, Americans violently resist the idea that they are brainwashed, and that their consciousness is unfree and controlled by the New World Order.

Media Monopoly

Since the 1980s, virtually all channels of our national media (radio, newspaper, television news, and gradually also the internet) are dominated by a few companies. Professor Bagdikian writes:

> Five global-dimension firms, operating with many of the characteristics of a cartel, own most of the newspapers, magazines, book publishers, motion picture studios, and radio and television stations in the United States. Each medium they own, whether magazines or broadcast stations, covers the entire country, and the owners prefer stories and programs that can be used everywhere and anywhere...These five conglomerates are Time Warner...; The Walt Disney Company; Murdoch's News Corporation...; Viacom; and Bertelsmann, based in Germany... This gives each of the five corporations and their leaders more communications power than was exercised by any despot or dictatorship in history....[55]

(There are a few exceptions to what Bagdikian says, which I will discuss shortly.)

Each of the leading media corporations is owned and controlled by ultramassive monopolistic corporations that profit heavily off of warfare and terrorism. But these militaristic corporatists, as Professor Bagdikian writes,

---

[55] *The New Media Monopoly*, Bagdikian 2004, 3-4.

"are American and foreign entrepreneurs whose corporate empires control every means by which the population learns of its society."[56] (There are exceptions but they are *very* few; one example is Lucasfilm, creator of the *Star Wars* films.) Consider what Professor Taylor tells us regarding these issues, in a passage about the brainwashing researcher and expert, Professor Robert Lifton:

> So how do totalitarian States, or individuals, try to implement their dreams of control? For governments, Robert Lifton... identifies eight psychological themes[57] characteristic of thought reform [i.e., brainwashing] and, he argues, of totalitarian ideologies in general,.... milieu control is the attempt to dominate not only the individual's communication with the outside (all that he sees and hears, reads and writes, experiences and expresses) but also — in its penetration of his inner life — over what we may speak of as his communication with himself.[58]

As stated above, by thoroughly controlling the environment corporatists have learned to control how people's minds develop: if you can control what the sensorium of a person gathers in, you can control the nature and structure of their consciousness. And if you can control their consciousness, you can control their behavior. And if you can control a person's consciousness and behavior, you can get them to do anything you with them to, including march into gunfire in oil-wars in distant lands, such as Iraq.

---

[56] 2004, 4.

[57] All of these are shown in this book to thoroughly apply to the US citizenry via the media.

[58] Taylor 2004, 16.

2. Brainwashing Understood by Example: A Case Study of "The Iraq Threat"[59]

"The Iraq Threat:" An Example of Brainwashing

I often hear or read people who tell us that "Americans are brainwashed," but they do not follow up this claim with clear, simple, empirical evidence that proves this. Proving that Americans are brainwashed is critically important, because the vast majority of Americans would likely disagree with the idea that they are brainwashed and unfree individuals. In the remainder of this first chapter, I will give clear proof that this is the case, so as to put this idea to rest.

I will do this by example, and the example I will use is the current war/occupation in Iraq. I fear that many readers will reject the idea that all-powerful Orwellian-level mass brainwashing is going on in America before seeing the evidence. The best way to specifically counter this unfounded doubt is by going straight into the core of the evidence with an example that all Americans are thoroughly familiar with.

In this chapter, I use data from opinion polls. I imagine that some readers of this book will find this problematical, since it's well known that opinion polls are often tampered with by the money-masters. This is of course true, and one must use caution in this chapter for that reason. But I trust that the opinion polls I am displaying in this chapter are reasonably true. I vividly remember the public sentiment on Iraq (and other countries, such as Iran) through the years, and how that sentiment changed, and that seems to be reflected precisely in the polls displayed below. Therefore, I have chosen to use them without reservation in this chapter; they simply match what I have seen occur in society through the past decades.

Iraq 1998

I will start my investigation of Iraq with a poll from 1998, which shows apparent animosity of US citizens toward Iraq. Interestingly, as far as I know, there was no real event of any sort in the years surrounding this poll that showed that Saddam or Iraq was a real threat to America.

CNN/USA *Today*/Gallup Poll. Nov. 13-15, 1998. N=1,039 adults nationwide: "Which one of the following possible goals do you think should be the specific goal of any U.S. attack on Iraq at this time: to pressure Iraq into complying with United Nations weapons inspections, OR, to remove Saddam Hussein from power?"

---

[59] All polls in this chapter were acquired from pollingreport.com

Pressure Iraq	25%
Remove Saddam	70%
Other (vol.)	3%
No opinion	2%

Gallup/CNN/USA Today Poll. Dec. 16, 1998, 6-9 PM EST. N=543 adults nationwide: "As you may know, the United Nations chief weapons inspector has reported that Iraq has not complied with its agreement to allow United Nations inspections of possible weapons facilities. In response, the United States and Britain have launched an air attack against Iraq this evening. Do you approve or disapprove of this attack?"

Approve	74%
Disapprove	13%
No opinion	13%

Since 70 percent of Americans favored the removal of Saddam, it is safe to assert that this same 70 percent believed Saddam was a threat to them, and hence their expression about removal, according to this sample in these polls. The second poll also shows support by Americans for the use of military action against Iraq in acts of war. Contrary to what politicians and news media told Americans throughout 2002 and up to the 2003 invasion, we now know that Saddam did not have weapons of mass destruction during that time — and even if he did, there was no evidence that the Iraqi government was going to use them against the United States.[60] Saddam Hussein and Iraq, therefore, were not a threat to America—*but it is very interesting to note how Americans appear to have believed they were a dire threat.* These two polls show how huge numbers of Americans can be fooled into fervently believing a blatant falsehood. That is the textbook definition of brainwashing: being tricked into believing a falsehood is the true reality.

> *These polls indicate huge support for military action by most Americans against Iraq, when there was no evidence of any sort of danger to these Americans: in the presence of no real threat, a threat was felt.*

In *actual reality*, the threat was nonexistent; but in *mental reality*, the threat was believed to be severe by 7 out of every 10 Americans, if these

---

[60] Some may say that Saddam Hussein's threats against the United States were evidence that he would use weapons against Americans, but of course that is not true, since saying something and doing something are entirely different things, and all sorts of threats are commonly made by dictators against the United States, and no actions follow, even in circumstances where actions could have been taken.

polls accurately mirror the sentiments of Americans. Americans were tricked into believing that a continual threat loomed over them from Iraq, spanning from 1990 to 2003. This is an astonishing, obvious, and masterful example of mass brainwashing. The brainwashing was so thorough, as we will see below, that Americans even felt they could send their children off to Iraq for a very dangerous invasion, war, and occupation from 2003 to 2007 (which was, and is, very profitable to the corporatists[61]).

The Fear and War Instrument: *Mass Media*

Where did this fear come from? How did this brainwashing occur? There can only be one answer: the propaganda machine of American media implanted this fear. Consider this hyped-up announcement by President Clinton, regarding the attack in Iraq on Wednesday, December 16, 1998, on the eve of his impeachment vote:

> Earlier today, I ordered America's armed forces to strike military and security targets in Iraq. They are joined by British forces. Their mission is to attack Iraq's nuclear, chemical and biological weapons programs and its military capacity to threaten its neighbors. Their purpose is to protect the national interest of the United States, and indeed the interests of people throughout the Middle East and around the world. Saddam Hussein must not be allowed to threaten his neighbors or the world with nuclear arms, poison gas or biological weapons... The international community had good reason to set this requirement. Other countries possess weapons of mass destruction and ballistic missiles. With Saddam, there is one big difference: He has used them. Not once, but repeatedly. Unleashing chemical weapons against Iranian troops during a decade-long war. Not only against soldiers, but against civilians, firing Scud missiles at the citizens of Israel, Saudi Arabia, Bahrain and Iran. And not only against a foreign enemy, but even against his own people, gassing Kurdish civilians in Northern Iraq.

Notice how Clinton lies outright (a key tactic in setting up fear-propaganda) when he says that Iraq under Saddam is the only country to use weapons of mass destruction and ballistic missiles more than once. Of course many examples prove Clinton wrong. There were Truman's *two* nuclear attacks on Japan, the *numerous* American Agent Orange chemical WMD (weapons of mass destruction) attacks on Vietnam, the small pox attacks US military soldiers carried out on the Indians,[62] and the pollution warfare of US corporations.[63] In the first Iraq War, the US used bunker buster bombs. These

---

[61] See Grupp 2007.
[62] Cole 1988, 12.
[63] See Grupp 2007, ch. 4.

contain "depleted" uranium, a WMD; specifically, so much uranium was used that it was the equivalent of 400,000 Hiroshima bombs.[64] The widely documented bombing and killing of civilians by Americans in World War II by various techniques,[65] and a plethora of other examples could be given.[66]

Clinton can tell this lie because he knows that the controlled media will not check him on this. He knows Americans, in general, will not know the difference since they know very little about history. Even if they did, with enough TV, beer, and hotdogs to continually fill them and sedate them in their evenings after work, they may not even have the ability to care.

Iraq 2002

Even though Iraq was absolutely no threat to America from 1998 to 2002, the polls indicated a continuous desire in the thoughts of Americans to use violence and acts of war against Iraq. Consider three polls on this issue:

CNN/*USA Today*/**Gallup Poll**. March 22-24, 2002. N=1,011 adults nationwide. MoE ± 3: "Turning to Iraq, would you favor or oppose the U.S. taking the following steps against Iraq? How about... ?"

Using military air strikes but no U.S. ground troops.

Favor	67%
Oppose	29%
Not Sure	4%

The Gallup Poll. June 17-19, 2002. N=1,005 adults nationwide. MoE ± 3 (total sample):

"Next, we'd like to ask you a few questions about Iraq. First, would you favor or oppose sending American troops back to the Persian Gulf in order to remove Saddam Hussein from power in Iraq?" Form A (N=519, MoE ± 5)

---

[64] See Brohy and Ungerman 2001 for more information on DU, and the talks from Doug Rokke and Leuren Moret on the Rense Radio Show archives (at www.rense.com) for the fall of 2006.

[65] This is clearly discussed by Robert McNamara early in the film documentary, the *Fog of War* (directed by Errol Morris, 2004, Sony Pictures). McNamara described how in World War II in Tokyo they burned/killed 100,000 civilians in one night. "We were... war criminals," he says.

[66] I have not even mentioned the following other events, which involved WMDs: the murder of 3-6 million civilians in the Vietnam War (where the WMD used was: the US military), to slavery in the 1800s (the WMD used was slavery), and the Native American genocide (there were many WMDs used in this case). The list of WMD attacks that could be listed is very long.

	Favor	Oppose	No Opinion
	%	%	%
6/02	59	34	7
11/01	74	20	6
2/01	52	42	6
6/93	70	27	3

Los Angeles Times Poll. Aug. 22-25, 2002. N=1,372 adults nationwide. MoE ± 3 (total sample).

	ALL	Demo-crats	Indepen-dents	Repub-licans
	%	%	%	%

"Do you think the United States should take military action in order to remove Saddam Hussein from power in Iraq, or not?"

	ALL	Demo-crats	Indepen-dents	Repub-licans
Should	59	53	53	73
Should not	29	36	32	15
Don't know	12	11	15	12

"Do you agree or disagree with the following statement? The United States should take military action against Iraq only if that military action has the support of the international community."

	ALL	Demo-crats	Indepen-dents	Repub-licans
Agree	65	74	70	51
Disagree	27	18	25	41
Don't know	8	8	5	8

What I find most interesting about these polls is that 9/11 did not significantly change the poll numbers in any permanent way from 1998 to after 9/11. 9/11 may not have even been needed for the invasion of Iraq, according to these polls (in other words, the corporatists did not even have to carry out the false flag event of 9/11[67] to get support for the March 2003 invasion of Iraq). All that was needed was the fabrication of a threat (a false threat) via the mass media.

Mass Media's Secret Conspiracy and Agenda

Readers of this book who are not familiar with the controlled, fabricated, brainwashing nature of the mass media might be surprised at the findings of the previous four sections, and the sections that follow this one. They may say, "I just can't believe that the mass media is involved in a secret plot to

---

[67] For reasons why 9/11 was a false-flag event (a staged terror attack), see Grupp 2007, ch. 1 and 4.

control all information for sadistic goals. How could they be so perfectly aligned and in unison? How could they be so cruel?"

To this sort of a comment, I can make the following reply: If one simply goes and watches the news, one finds that the very nature of the mass media proves that *there is a secret plot by the mass media to not report on important information that helps the people, and to only report on insignificant, distracting issues, or on issues that promote agendas that the corporatists wish to have promoted.* For example, as I finalize this book for publication, the mass media just finished a month of continual news reporting on Paris Hilton being sent to prison. And before that, it was a month of Anna Nichole Smith. And before that, it was a month about Britney Spears shaving her head and seeking some sort of drug rehab for her problems, whatever they might have been. Do you all remember how for an entire summer a few years back, the mass media endlessly talked about scandals to do with Michael Jackson, Coby Bryant, and Martha Stewart? Those stories utterly filled the media wires, while the mass media never once reported on depleted uranium contamination of the globe, corporate pollution, or the utter poverty that exists and which has been caused by monopolistic mega-corporations in Africa, Asia, South America, the Caribbean, and Mexico. I could go on, stretching back in time, to show how the news media are dominated by less-than-tabloid trash stories, while ignoring all the stories that matter to humanity. The point is this: the media will not report on critically important issues, which are too numerous to mention here (but I will throughout this book), and for that reason, they fill the minds of Americans with wasteful, distracting information.

As far as the question of whether or not this is a deliberate conspiracy on the part of the Big Media corporatists, we can see that it indeed can only be the case, as only a few examples that I will give next will show.

Notice how the corporatist mass media exists in astounding unison: *all* mass media was flooded for a month with "news" about Paris Hilton. Why didn't one news corporation, say, CBS, decide that stories about Paris Hilton did not hold real news value, and instead, something else must be reported on for a month—such as, for example, the fact that Iran has submarines all over the Atlantic ocean,[68] and if the US strikes Iran with acts of war, as the US leaders have been threatening for years, Iran could decimate the coastal cities of the USA?

The idea that the corporatist media are in perfect unison is not just possible, it is *provable,* by the few examples I have already given in this

---

[68] See "Iran Begins Building First Locally-Built Submarine," Tehran (AFP), published by NewsMax.com, May 11, 2005.

section. Here are a few more examples. Near the start of the Iraq war, it was caught on film how the US military attacked and killed members of the Arab news agency, Al-Jazeera.[69] This story was widely reported on outside of the USA, but it was not reported in the United States. In the infamous "Battle of Fallujah" in 2004 during the Iraq war, Americans used chemical weapons against the Iraqis.[70] In other words, the US Administration accused the Iraqi government throughout 2002 and into 2003 up to the March 2003 invasion of having ready-to-fire chemical weapons of mass destruction, which they did not, and instead the US administration used chemical weapons of mass destruction *on Iraq*. This is an example of the inversion of reality that the typical American is taught by their news media: if x is actually true, the mass media in the USA will tell the American citizenry that not-x is true. This story of the chemical attack in Fallujah was widely reported on outside of the USA, but was virtually never reported on in the USA.

And here's another example: US Steel, which is near Indiana University Northwest, where I taught until June 2007, is pumping out hazardous chemicals all over Lake Michigan, and downwind are all sorts of towns (Kalamazoo, Holland, Benton Harbor, Ann Arbor, etc.), and it is virtually never reported on. Given the catastrophe that mercury can cause to children and fetuses, this story may contain as much murder and slaughter as a typical Iraq war story might have, but no news coverage on it can be found *anywhere*.[71]

Here's another example of the way the media is always in unison. Why in November of 2000, deep into the night after the day of the Presidential election, did *all* the networks start calling the election for Bush, when

---

[69] For more information, see the film, *Control Room*. 2004. Director: Jehane Noujam. Studio: Lion's Gate.

[70] There are many news stories covering this outside of the United States. For example, see "White Phosphorous: Weapons on the Edge," by Paul Reynolds, November 16, 2005, *BBC News*. The only news coverage I know of associated with a US news agency was the *Washington Post Foreign News* Service: "U.S. Forces Battle Into Heart of Fallujah - Units Meet Scattered Resistance; Attacks Continue Elsewhere," by Jackie Spinner, Karl Vick and Omar Fekeiki, November 10, 2004, *Washington Post Foreign Service*, page A01.

[71] Interestingly, America is also undergoing an autism epidemic, where in just a decade autism went from being a not-so-common ailment among children to being one of the most frequent among children. Mercury is, to my knowledge, a top candidate for being the cause of this epidemic. Yet, no news media coverage exists of US Steel, one of the leading mercury polluters. See the Introduction and Prologue of Kirby 2005, which appears to prove that the autism epidemic is caused by the mercury in vaccines. Also see Ayoub (2005, 2006) for definite proof that mercury in vaccines is causing the autism epidemic.

obviously no such claim could be made yet, given the fact that there was no evidence and all the votes had not been counted?

Another example: Why did the mass media fail to report on the UN conferences that top US leaders (such as Al Gore in the 1990s) have attended, where they would discuss how the sovereignty of the US must be dissolved into a world government, and how sexuality should be promoted to children worldwide?[72] In all the Presidential race coverage in 2000, Al Gore's participation in such conferences *never* made the news media. Americans only know of these issues (for those that do know) because Joan Veon attended the conference and then put it in her book, *The United Nations Global Straightjacket*.

Examples of the unison of the news media are nearly countless. Here is another story that has literally never been reported in the United States: the US-led sanctions on Iraq that started in the early 1990s and which, without reason or justification, were never lifted; this resulted in, at the very least, 1 million Iraqi civilian deaths.[73] 300 million Americans have no idea that this happened, because of the amazingly well coordinated and synchronized news media, which are obviously more than capable of keeping this secret. Also, it is amazing that almost no Americans know what the over 150,000 American troops in Iraq have been actually doing over there in Iraq from day-to-day from 2003 to 2007, since it is never reported on.[74]

Iraq 2003

Now, interestingly, while Iraq remained no threat at all, from spring/summer of 2002 to spring/summer of 2003, polls showed an *increase* in support for an invasion of Iraq. Consider the following 2003 poll taken right around the start of (or, really, continuation of) the Iraq War ("Shock and Awe") in March 2003, where support and approval for the war hit an astonishing *80 percent*:

---

[72] See Veon 1999 (2000), chapters 1 and 2. This issue about sexuality among children was heralded in Huxley's *Brave New World*.

[73] For more information see Brohy and Ungerman 2001; Felton 2005, chapter 13.

[74] Here is a sample of what they are doing. They are practicing old-fashioned (and what could even be called Nazi-style) intimidation tactics: trying to act intimidating, to make their forces look bigger than what they are. Another thing they are doing is breaking into peaceful family homes during the middle of the night, often barging right into small children's rooms, pulverizing them with fear, then rummaging through their belongings. For footage of this, see Olds and Scott 2005, and Langan 2003. Students who are soldiers, who have been in my classes at three of the universities I have taught at, also confirm with me that this breaking-and-entering is a dominant part of what the troops are doing in Iraq on a daily (and nightly) basis.

CBS News Poll. March 26-27, 2003. N=868 adults nationwide. MoE ± 3.

"Do you approve or disapprove of the United States taking military action against Iraq to try to remove Saddam Hussein from power?"

	Approve	Disapprove	Don't Know
	%	%	%
3/26-27/03	77	19	4
3/24/03	75	23	2
3/23/03	80	17	3
3/22/03	76	22	2
3/20-21/03	76	20	4

This was the high point of the period when Americans were being told continually how Saddam is an imminent threat to attack the United States with his WMDs (weapons of mass destruction).

In Karel 2004, it is pointed out how Americans were tricked into believing that Saddam was like Osama. For example, only vague statements would be given about Iraq: "This [Iraq] is a regime with something to hide!"[75] Americans, still traumatized by 9/11, merely made the association and connection between Saddam and terrorism.

By March of 2003, days before the start of the Iraq War, it was firmly set in the minds of Americans that the terrorist-Saddam link was made. With no proof of an Iraq threat, only hours before the Iraq invasion of March 2003, George W. Bush told Americans in a tense, nationally televised speech that announced upcoming war (e.g., "journalists, please leave Iraq now!") the following, which includes the (false) claim that there is proof of an Iraq threat:

> The only way to reduce the harm and duration of war is to apply the full force and might of our military, and we are prepared to do so. If Saddam Hussein attempts to cling to power, he will remain a deadly foe until the end. In desperation, he and terrorists groups might try to conduct terrorist operations against the American people and our friends. These attacks are not inevitable. They are, however, possible. And this very fact underscores the reason we cannot live under the threat of blackmail. The terrorist threat to America and the world will be diminished the moment that Saddam Hussein is disarmed. (President Bush, March 17, 2003, on prime time television, addressing Americans.)

Now, consider the following 2003 CNN poll, a week after the Iraq War started, that showed that over 80 percent of Americans held very high

---

[75] State of the Union Address, January 29, 2002

confidence in their new war — even higher than the cherished Second World War, which it seems most Americans still believe was a "just" war.

CNN/USA Today/Gallup Poll. March 29-30, 2003. N=1,012 adults nationwide. MoE ± 3 (total sample).

"Do you feel that you have a clear idea of what this war is all about — that is, what we are fighting for?"

	Yes	No	No Opinion
	%	%	%
3/29-30/03 [War with Iraq]	81	18	1
11/01 [War on Terrorism]	89	10	1
12/90 [Persian Gulf War]	74	24	2
5/67 [Vietnam War]	49	48	3
11/42 [World War II]	73	27	-

As this poll was tabulated, a week into the Iraq War, Americans had seen on their televisions cataclysmic bombs destroying, detonating and igniting the Baghdad night like ultramassive lightning blasts. But nevertheless, Americans definitely supported the blood-misery, as the 80 percent level poll revealed. They even thought the war was all, in actual reality, only for an abstract idea (the "Iraq threat"): nobody had seen WMDs, there was no evidence for their existence,[76] and they were as nonexistent as unicorns. But the telescreen world told them these unicorns (WMDs) existed, and thus Americans believed it.

This "noble war" (as Americans apparently thought it was) was based on an unverifiable idea. This is an example of how uncritical, non-rational, and unscientific in their thinking Americans are. The education system does not teach them to be scientists and poets in schooling from kindergarten through college, but rather it teaches them to follow what the teachers say by fiat, lest you get an F, and fail out of school. The poll appears to show that the majority of Americans may not even have cared about evidence of an imminent threat at all: no evidence existed for an Iraq threat, but Americans nevertheless were as inspired as they were for World War II.

---

[76] Some politicians and media personalities have attempted to argue that WMDs have been found in Iraq since the March 2003 invasion, because old pre-1990 chemical and biological WMDs were found in Iraq. But these are not the WMDs that Bush, Powell, Rumsfeld, Cheney, and others told the nation about before the March 2003 invasion. Also, it is it not surprising that those weapons were found (the US gave them to Saddam), but they were not effective any more, since chemical weapons do not have long "shelf lives."

The following Fox News poll appears to indicate that Americans were also geared up for the genocide of civilians, indicating that the brainwashing was extreme enough to lead to the endorsement of mass murder of non-soldiers.[77]

FOX News/Opinion Dynamics Poll. March 11-12, 2003. N=900 registered voters nationwide. MoE ± 3.

"If Iraq were to use weapons of mass destruction against U.S. troops or a neighboring country, would you support or oppose the United States using weapons of mass destruction in response?"

Support	65%
Oppose	23%
Not sure	12%

Returning to the issue of evidence, next I will give a poll from early 2003 about how much *evidence* the Bush Administration had presented against Iraq. This shows precisely how misled the American citizenry can be as to what is actually going on in world affairs, since the Bush Administration did not present any evidence at all. For that reason, it is somewhat amazing that such a poll as this next one could even exist. It is not an exaggeration to suggest that this is analogous to having a poll about how much evidence the government has given that unicorns exist in the Yukon, since that too is merely a poll about something that there is no evidence for. Here's the poll:

ABC News/Washington Post Poll. Jan. 30-Feb. 1, 2003. N=855 adults nationwide. MoE ± 3.5. Fieldwork by TNS Intersearch.

"Do you think Bush has presented enough evidence showing why the United States should use military force to remove Saddam Hussein from power, or would you like him to present more evidence?" Asked of half the sample

	Has Presented Enough	Would Like More	No Opinion
	%	%	%
1/30 - 2/1/03	42	57	1
1/28/03	42	56	2

---

[77] Lifton (1989, ix) discusses how Nazi brainwashing, similarly, led "very ordinary people into murderous activities." And, also relevant to our discussion here of Americans, as compared to Nazis, Lifton writes: "I have been... concerned with a contemporary category of fundamentalism that could contribute to killing on so great a scale as to dwarf even what the Nazis did, that associated with a nuclear threat." (1989, ix)

1/27/03	36	60	3
1/16-20/03	39	58	2
12/02	40	58	2
9/02	48	50	2

The poll just given appears to be an ideal example of the power of propaganda success in the telescreen world: it is a poll about the *evidence* for something that has *never been observed*. This is like having a poll where the pollers are asked if they have ever *seen* an invisible man. But the Orwellian nature of telescreen information desensitizes people to the continual absurdism of telescreen world information, and nobody seems to much notice that, well, there are no unicorns and invisible men (that is, no WMDs or scary Iraq threats).

Many Americans thought Colin Powell was presenting evidence at the UN for the existence of weapons of mass destruction in Iraq. But Powell was showing the UN pictures from *before* 1990 of weapons of mass destruction that would have long lost their chemical structure and thus their status as weapons. In Greenwald,[78] there is a clear discussion of the details of the "evidence" (non-evidence) that Colin Powell presented about "Iraqi WMDs" before the March 2003 invasion. In the words of former CIA analyst Ray McGovern, this was "embarrassing," and "a masterful performance [of acting]." I think I can correctly write that what McGovern is getting at is that Powell's presentation was almost a "theater of the absurd." In Greenwald's film, experts discuss how literally all of this "evidence" was utterly ridiculous, and "complete nonsense," according to David Albright (a physicist). One example of this is how Powell took photos from before 1990 and said they showed nuclear weapons construction going on around the time of Powell's presentation. These absurdities were not discussed at any length in the national media, but nevertheless, the mass media presented it as evidence to the American citizens.

This next poll shows how the levels of support by Americans for the Iraq War diminished dramatically, after 2004, after many Americans began to figure out the ruse.

ABC News/Washington Post Poll. May 11-15, 2006. N=1,103 adults nationwide. MoE ± 3. Fieldwork by TNS. RV = registered voters.

"Do you approve or disapprove of the way Bush is handling the situation in Iraq?"

---

[78] 2004.

	Approve	Disapprove	Unsure
	%	%	%
5/11-15/06	32	66	1
4/6-9/06	37	62	1
3/2-5/06	40	59	-
1/23-26/06	39	60	1
12/15-18/05	46	53	1
10/30 - 11/2/05	36	64	1
9/8-11/05	38	62	1
8/25-28/05	42	57	1
6/23-26/05	43	56	1
6/2-5/05	41	58	1
4/21-24/05	42	56	2
3/10-13/05	39	57	4
1/12-16/05	40	58	2
12/16-19/04	42	57	1
9/23-26/04 RV	47	50	3
8/26-29/04 RV	47	51	2
7/22-25/04	45	53	2
6/17-20/04	44	55	2
5/20-23/04	40	58	2
4/15-18/04	45	54	1
3/4-7/04	46	53	1
2/10-11/04	47	52	1
1/15-18/04	55	42	2
12/18-21/03	60	39	2
12/14/03	58	38	4
11/12-16/03	48	48	4
10/26-29/03	47	51	2
10/9-13/03	51	47	2
9/26-29/03	50	47	3
9/10-13/03	52	46	2
9/4-7/03	49	47	4
8/20-24/03	56	37	7
7/9-10/03	58	41	2
6/18-22/03	67	30	2
4/27-30/03	75	22	2

It ("the Iraq threat") was all a dream, due to the endless inundation of auto-suggestion and conditioning from the politicians and the national media. I think it could even be argued that the dream almost made Americans become complicit in mass murder, if it were not the case that they were obviously *tricked* (by the New World Order) into supporting the slaughter of the people of Iraq.

America: Land of the Brainwashed, Home of the Nazis

Americans, in general, are prone to holding the belief that the spooky socialist tyrannies, such as the Nazi regime,[79] are the regimes that have brainwashed, warmongering citizens, whereas America consists of more peaceful citizens who are not brainwashed. Americans seem to perceive spooky socialist tyrannies as full of citizens who want kill for false and irrational ideas. But how do we *avoid* coming to the same conclusions about Americans, given the data above about how the governing corporatists create reality for the citizenry, fooling them into doing whatever the corporatists desire? The brainwashing expert Taylor writes that

> The Party creates its own reality, which may nave little or nothing to do with what is actually happening in the world... Victims of ... brainwashing... may appear disconnected when dealing with relatives or outsiders, or they may react with strong hostility to any challenge to the new beliefs."[80]

Many American corporatists are descendants of Nazis, or people who collaborated with the Nazis, such as the Bush family,[81] IBM,[82] numerous big pharmaceutical companies,[83] Rockefeller's Standard Oil,[84] the Federal Reserve,[85] which was run by Warburg when that corporation collaborated with the Nazis, among several others. Like them, Hitler also used false flag terror (creating fake incidents to make it look like Poland was carrying out murderous aggression against Germany in 1939[86]). He and his associates controlled the media to spread disinformation so that the German citizenry would not know reality, and instead would believe in a false reality—which is what brainwashing is. Citizens across the world outside of the United States at the time of the invasion of Iraq (and after) protested American plans

---

[79] Nazi brainwashing was so powerful that in his classic work on the brainwashing campaigns in China, Lifton (1989, viii-ix), compares the dramatically powerful Chinese brainwashing of the 20th century (discussed elsewhere in this book) to Nazi brainwashing.

[80] Taylor 2004, 22-23.

[81] See Tarpley 2004.

[82] See Black 2001.

[83] See Horowitz 2001, chapter 1.

[84] Ibid.

[85] Ibid.

[86] I discussed this in the last chapter of this book. Tarpley 2006, 67-68. This was a staged event that really got much of World War II going.

for invasion into Iraq.[87] I remember on the evening of the invasion of Iraq seeing on the news that a McDonalds in Paris was heavily vandalized by protestors against the American assault.[88] McDonalds is an international symbol of Americanism, apparently. This is a major *disconnect*, to use Taylor's word, from the confident war mood in America, where war fever was so great that belief in the war mission was even greater than in World War II. But Americans could only be blinded due to the uniformity of the American national media and government, which were replete with persons who would profit wildly from this war. Just after the initial March 2003 invasions, in response to the opposition to the war around Europe, anti-France and anti-German sentiments in the United States were quite high. There was even a fair degree of support among Americans for boycotting French and German products. Consider this poll from just over a week before the initial invasion of Iraq:

FOX News/Opinion Dynamics Poll. March 11-12, 2003. N=900 registered voters nationwide. MoE ± 3.

---

[87] Consider this passage from an article titled "Start of War Changes Few Minds About Wisdom of Attacking Iraq" (Emphasis added), March 21, 2003, Robert Barr, *Associated Press*.

The first shots of war set off global protests on the streets and drew dismayed responses from world leaders Thursday. President Bush's main allies stood firmly by him as U.S. flags burned from Berlin to Bangladesh. A world woven together by satellite TV watched the opening salvos of the war, and responses ranged from gasoline hoarding in Katmandu to cheers for Saddam Hussein in Kashmir. "The wrong decision has been taken. The war has begun. It must be ended as quickly as possible," German Chancellor Gerhard Schroeder, a staunch anti-war voice, said in a televised address. "The threat of terrorism is a fact," said Polish President Aleksander Kwasniewski, whose country backs Bush. "The world bears the joint responsibility and should show solidarity in fighting terrorism and proliferation of weapons of mass destruction." "Patience, patience, O Bush, tomorrow the Muslims will dig your grave," demonstrators chanted in Cairo, where police used water cannons to keep protesters away from the U.S. Embassy... Protesters banged pots in Manila and daubed "Bush, your empire will eventually crumble" on walls in Caracas. They trashed a McDonalds restaurant in the Montparnasse district of Paris. They stoned the U.S. Embassy in Brussels, and threw bricks and eggs at a local party office of Spanish Prime Minister and Bush ally, Jose Maria Aznar. In Srinagar, capital of heavily Muslim Kashmir, schoolboys watched TV footage of explosions in Baghdad and cheered when Iraqi President Saddam Hussein appeared. "Stupid war, mindless violence," said a placard in a sea of 50,000 anti-war demonstrators converging on Berlin's Brandenburg Gate.

[88] "Start of War Changes Few Minds About Wisdom of Attacking Iraq," March 21, 2003, Robert Barr, Associated Press.

"Do you favor or oppose boycotting products from France and Germany for opposing the U.S. position on Iraq?"

	%
Favor	40
Oppose	47
Not sure	13

This poll indicates that nearly half of Americans were in favor of retaliatory action against our traditional allies in Europe, just because they were not in agreement with the American position.

The polls and information of this chapter show how rather simple it is to carry out mass brainwashing when a well-organized secret corporatist government commands the military, the media, and false-flag terror. In his classic text, *Ordinary Men*, Browning discusses "how a unit of average, middle-aged Germans became the cold-blooded murderers of tens of thousands of Jews" (as described on the back cover.) "Middle-aged family men of working- and lower-middle-class background from the city of Hamburg,"[89] who were reminded that "in Germany the bombs were falling on women and children,"[90] were "ordered to round up Jews... the women, children, and elderly... to be shot on-the-spot...."[91] Similarly, American soldiers and warmongers have killed over a million Iraqi civilians,[92] as I have discussed elsewhere in this book.

In a recent popular documentary film, a father of a 9/11 victim discussed what he was thinking when he was first told, not long after 9/11, that Saddam and Osama had connections. "I was so insane with wanting to get even, that I was willing to believe anything."[93] This is successful brainwashing. This father used the word "insane," indicating his absence of critical, rational thought. Are there many other ways that Americans are unknowingly brainwashed? We will find out that there are a surprisingly large number. I will next discuss the story that was inundating the mass media news as I wrote this book: *Iran*.

---

[89] Page 1.
[90] Page 2.
[91] Page 2.
[92] Brohy and Ungerman 2001; Lando 2007.
[93] In Jarecki 2005.

The Mystery of Hezbollah[94]

As I write these words in early 2009, I can see that all the things you have just read about in this chapter about Iraq, are about to repeat with respect to Iran. In other words, Americans were told that Iraq had WMDs pointed at Americans, and that provoked a war. Now, again, in 2006-2009 Americans are being told that Iran has WMDs that are pointed at us. Again, as with Iraq, we are never actually shown the WMDs. It appears that everything you just read about in this chapter is about to repeat. It's as if Americans have forgotten everything I have just discussed about Iraq.

Back in 2006, it appeared that the CIA would use Hezbollah for an invasion of oil-rich Iran in the same way they used al-Qaeda to invade oil-rich Iraq. Hezbollah was to be a threat in order to stir the American people into an invasion of Iran (which could likely ignite World War III, since Iran is an ally of Russia and an oil supplier of China[95]). In July 2006, there was a one-month war between Hezbollah and Israel. The American national news media constantly told Americans during this time that there was a secret force behind Hezbollah and which threatened the US: *Iran*. Even "intellectuals" marched onto the Fox News Channel and said things like, "I believe Iran is involved in this…", as Joseph Cirincione did on July 16, 2006, without stating any evidence.

It is difficult to believe that Hezbollah could be genuinely financed by Iran, and could genuinely be a terrorist group (i.e., a terrorist group that is not created by the New World Order[96]), *because it can be shown that Hezbollah is a CIA-created army*, like al-Qaeda, for reasons I will explain next.

As shown at great length in Grupp 2007, al-Qaeda is merely a branch of the CIA, most likely some sort of PMF (privatized military force[97]). Now add to this that Hezbollah is greatly influenced by al-Qaeda and, suspiciously, *they even were created as one unit*—co-originated—as the mass media has made sure we are well aware of:

> The Lebanon-based Hezbollah organization, one of the world's most formidable terrorist groups, is increasingly teaming up with al Qaeda on logistics and training for terrorist operations, according to U.S. and European intelligence officials and terrorism experts. The new cooperation, which is ad hoc and tactical and involves mid- and low-level operatives, mutes years of rivalry between Hezbollah, which draws its support primarily from Shiite Muslims, and al Qaeda, which is

---

[94] All records of these polls were acquired from pollingreport.com

[95] See Grupp 2007.

[96] See Grupp 2007 for more information.

[97] This is a private army hired by a corporation.

predominantly Sunni. It includes coordination on explosives and tactics training, money laundering, weapons smuggling and acquiring forged documents, according to knowledgeable sources. This new alliance, even if informal, has greatly concerned U.S. officials in Washington and intelligence operatives abroad who believe the assets and organization of Hezbollah's formidable militant wing will enable a hobbled al Qaeda network to increase its ability to launch attacks against American targets. Hezbollah, which was founded by Lebanese clerics in 1982, has two wings. One is political and social, and its vibrant political party holds nine seats in the Lebanese parliament. The other wing is a guerrilla military force. The United States put Hezbollah on its terrorist list in 1997.[98]

Fox News even has tried to suggest that Hezbollah, and therefore Iran, are responsible for 9/11, due to the cognate nature of Hezbollah and al-Qaeda:

While the Sept. 11 commission found that contacts between Al Qaeda and Iraq existed in the past, it also pointed to another country with potential ties to the terror network: Iran. The report released Thursday by the National Commission on Terrorist Attacks Upon the United States says that detained terrorists, possibly including Al Qaeda operational planners Khalid Shaikh Mohammed and Ramzi Binalshibh, confirmed that several of the Sept. 11 hijackers traveled through Iran en route to or from Afghanistan. At least eight of the hijackers took advantage of the Iranian practice of not stamping Saudi passports, the captured terror suspects allegedly said. They denied any other reason for the hijackers' travel through Iran... Binalshibh is a suspected coordinator of the Sept. 11 attacks on the United States and has acknowledged meeting with Mohamed Atta, the leader of the hijackers and pilot of one of the commercial jetliners that demolished the World Trade Center's twin towers. Binalshibh and Atta, an Egyptian, met in July 2001. Shaikh Mohammed reportedly was the head of Usama bin Laden's terror operations and was the mastermind of the Sept. 11 attacks, the 1998 U.S. embassy bombings in Kenya, the Bali nightclub bombings, the murder of Wall Street Journal reporter Daniel Pearl and other Al Qaeda attacks. The two captured terrorists denied any relationship between the hijackers and Lebanese Hezbollah, the Iranian-sponsored Shiite militant organization that is on the U.S. State Department list of terrorist groups,

---

[98] This is from, "Terror Alliance Has U.S. Worried: Hezbollah, Al Qaeda Seen Joining Forces," Washington Post, Dana priest and Douglas Farah, June 30, 2002, front page. These Hezbollah-al-Qaeda alliance allegations started right after 9/11. For example: "Terror Network Travels Under Many Names," The Record (New Jersey) (Knight-Ridder Newspapers), John Dorschner, Sept. 28, 2001, page A23.

according to the Sept. 11 commission's report... There is strong evidence that Iran facilitated the transit of Al Qaeda members into and out of Afghanistan before Sept. 11; some were future 9/11 hijackers, the report concluded. There is also circumstantial evidence that senior Lebanese Hezbollah operatives were closely tracking the travel of some of the hijackers into Iran in November 2000. [99]

Thus, the question is: Since al-Qaeda is a CIA PMF, is it better to believe that (a) Hezbollah is influenced by the CIA, or (b) not influenced by the CIA? Obviously the most rational decision is to assert that there *is influence* on Hezbollah by the CIA. How can groups that interact *not* influence one another? If the groups are so closely interrelated and perhaps amalgamated, as to even have co-origination, how *can't* they have influence? If CIA/al-Qaeda influences Hezbollah, then the two are not entirely separate, and thus Hezbollah is to some greater or lesser degree a CIA operation. But CIA influence can only be for CIA operations. For these reasons, our best analysis of Hezbollah is to conclude that first-and-foremost, they are CIA, not non-CIA.

It all however died away (at least in the mass media). And instead, we are now, in 2009, being delivered a much more straightforward Iraq-like WMD-scare-story, just as we were leading up to the 2003 Iraq invasion. Again, as I said, it seems like history is about to repeat, and it's simply amazing that Americans have so little memory and analytical skills that they can't pick up on this.

Iran: Stepping-Stone to World War III

James Woolsey, PNAC member[100], and former director of the CIA during the Clinton Administration, interviewed by Sean Hannity on Fox News Channel on July 18, 2006 on the Hannity and Colmes Show, without any evidence, said that

Iran [is involved in a] coordinated attack on the West... We should not let this opportunity go by... We should not stand here and wait... We would be not stretching at all... Strike from the air..."

In this section, I will discuss how this conflict—a conflict which will surely rage on after this book has gone to the publisher—like Iraq, is merely another preemptive war, based on no evidence, and on a false reality (which is the primary ingredient in brainwashing). But Iran is a weapons customer of Russia, and the principal oil source for China. Thus, the impending US invasion of Iran should quickly lead to the next staged, planned world war

---

[99] "What's Iran Got to Do With It?" Fox News, Liza Porteus, July 27, 2004.
[100] See Grupp 2007 for discussion of PNAC.

originated by the partnered heads of state, in this case Russia, China, Canada, Mexico, Iran,[101] and the United States.

Polls about the Iraq War in previous sections showed that support and faith in that war lost a lot of its strength after two years into the war. At that time of decreasing support for the Iraq war, scare-propaganda about Iran and North Korea began to fill the news media. Both were portrayed the same way and just as the Iraq war in 2002-2003: as seeking or having WMDs, with no question that they will at least have serious intentions of using them on Americans.[102]

---

[101] I cannot prove that Iran's head, President Mahmoud Ahmadinejad, is secretly working with PNAC, the CIA, Russia, China, and so on, in coordinating the impending World War III, but I hold that this is the better assertion than maintaining that Iran is genuinely an enemy of the USA—a spontaneous and accidental enemy rather than a planned enemy—due to the fact that the history of the CIA in Iran shows that this is how Iran often finds their leaders: US forces covertly implant them. See my discussion about SAVAK. Therefore, by induction, I am forced to hold the position that Iran is secretly staging tension with the US leaders rather than genuinely carrying it out. Furthermore, the Iranian government and what is perhaps the most powerful corporation of all in America, Halliburton, which is certainly a name synonymous with the phrase, "Iraq War," and appears to be the most powerful corporation of the military-industrial complex, *have a business partnership*, according to Reuters, the Washington Post, and other newspapers. See these citations: "Halliburton probed over Iran ties," Reuters, July 20, 2004; "Halliburton Doing Business With the 'Axis of Evil'," Washington Post, *Jefferson Morley,* February 3, 2005; "Doing Business With The Enemy," CBS, Aug. 29, 2004; "Halliburton Secretly Doing Business with Key Member of Iran's Nuclear Team," Globalresearch.ca, August 5, 2005, Jason Leopold; "Business As Usual? Halliburton's CEO says his company is pulling out of Iran. But a corporate subsidiary is still going ahead with a deal to develop Tehran's natural gas fields," Newsweek, Michael Isikoff and Mark Hosenball. There are many other accounts of this secret dealing. There are other issues also, such as the well-known facts that Iran has been given nuclear supplies by the US government. For example, see "George Bush insists that Iran must not be allowed to develop nuclear weapons. So why, six years ago, did the CIA give the Iranians blueprints to build a bomb?" London Guardian, James Risen, January 6 2006.

[102] As is well documented, the United States sold nuclear weapons arms and equipment to each of these countries. For example, Donald Rumsfeld worked for a company that sold nuclear reactors to North Korea Karel (2004). Also see the following articles from the national media: "Rummy's North Korea Connection - What did Donald Rumsfeld know about ABB's deal to build nuclear reactors there? And why won't he talk about it?", by Richard Behar Research Associate Brenda Cherry, May 12, 2003, *Fortune Magazine*, also posted at CNN Money on the Internet: http://money.cnn.com/magazines/fortune/fortune_archive/2003/05/12/

Americans are now told through their national American media that the biggest terrorist threat of all is Iran, and that Iranians have violently hated Americans for decades (specific news footage will be cited later in this section). News bombarded Americans with the story just after 9/11/2001 that *celebrations* over the dead in America were allegedly going on in some Arab regions.[103] In the years following 9/11, Americans have been fooled into believing that "Iranians hate Americans," to put it in the way that media actors, such as Newt Gingrich, David Horowitz, and countless others put it, and thus some Iranians may have "cheered" on 9/11. But we find that on September 14, 2001, in a *far* less reported story, and in respect for the dead of the 9/11 terrorist event, 60,000 fans at the World Cup game in Tehran observed a full minute of silence for the victims of the 9/11 attacks.[104] We also find that the Iranian government in Tehran denounced the September 11 attacks.[105] Yet we are told that Iranians hate Americans, and are eager for the deaths of Americans? Not even four months passed from the time of the September 14, 2001 minute of silence by 60,000 Iranian citizens, before President Bush told Americans the following in his 2002 State of the Union speech:

Iran aggressively pursues these weapons and exports terror, while an unelected few repress the Iranian people's hope for freedom... States like these, and their terrorist allies, constitute an axis of evil, arming to threaten the peace of the world. By seeking weapons of mass destruction, these regimes pose a grave and growing danger. They could provide these arms to terrorists, giving them the means to match their hatred. They could attack our allies or attempt to blackmail the United

---

342316/index.htm. See also Newsweek, February 17, 2003. As for Iran, see a footnote just given.

[103] See "While Some Arabs Rejoice at Attack on America, Others Pause to Reflect," Associated Press, Donna Bryson, September 12, 2001.

[104] "Congress Approves Use of Force; Military Patrols Cities and Ports, Bush Rallies Nation, Tours Disaster Area," by David Von Drehle, Washington Post, page A1, September 15, 2001. And according to the Associated Press article, "Iran Holds Minute of Silence for Attack Victims," on September 14, 2001:

Iran held a minute of silence before Friday's World Cup qualifier against Bahrain to honor those killed in terrorist attacks in the United States. The crowd of about 60,000 sat quietly, players stood on the field and TV announcers kept silent. Sixty seconds later, the referee's whistle signaled the start of play.

[105] While Some Arabs Rejoice at Attack on America, Others Pause to Reflect," September 12, 2001, by Donna Bryson, Associated Press. Also see: "Iranian Parliament Leader Condemns Attacks on US," in "Vision of the Islamic Republic of Iran, Network 1," September 13, 2001.

States. In any of these cases, the price of indifference would be catastrophic. (President George W. Bush, January 29, 2002)

And here is what one American citizen said on a CBS news station, in a news story about how researchers wanted to go into Iran in order to dig up Biblical archaeological items there: "'I really didn't think we were going to get into Iran. What are the chances that ground zero, the country that hates America the most, that we could get in?' said Texan Arch Bonnema."[106] Notice how no evidence is presented, just a vague claim of a threat, which has not been verified, and which cannot be verified.

Iran 2003

Next I will discuss the evolution of this propaganda campaign against Iran, which started even before the American military preemptively launched attacks on Iraq. Consider a set of CNN/USA Today polls that are from three months after the March 2003 Iraq invasion ("Shock and Awe"), and long before the barrage of propaganda about the "Iran threat" that constantly hit the wires in 2005:

CNN/USA Today/Gallup Poll. June 27-29, 2003. Nationwide:

"Thinking for a moment about Iran: As you may know, the U.S. believes Iran is either providing assistance to terrorists or attempting to develop weapons of mass destruction. Do you think the United States should or should not go to war with Iran?" Form A (N=483, MoE ± 5)

Should:	27%
Should Not:	67%
No Opinion:	6%

"How likely do you think it is that Iran is developing weapons of mass destruction: very likely, somewhat likely, not too likely, or not at all likely?" Options rotated; Form B (N=520, MoE ± 5)

Very Likely:	46%
Somewhat Likely:	38%
Not Too Likely:	11%
Not At All Likely:	2%
No Opinion:	3%

---

[106] This came from a segment called "Texans Part Of Possible Noah's Ark Discovery," Brooke Richie reporting, June 26, 2006, CBS 11 news, Dallas. As of July 16, 2006, this story was located at http://cbs11tv.com/topstories/local_story_177234625.html.

"How likely do you think it is that Iran is providing assistance to terrorists: very likely, somewhat likely, not too likely, or not at all likely?" Options rotated; Form B (N=520, MoE ± 5)

Very Likely:	58%
Somewhat Likely:	31%
Not Too Likely:	4%
Not At All Likely:	3%
No Opinion:	4%

These polls show that on the one hand, Americans had no desire to enter another war. On the other hand, the vast majority thought that Iran was developing weapons of mass destruction, even though no proof had been presented (just as in the case of the nonexistent WMDs in Iraq). More interestingly, nearly all Americans drew a connection between terrorists and Iran, where the relationship was a threatening one in the eyes of Americans—again, no proof for this whatsoever had been established or put forth.

Proof is proof, and there is no grey area between proof and not-proof. It is not "somewhat likely," to use the words that the polls uses, that the sky is blue; it either is or is not blue; and to verify this, all one needs to do is look up. If CNN and USA Today gave a poll that asked, "Please give us your opinion on whether or not the sky is blue," on a sunny day the poll would result in 100 percent affirmative that it is, because it is merely a proven fact that it is, and the polled people would have seen it is so with their own eyes. There is no guessing or opinion about this issue, and about any issues that are proven. And, in fact, there needn't be any poll that asks whether or not the sky is blue, because everybody knows it is.

These issues get at the real absurdity of the polls, since they ask the polled people to give an opinion as to whether or not there is proof, which is Orwellian doublespeak. You can't give your *opinion* on something that is provable: you can't give your opinion on whether or not you believe that the sky is blue, that humans have two eyes and four limbs, and on whether or not the earth exists. Those are just facts, and thus they are not in the domain of opinion. Asking the polled people to give their opinion on whether or not there is proof on something is like asking them this (using the wording found in the poll): Is it "somewhat likely" we have proof that the sky is blue?

These polls occurred during the high time for American support of the Iraq War, a time when Americans had the "Axis of Evil" implanted in their minds as a "grave threat," when Americans largely were not focused at all on having actual evidence presented to them before answering polls questions.

We have just seen that in 2003, Americans apparently were against war with Iran, but the CNN/USA Today polls surprisingly indicate that at the same time a preference for *military action* against Iran.

The Los Angeles Times Poll. April 2-3, 2003. N=745 adults nationwide. MoE ± 4 (total sample).

"There is evidence that Iran is developing nuclear weapons and other weapons of mass destruction. Do you think the U.S. should or should not take military action against Iran if they continue to develop these weapons?"

	Should %	Should Not %	Don't Know %
ALL	50	36	14
Democrats	52	38	10
Independents	45	44	11
Republicans	59	30	11

The difference in language, "war" vs. "military action," is not clarified in the poll's question, but I presume that to the Americans who took these polls in 2003, "military action" just means something like "one day offensives," whereas "war" would appear to mean something like the occupation of Iraq.

Conclusion: Brainwashing by the Drip Method

On January 21, 2006, at 4:40 pm EST, on the Fox News Channel, Lt. Gen. Thomas McInerney told the viewers that "there is strong evidence that Osama has forged an alliance with Iran." Now it is critically important to note that *there was no presentation of what this evidence is.* Then McInerney told his viewers about Iran's relations with Syria and North Korea, and how he believed Osama could get, or has, nuclear, chemical, or biological WMDs. He said we need to be "very concerned." On May 31, 2006, on the "The Factor" on the Fox News Channel, Bill O'Reilly held an extensive interview Condoleeza Rice. This interview started off with Bill O'Reilly informing the audience that China and Russia don't want to help Americans out with the "Iran threat," and shortly after that comment O'Reilly said that "if Iran gets a bomb, that's the end of all nuclear restraint in the world." And shortly after that, after, Rice maintained that Russia and China have to "make a choice." And she further stated that "Iran having a nuclear weapon would be *devastating.*"

The New York Times, on May 19, 2006, exhibited a huge front page story describing how Iran was not cooperating with weapons inspectors—just like the stories about Iraq giving trouble to "the inspectors," in 1997, or 2002, or some other time. The Times article also involved the following passage:

As a result, the world is losing much of its ability to answer pressing questions about Iran's nuclear ambitions: how fast Tehran could make an atom bomb, and whether it harbors a program to do so.[107]

Notice that this is an admission that nobody knows whether or not there is a "spooky" Iranian "nuke the USA" program.

The "Iran threat" has been built up over time, gradually, via the corporatist US media system, to the point where it is very solidly locked into the mind of the average American. Consider what scientists say about "dripping" of information periodically to the citizenry accomplishes:

> ...television often influences viewers by what [is called] the "drip" model, a process of subtle and gradual incorporation of frequent and repeated messages. Because many effects of television on beliefs and attitudes occur in accretions over time, the fantasy world of television can cultivate a subtly pervasive view of the real world, in which television images are blended inextricably with other sources of information. This assumption is supported by the finding in many studies that the more television individuals watch, the more they believe and accept its messages about society. Gradual cumulative influences of the medium are difficult to measure with available social-science methods; therefore, we find ourselves in the position of having a plausible but not proven set of conclusion about the influence of television on many of the domains of interest in this volume.[108]

The steady stream of information through the Big Media about the so-called "Iran threat" is to be expected in a corporatist nation, since corporatists profit off of the chaos of war. Television creates a fantasy world; an unrealistic cinema about non-reality, which citizens are tricked into believing is reality. Since the mass of Americans think the unreal cinema is real, there is little choice but to label this as mass brainwashing. A fantasy world is a world of invisible mental things, of things that do not exist, like unicorns, Santa Claus, and round squares. But nevertheless, the average telescreen-world American has been tricked into believing that make-believe is true reality: they have been tricked into believing that what they cannot see is real, and what they can see is not real. They will learn to believe that al-Qaeda is real (even though they have never seen it, other than a few vague and contradictory pictures from CNN, for example), and that evolution correctly describes humanity (even though they have no evidence they have

---

[107] "Iran's Secrecy Widens Gap in Nuclear Intelligence," New York Times, Friday May 19, front page.
[108] Huston, Donnerstein, Fairchild, Feshbach, Katz, Murray, Rubinstein, Wilcox, and Zuckerman 1992, 6.

ever seen that this is the case). The average American learns to think that intangible abstractions are real, and that concrete fact is unreal.

On July 6, 2006, speaking on CNN's Larry King Live, President George Bush Jr. expressed his case against Iran:

> There's a lot of worries about them [Iran] having a nuclear weapon. There's a worry about political blackmail, there's a worry that they would harm our ally Israel; there's a series of worries. And the good news is, *Larry*, that most nations now understand the danger of the Iranians having a nuclear weapon.

All of these "reasons" presented by Bush Jr. are *abstractions*: no visible evidence can be given that any of these things will happen. This quote merely involves the ruse showing that the "Iran threat" is something to dread. It is part of false flag or fake war operations, and thus Bush can only talk in terms of abstraction and unverifiable issues (issues about non-reality), since no evidence of a threat exists.

The United States consists of 300 million people who have been raised on information about non-reality, and thus the US is a nation of people who live in the domain of the unreal, of make-believe, which is the matrix that I discussed at the start of this chapter. The evidence presented in this chapter is very simple, and it shows that the human consciousness of the average American has been destroyed, since it is based in a make-believe domain of fear and terror that the telescreen infuses, rather than in the poetics of the natural world.

3. The New Propaganda: "Educational TV"

The History Channel: "Iran: the Next Iraq?"

Often "educational" channels that are part of American cable networks are viewed to be good sources of information. It is my understanding that many American academics are not afraid to view these channels, and perhaps often even believe they are getting reliable information, and sometimes almost unquestioningly believing that they are getting the opinions and positions of experts, where not a lot of questioning is needed. I even see my colleagues in the universities I have taught at use material from the History Channel, National Geographic Channel, and so on, as lecture material in their classes. My students in my classes very typically will freely quote and cite information from these channels: "I saw on *The History Channel* that …"

In this chapter I will show how these channels—such as *The Discovery Channel*,[109] *The History Channel*,[110] *The National Geographic Channel*,[111] and so on[112]—are merely part of the propaganda network of the telescreen world discussed in chapter 1, since the corporatist media operate and control these channels. Thus any information that comes out of them is to be considered information as pre-approved by a communist,[113] corporatist

---

[109] Owned by Discovery Communications Inc., a supermassive 100+ channel global media megalith including The Science Channel, Discovery Kids, The Military Channel, The Learning Channel, and The Travel Channel. Discovery Communications Inc. is owned by

Discovery Holding Company, whose CEO is John C. Malone, whom Al Gore called the "Darth Vader of cable," and who has ties to News Corp and Rupert Murdoch. He is also CEO of several other media companies, including Liberty Media.

1. Cox Communications, which is controlled by the daughters of James Middleton Cox, who are two of the richest people in the world.

2. Advance/Newhouse Communications, a titanic media enterprise.

3. John S. Hendricks, CEO of Discovery Communications Inc.

[110] Owned by A&E Television Networks, which owns The Military History Channel (different from The Military Channel), to name one of many. A&E is owned by (a) The Walt Disney Company, (b) The Hearst Corporation, and (c) NBC Universal, which is a merger of GE's NBC with Vivendi, a French company.

[111] Partially owned by Rupert Murdoch.

[112] The previous few footnotes, documenting how enmeshed and massive the media industry is, give some indication as to its unification and oneness. For example, The Walt Disney Company owns ABC, is partial owner of ESPN, A&E (and thus the History Channel), Lifetime, just to name a few.

[113] See Grupp 2007, chapter 3, for reasons why corporatists systems, such as the US, are communistic systems.

system. This "educational television" is a nearly unimaginably powerful propaganda tool since, as just mentioned, it is ubiquitously believed to be genuine educational television by Americans.

We can get a real indication of how powerful corporatist-owned "educational TV" is if we look at a few polls[114]:

The Harris Poll. Nov. 14-18, 2002. N=1,010 adults nationwide. MoE ± 3: "Would you generally trust each of the following types of people to tell the truth, or not?" Percentage who would be trusted.

	2002	2001	1998
	%	%	%
Teachers	80	88	86
Doctors	77	84	83
Professors	75	77	77
Police officers	69	78	75
Scientists	68	76	79
The President	65	79	54
Judges	65	75	79
The ordinary man or woman	65	74	71
Civil servants	65	71	70
Clergymen or priests	64	90	85
Military officers	64	67	*
Accountants	55	*	*
Bankers	51	*	*
TV newscasters	46	54	44
Pollsters	44	51	55
Journalists	39	49	43
Members of Congress	35	42	46
Trade union leaders	30	37	37
Lawyers	24	*	*
Stockbrokers	23	*	*
Business leaders	*	43	49

Gallup Poll. Nov. 17-20, 2005. N=1,002 adults nationwide. MoE ± 3: "Please tell me how you would rate the honesty and ethical standards of people in these different fields: very high, high, average, low, or very low?"

---

[114] These polls are from pollingreport.com.

Nurses	82	Building contractors	20
Druggists, pharmacists	67	Lawyers	18
Medical doctors	65	Labor union leaders	16
High school teachers	64	Business executives	16
Policemen	61	Stockbrokers	16
Clergy	54	Senators	16
Funeral directors	44	Congressmen	14
Bankers	41	Advertising practitioners	11
Accountants	39	Car salesmen	8
Journalists	28	Telemarketers	7
Real estate agents	20		

Notice how the polls indicate that public trust in people seems to be highest for teachers and professors (and, for example, nurses), but trust in the corporatists and similar people (stockbrokers, etc.) is consistently at the lowest end. Now, here is the interesting issue that arises with so-called "educational television:"

Teachers and professors (highly trusted) are commonly presented on "educational television," but they present information on corporatist (highly distrusted) shows ("educational television"). Thus the corporatists are *hidden behind* what appear to be teachers and intellectuals (since educational television shows consistently use quotes and work from specific selected academics), sending out corporatist-approved information through them. So some of the most trusted group of persons in society (professors, teachers) are conveying information that is really from the least trusted group of persons in society (corporatists).

To see what this leads to, I will consider a few examples.

First I will consider The History Channel's hour-long show that aired on June 16, 2006, called "Iran: The Next Iraq?" The title indicates the agenda that this documentary wants to instill in the minds of Americans. The documentary consisted of a continual stream of discussion of Iranian hate for Americans (which we saw in the last chapter does not exist[115]), about how a ground-war is impossible in Iran (since, the documentary claimed, Iran has over seven million troops), about Iran acquiring a nuclear bomb and sending it in the direction of the United States to a city near you, and so on.

From what I could tell, the information in this documentary was indistinguishable from the corporatist news media (Fox News, CNN, etc.) of the same time in 2006. For example, the documentary claimed that Iran is "a

---

[115] Also, interestingly, on the Alex Jones radio show, on July 2, 2007, Jones interviewed an Iranian who reported that the Iranian people are actually pro-USA, and they were totally confused as to why the US wanted to invade their country!

radical Islamic republic," which means it is a *terrorist state*, since "radical Islam" in the mainstream American corporatist media in 2006 equals "terrorism." This is an example of an "educational television" channel labeling an entire nation (and apparently the civilians included in this) as "terrorist," which was standard in the corporatist media during the time that I wrote in this book.

"Experts" in the documentary repeatedly claimed that: Iran is intent on "getting a bomb" (a nuclear bomb); US intelligence agencies must assume that Iran "will be a nuclear nation in five years;" and there is evidence they are going to use the bomb, most likely on the United States. However, evidence for any of these claims was never presented. It was therefore hard to distinguish this "educational documentary" from the news media's din in 2002 and up to the invasion of Iraq in March 2003, their roar and din telling the American citizenry how Iraq is a dangerous threat, with no evidence supplied (see chapter 1). It is therefore difficult to see how this *History Channel* "educational television documentary" was any different from that non-evidential, corporatist warmongering media propaganda. Put another way, it is tough to see how this *History Channel* documentary was anything other than an advertisement and propaganda film for the next Bush-esque pre-emptive warfare.

Add to this that the documentary also actually claimed that it is likely that Iran would retaliate against us by carrying out *terrorist attacks against elementary schools in the Midwest*, with no evidence for why this claim was presented. The documentary included countless fast-paced images of nuclear bombs going off, flashing skulls, cartoon images of horror and terror, etc. Also in this documentary there were "experts" showing us pictures from US satellites or planes of supposed nuclear sites in Iran. These were astonishingly reminiscent of the famous episode discussed in chapter 1: Colin Powell at the UN leading up to the start of the Iraq War, showing pictures of Iraq's supposed WMD sites. Those pictures were all in some way or another fraudulent and bogus, such as being animation rather than photos, or photos from the late 1980s of long-expired weapons that the *United States* had provided to Iraq.

On a given evening, prime-time viewing for the aforementioned and other "educational TV" channels will typically be dominated, without exaggerating, by pro-military, anti-scientific, superstitious, pseudo-intellectual, and propagandistic material—all presented with the attempt to *appear* as academic, intellectual, scientific material. In May and June of 2006, I noticed that the typical prime-time shows on these channels had the following titles: "Big Oil Rigs," "Bible Prophecy," "The Science of the Bible," "Megastructures," "Banned from the Bible," "Dog Whisperer,"

"Crop Circles," "I Shouldn't be Alive," "Bible Code," "Armageddon," and, of course, "Iran: The Next Iraq?"

National Geographic's "Shock and Awe"

Next I will discuss another documentary on "educational cable TV" that appeared on the National Geographic Channel, called "Shock and Awe." The creators of this documentary continually informed the viewer about the magnificence, virtue, and glory of the initial 48-hour invasion and massacre (hence the name, "Shock and Awe") of Iraq in March 2003. This documentary does not mention that the initiators of this war—PNAC and the corporatist New World Order proponents[116]—blatantly lied to the American people in order to start this war. For instance, Colin Powell in Cincinnati on October 7, 2002: "the risk is simply too great that Saddam Hussein will use instruments of mass death and destruction, or provide them to a terror network."[117] And consider President Bush's radio address on February 8, 2003:

> The Iraqi regime's violations of Security Council Resolutions are evident, they are dangerous to America and the world, and they continue to this hour. The regime has never accounted for a vast arsenal of deadly, biological and chemical weapons. To the contrary, the regime is pursuing an elaborate campaign to conceal its weapons materials and to hide or intimidate key experts and scientists. This effort of deception is directed from the highest levels of the Iraqi regime, including Saddam Hussein, his son, Iraq's vice president, and the very official responsible for cooperating with inspectors. The Iraqi regime has actively and secretly attempted to obtain equipment needed to produce chemical, biological and nuclear weapons. Firsthand witnesses have informed us that Iraq has at least seven mobile factories for the production of biological agents — equipment mounted on trucks and rails to evade discovery. The Iraqi regime has acquired and tested the means to deliver weapons of mass destruction. It has never accounted for thousands of bombs and shells capable of delivering chemical weapons. It is actively pursuing components for prohibited ballistic missiles. And we have sources that tell us that Saddam Hussein recently authorized Iraqi field commanders to use chemical weapons — the very weapons the dictator tells us he does not have.

---

[116] See Grupp 2007

[117] "MEMORANDUM FOR: The President FROM: Veteran Intelligence Professionals for Sanity," February 7, 2003, CommonDreams.org. http://www.commondreams.org/views03/0207-04.htm.

The Invasion of Iraq was based on this sort of falsehood. It is easy to see that the Administration knew they were falsehoods, and deliberately ridiculed any persons who stood in their way (such as the weapons inspector, Blix, who turned out to be correct.) Clearly, the administration criminally acted to fool the American people.[118] Thus, this National Geographic documentary from Rupert Murdoch's News Corp. (majority owner of the National Geographic Channel), can only be considered part of the propaganda network. The conclusion is that like the History Channel, the National Geographic Channel functions as a propaganda network disguised as "educational television."

This National Geographic Channel documentary is also replete with untruths, impossibilities, absurdities, and is virtually indistinguishable from the news (e.g., Fox News) of the mass media that was complicit in brainwashing Americans into the Iraq War, as showed in chapter 1. The film refers to the US military force as "the greatest force of destruction in history." The documentary holds the very same appearance as the corporate news of the mass media, in being a sort of Orwellian war cinema. It looks just like a Hollywood action film with endless military action: fast planes, perpetual explosions, red fire shooting out of planes taking off, missiles launching like lightning, dazzling night-vision lighted warfare, fast tanks, even nukes going off in Japan at the end of World War II.

The greatest bit of propaganda and blatant untruth about this film is its repeated reference to how the "Shock and Awe" campaign was meant to not harm civilians. US military leaders had as a primary objective to design what amounted to a Nazi "scare invasion" or *Blitzkrieg* (hence the name "Shock and Awe." This comes from the Nazi military philosophy: bombard and obliterate the opponent with such a horrific display of military force that the opponent will be prompted to just give up.

I document in detail elsewhere in this book (and in Grupp 2007) that the aforementioned civilian protection did not occur. One million Iraqi civilians had already been killed from Gulf War I (Desert Storm) up to the March 2003 invasion[119] by unjust US-led sanctions on Iraq. The Lancet, a leading medical journal, came out with a study that showed that over 660,000 were killed in Iraq from the March 2003 invasion through the beginning of 2006.

At 15 minutes into the National Geographic "Shock and Awe" documentary, the narrators tells the viewers that "thousands of civilians were

---

[118] See Karel 2004 for interviews with Blix and many other experts and for excellent analysis of the way that the Bush Administration and the military connected to it have acted criminally to bring about this war.

[119] See Landon 2007; Brohy and Ungerman 2001.

killed in Japan in World War II." This is not necessarily a lie, but it is said in a way that gives a false impression, and makes it appear that the documentary is lying to the viewer. This is because the word "thousands" usually is meant to refer to, say, under 5 thousand, 9 thousand, or perhaps 12 thousand, since if one is talking about 30 thousand or more, one would say, "tens of thousands," not "thousands." Now the fact is that narrator forgets to inform the viewer that, according to General McNamara (Secretary of Defense during the Vietnam War), there were episodes during World War II when American forces killed *100,000 Japanese civilians in just one night!*[120] Maintaining that "thousands of civilians were killed in Japan in World War II" is not a lie, I suppose, but it is a *Fox News* way of putting things, that certainly makes things appear different than they are.

The National Geographic Channel's "Shock and Awe" documentary glorifies war, making it appear like necessary, inevitable, and even sporty theater, rather than a fabricated, deceptive, and deliberately staged profiteering enterprise by corporatists.[121] It makes war appear MTV-like, like a football game, a natural part of human behavior, rather than a product of brainwashing. Going to war is not a natural behavior by volition, but rather is a trick to get people to act in an irrational and suicidal way, to forgo their dreams in life in order to go and kill people they do not know, and who have never been shown concretely to be any sort of threat to them.

Information Warfare

Educational television appears to be part of a larger plan by the corporatists: to use psychological warfare against Americans.

One tactic of psychological warfare is to spray all sorts of easily accessible information at people from apparently credible sources, but which involve diametrically opposed (contradictory) messages. For example, one doctor who is very respectable will show conclusively that vaccines are harmful to children, but then the FDA (which is a government agency) will show concretely that vaccines are safe. When encountering this sort of informational contradiction, the average busy American, who does not have time to figure out what is going on, who is lying and who is telling the truth, will merely give up, not knowing what to believe. They will not be inclined to believe that the "prestigious" FDA is lying, and they will not be inclined to believe that the prestigious doctor is lying either. Thus they will have no idea what to believe at all, and will most likely just put it out of their mind, give up, and merely do whatever everybody else does, naturally conforming their

---

[120] This is according to an interview with McNamara in Morris 2004.

[121] See Grupp 2007 for more information.

behavior to the group ("group think") rather than using intellect and reason to figure the issue out.

This spontaneous conformity that humans exhibit is one of the primary reasons that secret governmental operations work so successfully. Millions of Americans can, for example, be taught to go along with things like the mass murder in Iraq, abortion, the battle of the sexes, consumerism, organized non-experiential [conformity-based rather than experience-based] religion, and so on. A sort of psychological warfare can be observed to pervade American information: college textbooks, mass media, educational television, church information, and so on. Each of these segments of society has been thoroughly infiltrated by the corporatists and their secret lobbyists, think tanks, intelligence agencies (CIA, etc.), and other corporate research organizations,[122] all in order to control and confuse Americans so as to shape their behavior and consciousness in a desired, yet denigrated, way.

The United States is currently a domain of information war. This is not necessarily a new sort of warfare, but it is at a level never seen before. It consists of bombarding the citizenry with so much conflicting but seemingly credible information that they cannot know anything at all, and are left helpless ("the people perish for lack of knowledge," as the saying goes). This is *information war*, and we can verify that it is a deliberate war against We the People. It has been documented as a Pentagon priority, as in Rumsfeld's *The Information Operations Roadmap*, a recently declassified 78-page document which gives some detail about the Pentagon's plans. Here are the first few pages out of that hard-to-follow, murkily written, declassified document, with many blacked-out parts:

B. Key Assumptions and Objective (U)

- (U) Key assumptions. Information, always important in warfare, is now critical to military success and will only become more so in the foreseeable future. Three key assumptions underscore the growing importance of information:

    - (U) Effectively communicating U.S. Government (USG) capabilities and intentions is an important means of combating the plans of our adversaries. The ability to rapidly disseminate persuasive information to diverse audiences in order

* The 15 supporting study efforts reflected 2004 DPG guidance. They were as follows: Overarching Information Operations Roadmap Requirements; Policies & Procedural Controls; Relation of IO with Public Diplomacy and Public Affairs; IO Organization; IO Career Force; IO Education and Training; IO Analytic Support; Computer Network Attack; Computer Network Defenses; Computer Network Defense Threat Attribution; Computer Network Insider Threats; Electronic-Space Analysis Center; Transforming Electronic Warfare Capabilities; Psychological Operations; Operations Security.

SECRET//NOFORN   3

---

[122] See Grupp 2007, and Rampton and Stauber 2001, for more information on this infiltration, and on this secretive nature of the secret groups that work for the corporatists in order to control thought.

SECRET//NOFORN

3. Executive Summary (U)

A. Conclusions (U)

- (U) The IO Roadmap participants collectively identified three matters of key importance that require immediate attention:

- (S) We Must Fight the Net. DoD is building an information-centric force. Networks are increasingly the operational center of gravity, and the Department must be prepared to "fight the net." ████████████████████████████████ but be fully prepared to ensure critical warfighting network functionality and to ███████████████████████████████████████

  - (S) However, networks are vulnerable now, and barring significant attention, will become increasingly more vulnerable. ████████████████████████
  ███

  - (S) The recommendations of this report offer a good start point for remedial action for network security to maintain decision superiority. A robust, layered, defense in depth strategy is the next necessary step in providing Combatant Commanders with the tools necessary to preserve warfighting capability.

- (U) We Must Improve PSYOP. Military forces must be better prepared to use PSYOP in support of military operations and the themes and messages employed in a PSYOP campaign must be consistent with the broader national security objectives and national-level themes and messages. Currently, however, our PSYOP campaigns are often reactive and not well organized for maximum impact.

  - (U) PSYOP enhancements outlined in this report, and clarification of the respective responsibilities and tasks associated with PSYOP, DoD support to public diplomacy and public affairs, will enhance DoD's ability to aggressively conduct IO and to do so fully consistent with broader national security objectives.

  - (U) In particular, PSYOP must be refocused on adversary decision-making, planning well in advance for aggressive behavior modification during times of conflict. PSYOP products must be based on in-depth knowledge of the audience's decision-making processes and the factors influencing his decisions, produced rapidly at the highest quality standards, and powerfully disseminated directly to targeted audiences throughout the area of operations.

- (U) We Must Improve Network and Electro-Magnetic Attack Capability. To prevail in an information-centric fight, it is increasingly important that our forces dominate the electromagnetic spectrum with attack capabilities.

SECRET//NOFORN   6

B. The Foundation for Building a Core Military Competency (U)

- (U) A uniform understanding and appreciation of IO should be based on a common DoD framework that includes a full spectrum concept of IO built upon three broad IO functions, five integrated core IO capabilities and a supporting definition as described below.

- (U) Three integrated IO functions. The Department's concept of IO should emphasize full spectrum IO that makes a potent contribution to effects based

SECRET//NOFORN   7

SECRET//NOFORN

operations across the full range of military operations during peace, crisis and war. The concept includes three integrated IO functions of overriding importance:

- (U) Deter, discourage, dissuade and direct an adversary, thereby disrupting his unity of command and purpose while preserving our own.

- (U) Protect our plans and misdirect theirs, thereby allowing our forces to mass their effects to maximum advantage while the adversary expends his resources to little effect.

- (U) Control adversarial communications and networks and protect ours, thereby crippling the enemy's ability to direct an organized defense while preserving effective command and control of our forces.

  • (U) By extension, when executed to maximum effect, seizing control of adversary communications and networks will allow Combatant Commanders to control the enemy's network and communications-dependent weapons, infrastructure, command and control and battlespace management functions.

• (U) Peacetime preparation. The Department's IO concept should emphasize that full-spectrum information operations are full-time operations requiring extensive preparation in peacetime.

  - (U) Well before crises develop, the IO battlespace should be prepared through intelligence, surveillance and reconnaissance and extensive planning activities.

    •

• (U) Similarly, considerable effort should be made to characterize potential adversary audiences, and particularly senior decision-makers and decision-making processes and priorities. If such human factors analysis is not conducted well in advance of the conflict, it will not be possible to craft PSYOP themes and messages that will be effective in modifying adversary behavior.

• (U) Computer Network Defense (CND) and OPSEC are vital capabilities in all phases of conflict, but should be given priority especially during peacetime to prevent adversaries from preparing effective information operations or exploiting vulnerabilities against our forces. Protecting our plans and networks

SECRET//NOFORN   8

The document goes on and on like this, and approximately 40 percent of it is blacked out (so much for the "Freedom of Information Act"), but never is "the enemy" specified in the document. At some places in the document, information about "the target" is curiously blocked out. Who is being warred against? Why is it a secret? Is it "the terrorists" that the mass media perpetually talks about? If so, then why block it out? Because it's not a secret that the US government says they are targeting "the terrorists." Thus it appears likely that "the terrorists" are not what is blackened out in "the target" part of the report.

A little logic can tell us who is likely "the target." Consider that 9/11 shows,[123] as does the contamination, weaponization, and militarization of

Food (MSG, aspartame, insecticides, pesticides, heavy metals)[124]

---

[123] See Grupp 2007, chapter 1 and 4.

Water (fluoride)[125]
Medicine and vaccines[126]
Information[127]
Education[128]

show, that the US corporatist government is out to hurt, injure, and torment the American citizenry.[129] Consider also that the American mass media exhibit elements of what is written in the Rumsfeld document. All these details lead us to the conclusion that We the People are "the target" that is blacked out in the document: the information warfare in the Rumsfeld document is certainly most likely declared against We the People (and all the peoples of the world).

This information warfare is visible throughout the mass media in the United States (even though the average American, with their denigrated/destroyed consciousness can't see it, can't put it together). The coverage of the 9/11 attacks in the government (corporatist) - owned media gives us good examples of this information warfare. The September 11, 2006 issue of *Time* magazine had an article about what the magazine called the "9/11 conspiracy myths" on the front cover. The word "myths" is telling the public that the "conspiracy theorists" are wrong, before evidence is presented in the article.

In the article itself, the evidence consists of little more than information war tactics. Right near the start of the article we find a paragraph about the blockbuster Internet film, *Loose Change* that reads as follows:

For all its amateur production values—it [the documentary *Loose Change Second Ed.*] was created by a pair of industrious twenty-somethings using a laptop, pizza money and footage scavenged from the Internet—Loose Change is a compelling experience. Take the section about the attack on the Pentagon. As the film points out—and this is a tent pole issue among 9/11 conspiracists—the crash site doesn't look right. There's not enough damage. The hole smashed in the Pentagon's outer wall was 75 ft. wide, but a Boeing 757 has a 124-ft. wingspan. Why wasn't the hole wider? Why does it look so neat?

---

[124] See Grupp 2007.
[125] Ibid.
[126] Ibid.
[127] See Chapter 1 above.
[128] See Grupp 2007, chapter 4..
[129] See Grupp 2007. for copious information on this issue.

This is info war. Why? Each sentence can be proven to be a misrepresentation, but the public, who has not looked into the issues about 9/11, would not know the difference. They will assume that big and grand *Time* magazine could never lie, and therefore, the "twenty-somethings using a laptop and pizza money" must be just silly kids. The passage makes it appear that the filmmakers merely surfed the internet, and then threw together, patchwork, a dumpy film that is devoid of any real evidence. But if one watches the film, one finds that actual video news footage from September 11, 2001 is used extensively for visual evidence. The filmmakers consult scientists and journalists, fireman, police, and so on.

I am however more concerned with the rest of the paragraph about the damage at the Pentagon. As mentioned in chapters above, there are the two phases of the Pentagon on 9/11: pre-collapse, and post-collapse 25 minutes after the initial explosion. The article covers up the first pre-collapse stage, as if there were only the second phase. This is agenda-cutting: deliberately withholding information in order to create a distortion of non-information.

I have researched the work of the 911 Truth movement, and of the 9/11 skeptics *extensively* for several years, perusing thousands of documents on these subjects. Never once have I ever come across a 9/11 skeptic discussing a 75-foot post-collapse hole at the Pentagon. The article makes it appear that the principal issue that "conspiracy theorists" are concerned with is the post-collapse 75-foot hole at the Pentagon, but literally none of them have ever been concerned with that.

This presents a great example of the information war. Unless you are familiar with all the details concerned with the issues being discussed, you will only be confused and not be able to conclude anything at all.

4. Telescreen Nation: Consciousness is the Telescreen-World

"Television is reality, and reality is less than television."
—Professor Brain Oblivion, character from the film *Videodrome*

"The force possessed by totalitarian propaganda—before the movements have the power to drop iron curtains to prevent anyone's disturbing, by the slightest reality, the gruesome quiet of an entirely imaginary world—lies in its inability to shut the masses off from the real world."[130]
—Hannah Arendt

Alex: "What exactly is the treatment here going to be then?" *Nurse*: "It's quite simple really, we just need to show you some films."
—From Stanley Kubrick's film, *A Clockwork Orange*

Introduction

There are only two ways you can put things into yourself:

i. you can put them into your *mind* (via information and experiences you take in by perception), or
ii. into your *body* (via food, vaccines, chemicals and substances, and so on).

The monopolistic-globalist corporatists I discussed in my previous book, *Corporatism: The Secret Government of the New World Order*, have a lock on the market for each of these. What we put into ourselves in either of these two ways is typically not of our own choice (for example, try to find chewing gum without the poisonous toxin aspartame, or try to find television that is not propagandistic). And we Americans typically have no idea as to the real nature of the items we are putting into ourselves. For example, aluminum goes into us via vaccines, soft drinks, baking pans, baking soda, deodorant, and so on, and how many Americans even know this, or know that aluminum is a severe brain toxin? Americans typically have no idea in the first place that harmful things are continually going into them via their minds and bodies. Also, the corporatists promote humans to put things into themselves that are poisonous and/or deadly. The corporatists do this in order to further their financial, economic, and feudal control, in order to keep the ordinary citizens subdued as much as possible.[131] One thing that corporatists need in order to have maximum control is dumb citizens, and that's why aluminum, for example, is put into so many products that enter into our bodies and minds.

---

[130] Cited in Goldberg 2006, pp 22-23.
[131] See Grupp 2007 for more information on these topics.

Not surprisingly, when one looks at the culture of the United States, there seem to be some real oddities concerning the intelligence level of the citizens. I am not just referring to the falling test scores and increasingly simple and pathetic curricula and courses of the elementary school and college students. What I mean is, loosely put, that American citizens do not seem to be intelligent, and it seems that they should be smarter than they are. Let me explain what I mean.

Given the power and size of a human brain, it is suspicious and surprising that American citizens can be observed to be principally and primarily *uncritical* thinkers. They are largely unintellectual, and almost exclusively interested in entertainment, shallow and unfulfilling pleasantries (cars, plasma TVs, cell phones, etc.) The brain power and size of the human allows it to create and compute mathematics that reveals the nature of the universe, and that is no small accomplishment. We have brains *far* larger than chimpanzees, but our behaviors are all too often *not* much more accomplished than chimpanzees. The ultramassive brain-power that humans have can only be there for a reason, and what other reason could there be than to understand reality as a whole. It is by such tasks as those that humans learn the best ways to survive and succeed in the world.

So why is this grand and noble quest virtually absent from the life of the contemporary American, when it was certainly *not* in any way absent in the minds of our primitive ancestors?[132] Why is the typical American instead fooled into believing that the normal life is one spent watching television (the telescreen), and working at unfulfilling, unenjoyable, often miserable jobs very long hours for insultingly low pay? Instead of doing what is innately joyful to us, which is participating in religion and religious experience,[133] farming, and caring for children? Why do Americans so readily accept that their lives will not be of this nature, and instead will be a quasi-concentration-camp sort of life as we have in workaholic America?[134] Why do they accept that as the normal life, rather than the life of a poet, philosopher or scientist, as was so spontaneous and innately natural for our ancestors?[135]

---

[132] See Radin. 1955 (1927). *Primitive Man as Philosopher*. New York: Dover. Also see *Lost Star*, by Walter Cruttenden, St. Lynn's Press. In my opinion, Cruttenden's book is the best book on prehistory that has ever been published.

[133] For more information on why I say this, see my radio shows from March to June 2009 at www.antimatterradio.com.

[134] For reasons why I describe America in this way, see Grupp 2007.

[135] Again, I refer you to the astounding book, *Lost Star*, by Walter Cruttenden, St. Lynn's Press.

In this chapter and the next two, we will see that America resembles a textbook case of mass brainwashing. In this chapter I will describe the basics of brainwashing (especially the specific American-style brainwashing), and I will give a few examples. We will also see that this brainwashing leads to tremendous suffering for Americans—it is a matter of life and death for all Americans, and all citizens of the world. I will show how the mass media are largely responsible for constructing the consciousness of the average person in American society, while the education system, churches, and general social dynamics in America are nearly as powerful in participating in our brainwashing. This culture-wide brainwashing process is *automatic*, meaning that it is a monster out of control that seemingly cannot be shut off, and which devours and crushes hearts and minds like a wild-fire: not in any ordinary citizen's control, turning everything into itself: an atomizing destructive force. And we will see that the nature of pervasive telescreen-world stimulation is addictive, and that addiction gives the tyrants of the New World Order total control over the deep aspects of a person's consciousness, will, and self. In the next two chapters, I will focus in on the specific mechanics of the media, and how they cohere as a unit to accomplish this amazingly well-organized feat.

Books about media corruption and the non-democratic nature of media corporations are many. In this book, I do not merely repeat and/or summarize what those books have said. Rather, these next two chapters are on issues I certainly have not seen anywhere. My thesis is that the din of the ubiquitous American telescreen-world, deafening, and blaring in our minds from almost the time of our birth, is a deliberate brainwashing tool (in the strongest sense of the word "brainwashing") which *constructs* human consciousness. It creates your soul.

The Very Basics of Brainwashing

What is brainwashing?

Brainwashing is the replacement of a person's innate and spiritual subjectivity and self with a different, despiritualized, non-natural subjectivity and self, where this is done by a deliberate implanting of the new subjectivity and self by another person or group in order to get the brainwashed persons to specifically believe with utter conviction in a false reality (i.e., a non-empirical reality), where the brainwashing occurs with specific techniques (for example: repetition, monopolization of information, fear techniques, etc.), and often to get the brainwashed to commit to or participate in atrocities of various sorts.

I think the strength of this definition is the use of the word "replacement." I have seen some of the philosophers who study the thought control issues in the books *Brave New World* and *1984* discuss brainwashing along these lines, where there is a subjectivity *replacement* going on: "...Winston Smith comes to love Big Brother, and thus *ceases to be himself...*"[136] (Italics mine)

Media and Brainwashing: News is *Created*, Not Discovered

In the film *Deep Impact*, there is a tenacious mass-media news reporter, who seems to have incredible conviction and passion, and who stops for nobody and nothing to get a story out for the American public. She uncovers an amazing story that the government is hiding, about a doomsday comet that is soon going to strike the earth. The film makes it look like her boss is pleased with her drive and inner fire to get to the truth of things. There is no question he will allow her to instantly report on it, no matter what, since it is just part of his job of getting the story out.

It is important for you to know, as I will show in explicit detail in this chapter and much more in the next chapter, that this self-flattering image is *sheer fiction*, preposterous and contradictory to reality. Nowhere in the mass media (including local news stations and newspapers) does anything like this exist. Even reporters and newspaper writers do not fully realize this, but if they stopped to analyze their jobs and what they are doing every day, they would notice. We can prove this merely by noting the types of stories in all the mass media, including local news and newspapers. All mass media sources are endlessly preoccupied with meaningless tabloid issues (Britney Spears, etc.), Obama, war, the stock market, sports (and just some sports, not all of them), their take on terrorism, or Iran. But why don't they ever report on issues like these: the money-powers behind Obama;[137] suicide and SSRI antidepressants; how guns in the hands of citizens reduce crime;[138] the money behind war; how the Pentagon on 9/11 did not even have broken windows in the first 25 minutes after something exploded there; depleted uranium; corporate pollution; or aluminum in vaccines. I could almost create an endless list here, since there are so many utterly critical issues that deeply affect all Americans — never mind comets — that no corporate mass media will cover.

The point is that *the mass media report on what they are supposed to, not on anything reporters choose to report on.* They report on what is "acceptable" to their advertisers, editors, money-bosses, and so on. They are very careful to obey the conformity of the culture, and make sure not to

---

[136] Gleason and Nussbum 2005, 1.

[137] For information on this, see Alex Jones's incredible film, *The Obama Deception*.

[138] See *More Guns, Less Crime*, by John Lott, University of Chicago Press.

report on anything too "over the top," as I am sure they would phrase it. For example, if the story about the Pentagon windows just mentioned were to show up on the front page of the New York Times tomorrow; millions of people would say, "oh, that newspaper is just lowering its standards", or something like that, rather than looking into this issue. That last point is really how the system works. Humans get themselves into these idea-traps, where everybody (due to telescreen persuasion) starts to think some ideas are only for weirdos, and everybody flees from them, and mocks anybody who believes them, and the mass media reporters simply will not "succumb" to such "quackery", as Bill O'Reilly typically phrases it. No evidence on these issues will be sought; rather, people will just be too scared to be associated with them. This is the utter power of human conformity that I analyzed in a previous chapter. The mass media cannot report on things outside the pathetic "status quo" in America (and that status quo is created by the telescreen world, as you will see in this chapter and the next two).

For reasons just given, we can conclude that media information is *created*, not discovered. It is *chosen*, not found. It is manufactured and fabricated, not simply reported and conveyed to the absorbing citizens. Many examples I give in this book support these claims. Tyrannies do not involve a free press,[139] but rather involve a highly controlled press that is deliberately meant to be a force of an indoctrinating propagandistic thought control,[140] all in order to control the citizenry so that they will fully support war, monopolization, domination, slavery, and oppression.

The Unfree Press

There are many obvious and hidden ways that the press (mass media) is unfree. As for examples of the overt ways, it was widely documented after 9/11 how journalists were being fired if they dissented from, or even slightly questioned, the official view of 9/11. These firings did not take place because the journalists published *non-facts*; but rather, they took place because the journalists merely asked simple questions, such as: Can you show us the specific evidence that Osama bin Laden was involved as a conspirator in the 9/11 events?[141] Tarpley writes:

In the immediate aftermath of 9/11, the US media were gripped by chauvinist hysteria and war psychosis. Two courageous editors, Ron Gutting of the Texas City *Sun* and Dan Guthrie of the Grants Pass,

---

[139] See Grupp 2007 for information as to why the United States is a tyrannical nation.

[140] Ibid.

[141] This was asked by many politicians and journalists around the world after Ari Fleischer officially declared to the nation on 9/24/2001 that the US government *will not release any such evidence.* (See Tarpley 2006, 26 and 38-43)

Oregon, *Daily Courier*, were fired... when they dared to criticize Bush...[142]

As we will see, information in the US media is just the voice of a few corporatists. Therefore, in the corporate mass media, information is really non-information. In other words, actual reality is not reported on, and instead, information is merely created, and is reported on *as if* it were real empirical information about actual reality. Iraq is a "threat due to WMDs," Iran is a "threat due to WMDs," Syria and Pakistan are "threats," North Korea is a "threat," Venezuela is a "threat." Oil is increasing in price because of supply and demand, and there is a "peak oil threat." Al-Qaeda has no ties to the CIA, and a jetliner hit the Pentagon on 9/11/2001. Genetically modified food is healthy (according to the FDA and the companies that create it), there is no evidence that vaccines are harmful, there is no cure for cancer, and the list is seemingly endless.[143]

The list of non-facts that Americans are spoon-fed, and the consequent brainwashing (believing in a reality that does not exist) that Americans endure, is staggering. It seems, however, that this is still not at all widely known by Americans. In other words, Americans still are, in general, living in a brainwashed state: a telescreen dream world.

A tyranny that is not direct—i.e., not controlled by soldiers, but rather by the telescreen—is the most efficient system of mass brainwashing. It can make synthetic terrorism (false-flag terrorism) look like the work of "people in caves" (Osama and al-Qaeda), and it can make the nations that do not have weapons of mass destruction look like they have chemical weapons pointed right at us. Propaganda only works in a climate where skepticism and critical doubt are derided and ridiculed. Through propaganda, a corporatist/ tyrannical state can make war look appealing and peace distasteful. *It makes what is good for the populace look bad.* And most of all, it makes the perspective of the ultra-rich look like the only perspective that makes sense — so why question it? Henry David Thoreau wrote about this in *Walden*, Ch. 1:

The greater part of what my neighbors call good I believe in my soul to be bad, and if I repent of anything, it is very likely to be my good behavior. What demon possessed me that I behaved so well?

---

[142] Tarpley 43, 2006.

[143] See Grupp 2007 for copious empirical information on each of these issues, and to see why each of these are non-facts.

The Exterior Creates the Interior

In this chapter (and the next) I discuss the two major techniques involved in the basic mechanics of brainwashing. In this chapter, the main issue will be how the mechanics of brainwashing derives from one simple principle that, amazingly, most people are oblivious too:

Consciousness is (largely) created by the outside world.

Most of our ordinary daily-life experience, our waking life in our ordinary consciousness (for example, in our "workaday life", and not in, say, a religious ecstasy or something higher than our workaday life consciousness), consists of focusing our attention on the world. Humans are made to navigate through their reality. All our faculties—our senses, our minds, our problem-solving apparatuses—are largely about the *outer world*, the world around us. When we are walking through forest, our senses are focused on the outer world: trees, birds, sky, and so on. These are the images that fill consciousness, that make up my conscious contents.

The significance of this is that these images from the *outer* world are largely responsible for creating and constructing what is *inner*: our consciousness. I believe that the trees, birds, and sky are outside of me, but they shape and construct, to a huge degree, my inner mind. In other words, *the world (environment) you inhabit creates your mind*: the exterior creates the interior. We perpetually use our consciousness to look out at the world, and thus the world creates our consciousness, and our consciousness does not create itself.[144]

A person *is* their consciousness (as I will discuss below). But since consciousness is created by the external world for the contemporary American, then a person is largely a creation of the external world. This issue becomes very significant when we understand that the modern human is a creature that has their entire world and surroundings dominated by media and "education" that is controlled by a few jingoistic New World Order controllers. This starts for the average American in their earliest days in kindergarten at five years old, or much earlier. The telescreen in Orwell's *1984* functioned in precisely the same way: the pervasive presence of the telescreen-created consciousness.

Now, in the United States, when one fills up their gas tank, music is usually blaring in an outdoor speaker system at the gas station. If one goes to the post office, CNN may be on in the lobby (as in the post office I often

---

[144] In higher states of consciousness, humans are not solely focused outwardly, as the typical American is, but rather are focused inwardly and outwardly, and where the two of these mesh together. See Grupp 2009. Also see Cruttenden 2005

visited near Purdue University Northcentral in Valparaiso, Indiana when I was still teaching there). One cannot buy a computer anymore that does not spy on you with a camera and microphone[145] in the same way that the telescreen does in Orwell's *1984*. And it is difficult to find households in the United States that do not have cable television with 900 channels, give or take a few.

Television is Consciousness

"It's funny how the colors of the real world only seem really real …
on the screen."

—Alex, in Stanley Kubrick's *A Clockwork Orange*

"The television screen has become the retina of the mind's eye."

—Brian Oblivion, character in the film *Videodrome*

In the film *The Cable Guy*, directed by Ben Stiller, the main character, "Chip," the cable guy, lives his life through TV. The sentences he says in daily life, the thoughts he has, and the mannerisms he acts out in his behavior, appear merely to be repetitions of what he's witnessed on TV and in the movies. Of course I am sure the average viewer of this film would imagine this is just part of the film for comic purposes. But is it?

Some readers may find the idea that "television is consciousness" is silly, and they may rejoinder: How can it be asserted that one's entire life and surroundings *are* television? People only watch television at night after work, in general, right?

The answer to this issue can be found by investigating two issues, which are needed to get a grasp on the utter power of telescreen stimulation.

1. *Life is repetition.* A huge percentage of human actions, when humans are not watching television, are entirely repetitious behaviors. This is true even in the case of our spontaneous and everyday behaviors, conversations, etc.[146] How many times have you found yourself talking about the weather with someone because there is nothing else to say, uttering the same words in virtually the same way as you did the day before, or hour before, with another person? How many times have you said or thought the same thing over and over? How many times have you said the same phrase over again from one day or hour to the next: "oh, that's life," "shit happens," "good morning," "thank God it's Friday," "honey, I'm home," "how's the family?"

---

[145] See "Google Developing Eavesdropping Software," *The Register* (UK), September 4, 2006.

[146] For more discussion of this repetition and programming of the everyday life of a human's behavior (including conversations), see Berne 1992, especially the Introduction.

If we analyze our language, it does not vary as much as we might think from day to day. How many times have you tried to solve a problem in the same way as you did in the past? You try to win a confrontation with another person by yelling back in the same way you always have, or by shutting up in the same way you always have. How many times have you tried to ignore problems in the same way over and over? How many times have you dreamed of winning the massive lottery jackpot in the same way you dreamed about it in the past? How many times have we acted out the same behavior, expression, laugh, emotional display, and the like in the same manner from day-to-day? How many times have we done fake little laughs, laughing at what people say just to be polite, but not really thinking what was said is funny in any way? So much of human behavior, and the conscious mental activity associated with our actions, are mere repetitions—as if one is on *autopilot*.

2. *Consciousness is external*. This is the idea that exteriority creates interiority. Consciousness, for the average American, is largely created from the world outside, the world all around.

In your daily life, what is your consciousness filled with? It is filled with images of the world *outside* of you. When you are walking through the park, you see images of trees and squirrels, which fill your mind, and thus your "inner mind" is filled with "outer stuff." It is a rather rare human activity for a human to take their "mind's eye" and watch their own thoughts and mental reality, effectively shutting out "external stuff."[147] This is a very rare activity, and so rare that perhaps we can consider Westernized consciousness to be largely devoid of this practice, and thus to be *externally generated*, where basically all of our waking life is externally focused.

If 1 and 2 are the case, if life is repetition and if consciousness is external, then it will be easy for me to show how your consciousness, quite literally, *is television*, where consciousness is constructed by media stimulation, for reasons I discuss next.

In situations of repetition (issue 1, above), the mind experiences boredom. Consider what the mind does in states of repetition: it feels boredom. If you doubt me, try watching *The Little Mermaid* 100 times. When a person gets bored, their mind wanders and drifts. A person can be at work engaged in an activity, and quite literally not be conscious of what they are doing—this is the autopilot life I mentioned at the end of point 1 above. This might be a rather normal work consciousness state. I have often heard people say that

---

[147] This practice is, in general, the basic principle of some varieties of Buddhist meditation: placing attention on the inner and not just the outer. See Hubert Benoit, 1990, *Zen and the Psychology of Transformation*, Inner Traditions Press.

their "mind is not *in* what they are doing." Even though one's actions may be engaged in some work activity, such as typing a memo or washing dishes, often one will find that their mind is "elsewhere," consumed with other issues. It may be safe to say that much of American life takes this form.

Now, consider this: television is nearly *never* repetitious, and thus it is very unlikely that one's mind will get bored (so long as they are watching something they are drawn to, which shouldn't be difficult if they have 900 cable channels, much of which is dedicated to scandal, sex, etc.). If one's mind *is* interested while viewing the television screen, one will not have a wandering-drifting mind and thoughts in the way just described above. In summary, in contemporary America, people will spontaneously find themselves in situations where in daily life they *are not* engaged in the activities of their daily life, but where they are *entirely* engaged by television.

Now consider the following question:

> *What might the workaday TVaholics in America daydream about during the utter repetition of their workaday lives when their minds are wandering?*

A good guess is this: the things that *fully engage* consciousness. Or put in other words, the things that are interesting to a person. For reasons just described, much of this engaging material that will enter into the daydreaming mind of the bored worker is the content of television and of the telescreen world.

How many of you have found yourselves daydreaming about last night's television shows repeatedly through the day while at work? How many of you have experienced this sort of "television daydreaming" when playing with your children, if you have children? This is what I mean when I say that, for the TV junkie, *television is consciousness.*

Effortlessly, the corporatists that create the television shows are responsible for constructing the consciousness of the average citizen, for reasons I am describing here. The mind is constructed and thus controlled with no struggle: hundreds of millions of Americans happily comply—they automatically, and perhaps often even *earnestly*, set themselves in front of television, and into the telescreen world overall, as much as possible: they seek out the non-boring televisual, consciousness-creating experience. Here is what Orwell wrote about these issues in *1984*:

> When finally you surrender to us, it must be of your own free will. We do not destroy the heretic because he resists us: so long as he resists us we never destroy him. We convert him, we capture his inner mind, we

reshape him... [W]e bring him over to our side not in appearance, but genuinely, heart and soul.[148]

Why does TV not give rise to the feelings of boredom mentioned above? Because television is different from real life and does not involve boredom-inducing repetition, the sort that millions might feel daily at their jobs, or at church or school. A *huge* percentage of the jobs in America very likely give rise to such boredom. Above I mentioned watching *The Little Mermaid* 100 times, but imagine flipping burgers in the very same place, or typing the same sorts of memos 1000 times. For that reason a psychology of "the bored person" might be considered a *normal* state of being, a normal psychological state, due to its pervasiveness in America. We all see/feel it in each other, and thus can't relate to a different psychology. With the incessant changing images and narratives of television, with the endless tabloid-like social dramas, the sports, the high-action of the cable news and their endless war coverage and fear mongering of the telescreen-world, with the elimination of repetition that the telescreen-world offers compared to the monotonous toil of the workaday life, there is little chance that one will grow tired of watching TV, or diving into the telescreen-world with maximum gusto. And this is precisely what we see going on in America, which means that a few people have the power to create all of our consciousnesses! The stimulation is so titillating compared to the non-stimulation (by comparison) of the workaday life.

> Through all the confusion [of media stimulation] we sense something like a unity at work. The torrent is seamless[149]: a collage of back-to-back stories, talk show banter, fragments of ads, and soundtracks of musical snippets. Even as we click around, something feels uniform—a relentless pace, a patter of interruption, a pressure toward unseriousness, a readiness for sensation, an anticipation of the next new things.[150]

Consider what the effects of such high stimulation are. The fast flashing of the images and content of the televisual presentation focus the attention and senses of the viewer fully fixed on the screen, gazing at it motionlessly. This is a common behavior in American culture, and it seems that Americans do not tend to think it is very odd. Americans are accustomed to the idea that all across America there are rooms full of people who all silently stare trance-like in one direction (i.e., staring at the telescreen), and thus this idea does not seem so strange to us. To an outsider, such as a Penan Indian, or an alien, such nationwide trance-behavior might appear peculiar to say the least, and might even immediately appear to a Penan or an alien to be a form of

---

[148] Cited in Taylor 2004, 24.
[149] I believe that what Professor Gitlin means by "seamless" is synonymous to "without gaps," "continuous,' or 'without dead-air"
[150] Gitlin 2002, 7.

mass hypnotism. But in America, how many of us telescreen-world-addicts believe that? Believe that they are being brainwashed so deeply? Telescreen-world addiction and devotion is such a pervasive behavior that it takes the appearance of being normalcy in America, so nobody has the time to take note if they have been brainwashed or not, and if their consciousness has been hijacked or not. Professor Miller discusses this mass hypnosis:

> [For] TV's overseasoned audiences… discontinuity, disjointedness are themselves the norm; a spectacle that no stark images could shatter because it comes already shattered. TV ceaselessly disrupts itself, not only through the sheer multiplicity of its offerings in the age of satellite and cable, but as a strategy to keep the viewer semi-hypnotized.[151]

Televisual and auditory media stimulation function as an antidote to the aforementioned boredom. And it would appear that this antidote will be more escapist the more titillating the media stimulus is. For example, boredom can set in during the 6th inning of a baseball game, or the third quarter of a football game, causing the antidote of media stimulation to lose its effect. Channel-switching will result, and the sports viewer will look for the antidote to do its job, and to really end the felt boredom creeping in during the 6th inning. The sports viewer will seek out the titillating televisual or media stimulus: a suspenseful football game, or a high-speed movie, pornography, or a mushy romantic comedy, for example. The more titillation the better the escape from the boredom of our mass-industrial, despiritualized, far-from-nature corporatist culture. When something like a "made-for-TV" war pervades the mass media, such as with the "Shock and Awe" slaughter of the March 2003 invasion of Iraq, this may bring a maximum level of titillation. Viewers will experience the media stimulus "fix," and take the addictive opiate to cover-up their bored, corporatized selves (i.e., their brainwashed/replaced selves, not their genuine, spiritual selves) to a maximum degree.

Ordinary life became less livable as the 1900s progressed and the telescreen-world stimulation-addiction was increasingly introduced into people's lives. People began to have the ability to make comparisons they previously could not make: ordinary life-experience versus the life portrayed on the telescreen, or ordinary life-experience versus the addict's life of sitting in front of the boob-tube, forgetting the boredom and shallowness of their industrial lives. Things were just more exciting, beautiful, and stylish in the world of the telescreen, and ordinary life suddenly became, well, *ordinary*. During the 1900s we also became more industrialized, overworked, removed from nature, distant from our families. These losses could have fueled the

---

[151] Miller 1989, 13.

yearning, the addiction that developed in people for the telescreen world, and which we now see has taken over human reality. Real life was hijacked and replaced by virtual reality.

Telescreen Addiction, Part 1

For reasons just discussed, the addiction-like qualities of the telescreen-world stimulation take over the interests of the person to some degree, and thus ordinary life experience suddenly is seen as having an alternative, and not being as appealing. The telescreen-world stimulation becomes important, and daily life less important (or unimportant). Telescreen-world stimulation becomes non-boredom, and daily life becomes boredom (again, this happens in industrialization, and I suspect that our ancestors, in their forests and savannas, imbued with their spiritualized shamanic ways of life were not bored. Modern humans are so removed from this that few of us in the contemporary corporatist, workaday, addiction-filled telescreen-world can understand this shamanic, primitive, non-boredom of people living under a religious high that[152]). And eventually, for some, corporatized daily life became undesirable, and the telescreen-world an addiction, perhaps having some similarities to what the cigarette means to the smoker or the heroin to the junkie. Life is pain, monotony, and drudgery to an addict between fixes. Addictive substances are used to break up the monotony of the corporatized, industrialized day, and to give a release from the corporatized life which is uneventful, boring, and often inhuman, for the addict and non-addict.

This occurs because, like the cigarette and heroin syringe, *telescreen-world hypnosis* (to approximate Professor Marc Miller's phraseology), is soothing and a sort of "release from it all." Professor Gitlin describes these issues in straightforward language:

> But we diminish the significance of media and our reliance on them in everyday life by classifying them as channels of information. Media today are occasions for and conduits of a way of life identified with rationality, technological achievement, and the quest for wealth, but also for something else entirely, something we call *fun, comfort, convenience,* or *pleasure*. We have come to care tremendously about how we feel and how readily we can change our feelings. Media are by inviting images and sounds into our lives, making them come and go with ease in a never-ending quest for stimulus and sensation. Our prevailing business is the business not of information but of satisfaction, the feeling of feelings, to which we give as much time as we can manage.[153]

---

[152] For more information on this, see Cruttenden 2005.
[153] Gitlin 2002, 5.

If telescreen-world stimulation was not an "escape from it all," people would not watch television, listen to the radio, read the papers, etc. And if there were more desirable or enjoyable things to do that were within one's grasp than expose oneself to telescreen-world stimulation, one would do them.

The time Americans devote to telescreen-world stimulation implies that media entertainment is of the *most enjoyable* things they engage in, which is why the telescreen-world entertainment is all so popular, so ubiquitous in American culture. Some researchers give the antidote to boredom a pseudo-nirvanic quality (that is, a *self-forgetting* quality):

> In the uses and gratification approach to studying television viewing..., [researchers have found that] children and adults have been surveyed to learn why, in general, they watch television..., the varieties of programs or genres watched... In most research, people report that the act of viewing television is motivated by both cognitive and affective concerns. Affective motivations include the desire for increased pleasurable arousal and the desire for decreased noxious arousal. People say they want to see something exciting or thrilling, to escape boredom, or to take their minds off their problems.[154]

With the television screen (or other media stimulants), one does not have to wait for the weekend or vacation to "get away from it all;" it occurs instantly any time one flips on the telescreen.

Americans are, in many ways, emotion-consumers: they are in the business of regulating their emotions, and will often pay big dollars to do so. There are many examples. One familiar one is the way that emotions can be altered through substances that a person takes into their body, such as beer, Prozac, junk food, tobacco, caffeine, and so on. Often it is standard for Americans to take in substances to change their emotions to some desired state. Putting the issue quite simply: on any given day, tens of millions of Americans will use beer, Prozac, Xanax, or wine to "feel better" (even if one is not knowingly less-than-happy in the first place).

Telescreen-world stimulation is also a means of emotion regulation, and one that often resembles a dependency. How often do people go to light romance films to "feel good", or watch the cable news channel's war coverage and feel excitement and suspense that is perhaps similar to a football game?

---

[154] Huston, Donnerstein, Fairchild, Feshbach, Katz, Murray, Rubinstein, Wilcox, and Zuckerman 1992, 41.

Emotional Regulation and Choosing

In addition to regulating emotions for addiction purposes, telescreen-world information also teaches emotional behavior and responses. Consider the way scientists discuss how emotions and emotional responses are learned, and how telescreen stimulation may be a primary source of this learning:

> Television is a potentially powerful teacher about social relationships, intimacy, conflict, and feelings. Family relations, emotion, sexuality, and violence are the stuff of entertainment television... Television is a subtle, continuous source for learning about the rules of life and society... Although we also know remarkably little about the nature of emotions displayed by television characters, there is evidence of viewers' emotional responses. People use television to deal with their emotional states—seeking arousal when they are bored and seeking reduced arousal when they are under stress. Children also learn about emotions from television. They learn what situations lead to what emotions and the social norms for expressing emotion.[155]

In a wide variety of ways, telescreen-world information is *exciting* to people. It regulates the emotions in ways that fulfill addictive tendencies for people. If one is feeling bored, one can turn on the television and suddenly one is not bored, and instead a person is instantly titillated. Even if one is not bored, and engaged in a rather enjoyable activity, such as sitting out on the porch listening to the wind, playing basketball, or spending time with the children, one may nevertheless abandon these, and turn to the telescreen-world stimulation in order to fulfill the desire for a different emotion than the porch, basketball, or child will give.

The Telescreen Domination of Consciousness

The human mind (specifically, the mind's eye), for the most part, can only be occupied by one thing at a time. In other words, a person can only concentrate on, or think about, one thing (one object, one scene, one emotion, etc.) at a time. For example, when you are concentrating on something and somebody tries to start talking to you, you will likely say, "wait a minute! I am thinking about something." You will say that because, as I just said, the "space" in your consciousness can only accommodate one activity or thing in any given moment, so if somebody else gets you to think about something else, you will forget the first thing you were thinking about. The point is this: if a person's thoughts and "mental space" are filled with something (such as the endless information streaming by on the addictive telescreen), then how

---

[155] Huston, Donnerstein, Fairchild, Feshbach, Katz, Murray, Rubinstein, Wilcox, and Zuckerman 1992, 57-58.

can they think about anything else? If mental space is taken up, how can anything else fit in? The answer is: *it can't.*

This leads to the following question: If so many Americans are consumed with telescreen-world stimulation,

> *then their mental space is constantly filled with that information* (whether they are watching TV or not, listening to the radio or not), and for the most part *their minds do not have any thoughts that are not constructed by media stimulation.*

This is another way to think of the way consciousness is constructed by media information: *the telescreen is consciousness.* From the chapters above, it can be concluded that this is no different from the idea that *consciousness is constructed by the monopolistic corporatists*:

> *Corporate fascism puts together and builds the self in a huge percentage of the citizens of the United States and the world.*

Consciousness is thus created not by anything like free will or innate inner human religious power in the American telescreen nation. Rather, consciousness is created by the in-formation available and which comes into consciousness, and which consists of the pervasive telescreen-world information. The addictive, overpowering telescreen-world is merely a high-tech propaganda film that generates complicity for wars, slavery, despiritualization, unintelligence, unhealthiness, and apathy. There is nothing innately spiritual or human about it, but it shapes us and becomes us. That is why I said in the first lines of this book that the telescreen-world is a world not of humans but of subhumans. In chapter 1 of *Walden*, Thoreau writes:

Only they who go to soirées and legislative halls must have new coats, coats to change as often as the man changes in them. But if my jacket and trousers, my hat and shoes, are fit to worship God in, they will do; will they not? ... Beware of all enterprises that require new clothes, and not rather a new wearer of clothes.

Thoreau is suggesting here that there is a tremendous reward in not focusing just on our external appearance, but rather in focusing on our innerness. A despiritualized culture focuses on the external, thinking that it is reality, never taking the time to notice that we have an entire inner world of thoughts, feelings, religiosity, and power. The telescreen culture does not even know what those words mean. But humanness is found in thoughts, feelings, religiosity, and inner power, and so the telescreen-addicted human is not truly human. Thoreau writes:

Most men... through mere ignorance and mistake, are so occupied with the factious cares and superfluous coarse labors of life that its finer fruits cannot be plucked by them... Actually, the laboring man has not leisure for a true integrity day by day; he cannot afford to sustain the manliest relations to men... He has no time to be anything but a machine.

The mass of men lead lives of quiet desperation. What is called resignation is confirmed desperation. From the desperate city you go into the desperate country... But it is characteristic of wisdom not to do desperate things.

Corporatist Media Creates the Drugged Self

TV and the addiction of telescreen-world stimulation is a dream come true for corporate tyrants, since with the media addiction, minds and selves are endlessly controlled into submission, and are drugged and soothed with pleasures that also bring submission. Going to an undesirable job where one is underpaid and unfulfilled is perhaps *much* more bearable if one has the telescreen to turn to nightly, after the work-day scene in the corporate communist world of mini-dictatorship.[156] If all throughout the day in the miniature communist dictatorship that is a corporation is[157] the laborer knows that after flipping the burgers, writing the memos, washing the dishes, writing the reports, and so on, there is a quite pleasurable "fix" available, then the focus turns to merely getting back to the fix, rather than getting to some other activity, such as more time with family, reading, meditation, etc. Much in the way religion (false religion, that is) is often considered the opiate of the people, as the old saying goes, this is probably much more true of the telescreen-world, which is the real opiate of the people. Consider what Professor Miller writes about these issues, where he uses the word "quasi-automatic" in place of my words "opiate" or "day-dreaming" that I used above:

> The arrival of the culture of TV [in the 1970s], then was the imperceptible result of many factors—material, commercial, demographic, technological. This culture, however, represents not only the convergence of those disparate developments, but also—or primarily—the fulfillment of an old managerial ideal: to exact universal assent, not through outright force, but by creating an environment that would make dissent impossible. Since World War I, such has been the enlightened aim of management for the workers in America's factories and office building; and such too has been the enlightened aim of advertising for as many years [such as the advertising on television or the internet]...

---

[156] See Grupp 2007 for more information as to why corporatist America is communistic.

[157] Ibid.

Like propaganda generally, advertising must thus pervade the atmosphere; for it wants, paradoxically, to startle its beholders without really being noticed by them. Its aim is to jolt us, not "into thinking,"... but specifically *away* from thought, into quasi-automatic action... This Pavlovian (or Oceanic) project requires that "the respondent" not be confronted by the message head-on and in an alien context, because so direct and vivid an approach might snap him out of his receptive trance and into an unprofitable meditation. Rather, advertising must come down on everybody like the scents of spring...

It has long been the aim of advertising to be everywhere... On (and as) TV, mass advertising is ubiquitous, and yet it also hides behind that very flagrancy, half-camouflaged within surroundings that offset it and yet also complement it.[158]

Americans generally work hard throughout their workday (or work-night), away from their families, with children in day-care, and they arrive home late to spend tired and distracted moments (if much time at all) with their children, whom they have not seen all day. Yet despite all that, they will likely spend copious amounts of time watching TV—who has energy to do much more than this?

Consider the still on-going Iraq war. The fact that Americans do not act against it, and instead they now are fooled into believing that Iran is a real threat, is a rather stunning testament to how efficient the propaganda machine is. America is not even finished with the war in Iraq, which was started on information now widely known by Americans to have been false propaganda. Yet the TV-drugged populace has apparently forgotten this, since they are now fooled into believing that Iran is also a threat, and could use "weapons of mass destruction" against the USA. Americans are fooled by the fear the media/telescreen puts into them, as exemplified in this news article:

Secretary of State Condoleezza Rice on Thursday accused Iran of "lying" about the aim of its nuclear program, saying there's no doubt Tehran wants the capability to produce nuclear weapons and has deceived the U.N.'s atomic watchdog about its intentions. "There is an Iranian history of obfuscation and, indeed, lying to the IAEA," she said, referring to the International Atomic Energy Agency. "There is a history of Iran not answering important questions about what is going on and there is Iran pursuing nuclear technologies that can lead to nuclear weapons-grade material," Rice told reporters aboard her plane as she headed to Moscow. U.S. officials have long accused Iran of trying to develop nuclear weapons behind the facade of a civil atomic energy program, charges that Tehran

---

[158] Miller 1989, 11.

denies. But Rice's strong words, including the blunt reference to Iranian "lying," come at a critical time in dealing with the matter.[159]

What the Americans who read this article do not understand is that the history of Iran was created by the United States' CIA, created using SAVAK, in the same way they have created and are currently using al-Qaeda.[160] Not only do Americans just not know about this history (since their elementary school, high school, and college education is devoid of any such information on Iran), but furthermore, a brainwashed TV-addicted culture can be led *to forget the past and believe in absurdities.* Americans can be right in the middle of an excruciating and failed war/occupation that is based on a false WMD threat (of which no evidence was provided in the first place), and be fooled into believing that Iran now is a WMD threat (again with no evidence provided).

The telescreen-world is consciousness in the despiritualized fully externalized American existence. And thus if the telescreen-world involves absurd and false information, then consciousness gets accustomed to it, and itself becomes absurdist. Perpetually believing in, and fighting for, a false reality that for the most part gives them hopelessness, confusion, and sadness, rather than spiritualization, interiority, satisfaction, power, and intelligence. I suspect our spiritualized ancestors were drunk with daily life in their vitalistic world of trees, plants, sky, wind, water, and wild animals. Consider what Thomas Jefferson wrote, which gives us a taste of this spiritualized existence that the telescreen-world robs us of:

> The object of walking is to relax the mind. You should therefore not permit yourself even to think while you walk; but divert yourself by the objects surrounding you. Walking is the best possible exercise. Habituate yourself to walk very far.[161]

Telescreen Addiction, Part 2

How important do you think the telescreen society is to Americans? From what has been written in this book, so far, it seems to be a national addiction and a national (false) "education". Psychologists call something an addiction when it cannot be given up *and* when it harms ordinary life by interfering with the daily responsibilities of life. Living means communication with family members about various things, taking care of children, reading, properly functioning at the job-site, taking time for hobbies and recreation,

---

[159] From "Rice Says Iran 'Lying' About Nukes," Associated Press, by Matthew Lee, October 11, 2007.

[160] See Jones 2006, Grupp 2007, and Tarpley 2006, for more information.

[161] Letter to Peter Carr, Paris, August 19, 1785.

bettering oneself overall, etc. As far as I can tell, it is not uncommon for parents to neglect their children, for children to avoid their schoolwork, for reading to be altogether abandoned (except for newspapers), family life largely abandoned, and so on, all in order to watch television and participate in the telescreen-life.

From my perspective, it is as if the ordinary aspects of life, such as communication, taking care of children, hobbies, art projects and outdoor playtime (especially for children), and reading, all have been largely *replaced* by immersion in the telescreen-world. It is important to note that, without exaggeration, this could not be better news for a monopolistic corporatist, who wants to control thought in order to produce "more efficient" workers (feudal slaves), warriors, or dutiful and distracted people filled with fear, confusion, entertainment-seeking, and hate.

As I will discuss, the average American is a bit like a drug addict. Schechter writes about issues similar to this, in his book on the news coverage surrounding 9/11:

We have more media and less understanding... [W]e are all exposed to information of all kinds, online and offline, analog and digital, broadband and satellite, in the traditional press and conventional television newscasts, as well as in a proliferating array of magazines, website, webzines, videos, and films. What is called "news" pours through us, mediated through yet more technologies and platforms than I can keep up with. There were even instances in this time of terror that the media seemed to terrorize us more than enlighten us. News about terror often became distancing and frightening, with alarmist reporting of an often unsubstantiated (if not misleading) kind of journalism, which resulted in a panicked response ... In many instances, the first stories and "breaking news" bulletins that forecast new attacks were proved wrong... *Much of the public became hooked, even addicted, to this ever-flowing digital news stream, tuned in and zoned out by the endless repetitive chatter of the twenty-four news channels...*[162] (Italics mine)

Addictions are very important in corporatist-communist America: *if an addiction can be created, then a dependency can be used to control thought and behavior, and to make profits.* If a social class of people can become addicted to junk food or cigarettes or the telescreen, and there is payment associated with this addiction, and if the product is controlled by just a few, then the addiction can become very profitable.

---

[162] Schechter 2002, xxv-xxvi.

If telescreen-world "information" is a national addiction, is it possible that *other* effects of addiction can be identified? For example, when addicts of dope are deprived of and not under the influence of their dope, they likely will become irritated and nervous to various degrees. Does that also happen with telescreen addicts? For example, when the majority of Americans are at work, do they long to leave work so that they can go home and put their feet up and watch the tube? This sounds reasonable, since so many jobs are dreaded. But do millions of Americans do the same thing when they are taking care of their children, eating, doing yard-work, walking the dog, or taking a shower? Are they more nervous and hasty during these times since, in the back of their minds, they are thinking, "I need to hurry so I can put my feet up, get a beer and see my favorite TV show"? Are there reasons why, for millions of Americans, the fast flashing of images on the television screen may titillate and stupefy and perhaps even hypnotize or soothe many people in a way that their jobs, taking care of children, doing yard-work, and so on, *cannot*? It seems that the telescreen-world stimulation is a true opiate and a reducer of consciousness,[163] just as the drug-addict's smack is. Thus we can expect the telescreen-world addict to be more jittery than he/she would normally be, since he/she goes through the day with "the big game tonight" in the back of their mind, never fully focusing on their life and family and soul.

Is the postmodern kaleidoscope of the television screen's hypnotism more titillating than playing with and taking care of one's own children? When millions of Americans go to the grocery store, are they subtly irritated since some of their thoughts are filled with ideas of hurrying to get home to relax "in front of the tube"? Do Americans endlessly have these sorts of ideas present in the "back of their mind when they are away from their "fix?" Do they think to themselves, "I would rather be doing something else (watching TV), so I need to get done with what I am doing, so I can go home and relax." Does this make millions of people hurried or jittery more than they would be if they were not addicted when they walk through the grocery store, do yard-work, take care of children, and so forth? Are there large numbers of

---

[163] See, "Early Television Exposure and Subsequent Attentional Problems in Children" Pediatrics, Vol. 113 No. 4 April 2004, pp. 708-713, by Dimitri A. Christakis, MD, MPH , Frederick J. Zimmerman, PhD, David L. DiGiuseppe, MSc and Carolyn A. McCarty, PhD; "Too much television can make children 'mentally ill'. Too much television and time spent on the internet can make children mentally ill, an in-depth report has concluded", London Telegraph, February 2, 2009; "Study: Hobbies can help slow Alzheimer's", USA Today, March 5, 2001(this article discusses a link between TV and Alzheimer's); "How Pokemon Shifts Brain Into Overdrive", Science (ScienceNOW), March 3, 2001, http://sciencenow.sciencemag. org/cgi/content/long/2000/303/3; "Cartoon-based illness mystifies Japan", December 17, 1997, CNN.com, http://www.cnn.com/WORLD/9712/17/japan.cartoon.

people who are regularly and unreasonably irritated toward and short with their children due to this subtle irritation that they may have in the background of their mind? Is this nervousness a reason why Americans so often use shopping and endless purchasing of things that they do not need as a hobby?

These words about *addiction*, I fear, will appear too dramatic for some readers of this book. For those readers, the issues just discussed can be conveyed in softer language, such as with the following passage, written by several academics who are experts in media and thought control:

> In its approximately 40 years as a part of American society, television has become an integral part of almost every home. It accompanies much of daily life, either as foreground or as background... Americans and people in most other countries spend many hours a week watching television. American children spend more time watching television than they do in school. Some of that "viewing" is accompanied by other activities—eating, playing, doing homework, and talking. Much of it occurs in the company of parents, siblings, and friends.[164]

There is Only One Stream of Information in the United States, and any Stream Outside of it is Considered Mental Illness

In his book about telescreen-world stimulation and American culture's obsession with it, Professor Miller discusses how this new telescreen-addict lifestyle of telescreen addiction was set up in America during the late 1960s and early 1970s:

> Here was the completion of an enormous transformation, all the more striking for the fact that no one was struck by it. Whereas the earlier critics could track the flagrant spread of advertising and its media through the cities and the countryside, and even into common consciousness, one could not now discern TV so clearly (if at all), because it was no longer a mere stain or imposition on some preexistent cultural environment, *but had itself become the environment. Its aim was to be everywhere*: not just to clutter our surroundings, but to become them; and this aim had suddenly been realized by TV, which was not only "on the air," but had become the very air we breathe.[165] (Italics mine)

It would seem safe to say that the information that the vast majority of Americans hear and experience, and which fills their minds, is predominantly

---

[164] Huston, Donnerstein, Fairchild, Feshbach, Katz, Murray, Rubinstein, Wilcox, and Zuckerman 1992, 1.
[165] Miller 1989, 8.

corporate media information. Regardless of whether or not they hear it from friends, neighbors, co-workers, in church, on the telescreen, or at school—all information channels are in agreement, reinforce one another, and create telescreen-world addiction. Taylor writes: "[It] is the ultimate totalitarian fantasy: not only behavior, but every single thought in every single brain in all the world conforming to a single ideological format."[166] The information is titillating, tabloid, ultra-violent, pornographic, pervasive, voyeuristic, fast, and ever-changing. For example, if a person hears something on Fox News, she will go and tell her friends about it, and will discuss it in church. Thus the information in the corporatist telescreen engulfs all of reality, all of consciousness, and creates consciousness, to a point that people's consciousness is not their own. Yet nearly no one has any idea of that, and has no idea that their worldview of reality was not created by them and has, literally, nothing to do with actual reality—it is telescreen-reality.

Even though it that the United States is a cornucopia of information and information sources, for reasons just given, there really is, for the most part, only one stream of information. All the same topics are discussed over-and-over (Oprah, Iran, terrorism, Britney, Obama, Madonna, Brad Pitt, Rush, etc.), rather than a true diversity of information that is outside of a pre-selected universe of discourse. So, whether it is in church, in the academic books, in school, in casual conversation, or on the telescreen, in all cases, the uncritical, false, absurdist *in-formation* creates a subhuman-level of consciousness in humanity, and reinforces itself in the quasi-consciousness of the citizenry. The citizenry in general does not notice that it is just one stream of information, and they, for example, mistakenly believe that Democrats say different things than Republicans do on various issues. The information is considered different sorts of information from the mainstream media. In addition to things like implanted fear, this is how dictators fool populations to believe whatever the dictators want them to believe. Americans are living in a dream-world they believe to be real.

---

[166] 2004, 24.

5. Totalism: There is Only the Telescreen

"The unexamined life is not worth living."
—Socrates (at the trial which led to his execution)

The Human Becomes a Self-destructive, Non-mental Subhuman

Following what was found in the previous chapter—that the telescreen *is consciousness*—I will now discuss more explicitly the mass American brainwashing that occurs from the telescreen. To get a handle on where I am going, consider another passage from Professor Taylor, which has a lot to do with the material from the last chapter:

One obvious conclusion which we can draw from the literature on brainwashing is that in its alleged status as a process—an evil and terrifying magic which turns free citizens into zombies—it is essentially a social process, requiring at least two participants. Brains are changed by signals from the world around them all the time... Since today we humans have been unable to change brains directly (except by crude methods like knives, bullets, drugs, and the odd lobotomy)... we have had to rely on indirect methods: changing the signals which the brain receives. This can only be done by manipulating the physical or social environment of the victim. Of course, changing other people's environment is something we all do: we are all influence technicians— but there are degrees. Brainwashing is extreme: the brainwasher aims for total control over his victim's world, in order that he may eventually control his victim's mind.[167]

And consider another passage from Professor Kathleen Taylor, which is about Orwell's *1984* and the telescreen:

Winston at the end of *Nineteen Eighty-Four* certainly seems a very different person from the restless protagonist of earlier in the book. The fire which sustained him in opposition days has gone out; his concerns have narrowed to the immediacies of everyday life. Out go truth, memory, history; in come the endless telescreen and the size of his drinks bill.[168]

This passage gives a sense of the *totality* of the alteration that occurs with brainwashing in the telescreen-world: it is as if the real/innate self does not have any common properties with the replaced/brainwashed self. They are different selves: one has been obliterated so that a constructed/corporatized self can exist.

---

[167] Taylor 2004, 15.
[168] Taylor 2004, 23.

The constructed/brainwashed self is typically *self-destructive* and *non-mental*, to various degrees. What do I mean by self-destructive? Since the real self of the brainwashed person is destroyed and/or replaced, the person becomes *a destroyed and/or absent person*—the human becomes a subhuman—and thus can only act in the way such a deformed person would.

A principal way a brainwashed person maintains her/his brainwashed state of being is by *not examining their self.* Such a process of self-examination, solitude, meditation, and/or shamanic quest is so rare in American culture that it almost seems to be considered strange, anti-social, or scary. If a brainwashed person/self merely took a look at their self, carefully noticing the "parts" and "structures" of the self, the brainwashed would notice what the self is really like, what its qualities are. To understand who you are as a person, you have to close your eyes and look in at your consciousness (your thoughts, feelings, and imaginings). But in doing this, and in noticing what the self's qualities are, in the case of a brainwashed, this would be to directly see and understand that the self is a brainwashed, artificial (replaced, corporatized, constructed) self (a deformed false self). To maintain and uphold their brainwashed status, therefore,

> *a brainwashed subhuman/replaced self cannot take her/his eyes, attention, and interest off of the world (i.e., the telescreen) and turn it inward to therein observe the self, and thus to find out what one really is made of deep inside, and to find what one's real desires, dreams, and true feelings are—lest the façade of the artificial self crumble.*

The replaced self cannot awaken, cannot question its construction, lest a breakdown of the false/replaced self happen, which would be a trauma that the corporatized addict would not find "pleasurable" compared to her/his daily engulfing into telescreen-addiction-world after long hours of work at the corporation.

If you are dreaming, and you suddenly realize that you are dreaming, you start to wake up. If you are brainwashed, and you look within yourself, you will see that you are not living a life in accord with your true self, and thus you will see the dream and wake up. Therefore, the brainwashed subhumans are responsible for keeping themselves in a state of deformity and totalism, by the very fact that they do not live what Socrates called "the examined life." They self-police themselves, making sure they don't stray into areas that will weaken the façade of the false/replaced self, such as by taking on a new paradigm, noticing the horrors of the wars they support, embarking into religious experience, or questioning anything about their daily life and their self.

For these reasons, the actions and activities of daily life of the brainwashed person can only be actions and activities that do not allow the brainwashed to take notice of the self, but rather they are actions and activities *that are meant to clear attention away from the self*. In other words, brainwashed persons do not have the ability to know themselves, take care of themselves, and genuinely express themselves. This is why the United States is involved in an epidemic of Prozac, Ritalin, Xanax, psychotherapy, despiritualization, and it is why the counseling psychology industry is booming.[169]

One effective way for a brainwashed person to keep distracted from paying attention to her real self is through the various distractions that the culture offers, which the telescreen-world fulfills (as does consumerism, the shallow churches all over, junk food, pornography, and so on). Distractions, as I have just defined them, are self-destructive behaviors: they are the behaviors carried out by those whose self has been destroyed. To be self-destructive is to destroy one's self. And since, as I just pointed out, it is ultimately the brainwashed who are keeping themselves in totalism, it is therefore they who destroy themselves: they keep their true self obliterated, and the false deformed subhuman brainwashed self in place. This is called self-destruction, and it is the heart of what it means to be a brainwashed person in the telescreen-world. The more extreme the brainwashing, the more extreme the destruction of the real self. It is true that citizens of the world are tricked into being brainwashed, but ultimately, the apparatus for brainwashing consists of the brainwashed initiate keeping the game of brainwashing going. The telescreen is the opiate that the drug dealer gives to the junkie, but the junkie must raise her hand and open her mouth.

Instead of being concerned with the issues to do with her/himself, the artificial and deformed self is not concerned with this sort of activity, *and thus can only remain a stranger to her/himself*—never knowing why she is confused, restless, or dejected. Indeed, self-reflection or self-examination appears spooky or ridiculous to the false brainwashed self. The brainwashed *cannot* look at her/himself, they cannot allow the real self to live freely, lest the façade break apart, as I mentioned. The artificial self, unable to be concerned with itself, unable to care for itself, unable to know itself, can then only participate in activities which support and do not conflict with the fascist state. It can only participate in activities (distractions) that keep attention away from knowledge of the real self and of actual reality.

These activities are, typically, *addictions*: TV, alcoholism, Prozac, food, emotion regulation, the façade of the pleasures of youthful recreations, and

---

[169] See Grupp 2007, ch. 4 (and, less so, chapter 2), for much more information on these issues.

so on. The reason the brainwashed addict can only carry out addiction-behaviors that are in line with the corporatist-telescreen empire is that the outward-focused, broken, brainwashed self *will only have as much knowledge as it has been given*, and that sort of information will be the corporatist-approved and corporatist-generated telescreen-based information. That information only teaches obedience to American communism, and thus instructs one only to do what is good for the fascist/corporatist state. And what is good for the fascist/corporatist state is to remain addicted to a substance or activity that promotes militarism, deformity, the Friedman/monetarist economics of rampant consumerism, and other Huxleyan or Orwellian themes.

Brainwashed Persons are Mere Reaction Machines

And what did I mean above when I said that the deformed brainwashed subhuman is *non-mental*? A destroyed self can only *react* to the world, and cannot look inward at itself. In simpler words: if the brainwashed self cannot focus on her/himself, there is only the world around left to focus her consciousness on. But that turns the brainwashed into what could be called a "reaction machine:" a self that is only operating in a one-way relationship *from* the world *to* the false self, where consciousness (subhuman consciousness) is just merely needed to respond to the world, not to deliberate with it. This is an *accidental life*, where the subhuman is merely aimlessly pushed around by the forces of life. It is not unleashing its real deep inner selfhood onto the world, in a relationship not going only *from* the world *to* the self, but also going *from* a real self *to* the world.

Take a look at your own inner/subjective world. Do it right now. Just close your eyes, and use your same mind's eye (the eye of your consciousness) that you use to look at the world with to look at your feelings, thoughts, and visualizations inside of you. A significant portion of this inner world just consists of an inner conversation, endlessly flowing and rambling in your head. This is actually needed for there to be thought: inner mental talk/conversation. The inner conversation is often about the world, about people that the person associates with, about things going on in one's life, about dreams and desires deep within you, and so on. This conversation can build up consciousness, since the more developed this inner conversation is, the more developed thought will be.

In any productive conversation, two conversing parties go back and forth, the subject-matter deepens, and thus learning comes out of this process. This is precisely what can and does go on in the minds and thoughts of people, and it only occurs by this *interacting*: your inner mind will have conversations with itself, bouncing ideas back and forth, learning from itself, and amplifying its intelligence. So your mind is largely an inner conversation, as if there are two (or more) people "in there" talking to one another. The more energy this conversation has, the more consciousness can be generated. But for the destroyed self (the brainwashed), the mind is not meant to interact with itself in this way, since its quality is to be pointed outward at the world.

When is the last time you went and talked to a philosopher or scientist, asked a hard question, and saw him or her say, "Okay, but let me think about that a minute." Then they sit there motionless in their chair thinking, as if that stillness is meant to be a way of subduing the interaction of self to the world, in order that the mind's resources can interact with themselves in thought to solve the problem? Therefore, it would seem that the brainwashed person is not allowing the inner thought dialogue to be strengthened, since productive thought is engaged in more rarely than with the inner-focused, self-critical, non-destroyed non-brainwashed self.

When the brainwashed person is totally controlled through totalist brainwashing, the brainwashed person becomes not only a destroyed self, but *ipso facto*, a thoughtless self, to some degree. This might help to explain the seemingly decreasing level of intelligence of Americans.

"The man in the street does not ordinarily trouble himself about what is 'real' to him and about what he 'knows'... He takes his 'reality' and his 'knowledge' for granted."[170] There is no reason whatsoever for the brainwashed person to question things, as long as their stomachs and minds are full of junk (junkie food or junkie telescreen information), which they will not understand is junk. Since the fascist state has constructed her/his consciousness and self, *to question something about the state would be to question the self.* This is impossible to do, however, if brainwashing is to remain in place. The telescreen acts as the total controller, to use Taylor's way of putting it, that the totalist brainwashers require.

> Milieu control is the attempt to dominate not only the individual's communication with the outside (all that he sees and hears, reads and writs, experiences and expresses), but also—in its penetration of his inner life—over what we may speak of as his communication with himself.[171]

What Taylor means by "communication with himself," I am describing as the *subduing of thought* and the *rejection of questioning, doubt, and skepticism.* This makes the brainwashed, for the most part, *non-mental.* This is the definition of totalism: the person's deepest inner self is constructed and controlled by the fascist powers, without the victim ever knowing.

---

[170] Berger and Luckmann, 1966, 2.
[171] Taylor 2004, 16.

Corporatist Totalism

TV and any media stimulation in the United States is amazingly "corporate friendly." Not too long ago, in the 1930s, there existed "mass animus against big business..."[172] But now, in the national media, one can go literally days or weeks without hearing a single negative word against controlling monopolistic corporatists. Not a negative word in any of the advertisements for the corporate media, not in any of the shows on television, not in the news shows. According to the national media defector, Charles Lewis, former producer of *60 Minutes*, "...I have to tell you, when we have investigated corporations, for some reason it just doesn't get covered."[173]

The false self referred to earlier in this chapter can also be considered a corporatized self: a self that is created by the corporatistic monopolists that control the telescreen (a detailed examination of them is given in the next chapter). The deformed and false corporatist self is corporatist friendly, and only by braving a very strong note of dissent from society would one deprogram and, for example, start questioning her false existence. This is why leaders such as Stalin have publicly said that they are unconcerned if much of the population wakes up and figures out what is really going on. A person dissenting from the brainwashing and from the corporatist society would, in the eyes of the masses of the brainwashed, appear as a threat, since they will threaten the existence of the false, deformed, corporatized self. That is why there is often such a violent reaction to the lone activist who is pointing to the "writing on the wall."

Interestingly, Americans are given endless criticism of the government in our media streams—occasionally even form the so-called "conservative" channels, like the Fox News Channel—and this gives us the illusion that media streams are full of balanced criticism of the controllers of the country. But in truth, the real controllers (the monopolistic corporatists) are never discussed and are virtually unknown.[174] These criticisms of government take two forms:

1. They involve pointless, distracting, unreal or false issues, such as how the government has not invaded Iran quickly enough, or how it has not given enough money to Israel or some other country.

---

[172] Miller 1989, 14. In this passage, Miller is talking about General Motors, in particular, in the 1930s.

[173] This quote is from Pappas 2003.

[174] This is discussed in great detail in the last section of ch. 7 below, and in Grupp 2007.

2. They are meant to pre-program the telescreen-world subhumans to their fate. Alan Watt,[175] a famous author and radio host, has called this predictive programming, meaning that the idea is implanted into your consciousness to get you used to it. If we are told over and over how ghastly the government is for invading our privacy, violating the Constitution, wasting money, causing wars, being inept, and so on, well, we all get used to the idea, it becomes normal and expected, and nobody is motivated to change it. The telescreen-world subhumans learn that "there is nothing they can do," because "it's just the way it is," as people so often tell me. Also, if the telescreen-world subhumans have enough telescreen-world stimulation to distract them, well, then who even cares about how tyrannical things get if you have the "fix" always present, always pumping into your subhuman "consciousness."

This "government criticism," then, is a wonderful corporatist trick, and it really makes the "news" shows of the telescreen look like real information. It's not, of course; it's more telescreen programming, but the dumbed-down subhuman population cannot tell the difference, even if it's pointed out to them. The government is a fall-guy for the global system of corporatist communism/fascism, and the media upholds this by keeping our attention away from the real controllers of the country. The creators of consciousness are never in sight.

Real information about government and the monopolistic corporatists that rule the world in secretly is actually *hidden* by the telescreen-world mass media, always keeping the real mechanics of the social world a secret, by merely not discussing it. When is the last time you heard Fox News talk about the Bilderberg Group,[176] the Bohemian Grove,[177] the trillions of dollars the Pentagon pilfered from taxpayers, how the General Motors "bailout" money of spring 2009 was to be used to move GM out of the country, how the US military killed millions of Iraqis from 1991-2009[178] (the telescreen-world mass media says thousands, not millions) — on and on and on I could go with this list. All these are undiscussed, and thus they become non-facts, since the American telescreen-world subhuman does not believe things are real unless they show up in the telescreen-world news. If you doubt this, go and tell somebody that Prozac is in their tap water,[179] watch them laugh at you, then pull the news articles about it, show them to the person, and you

---

[175] See his web site: www.cuttingthroughthematrix.com.
[176] See Jones 2006.
[177] See Jones 2005.
[178] See Grupp 2007.
[179] See Grupp 2007.

will see them transform from an unbeliever to a believer. But if you were to show them an article not from the mainstream news, but rather from a scientific journal, they still would not believe. It has to be in the mass telescreen-world media for it to be real to the telescreen-world subhumans of America.

The telescreen-world creates consciousness in a way that teaches us that communistic corporations of America are inevitable and good entities, when in reality they keep us poor, keep us from our families, teach us to be un-Constitutional, teach us to live like feudal subjects, and so on. Through endless conditioning and auto-suggestion of television advertisements and so on, there is literally a stream of images and information via advertising, about corporations being fantastical lands of happiness and sophistication. Commercials are set to wonderful music, showing smiling people working in investment firms, in factories, in fast food restaurants, banks, car dealerships, and so on. It is as if the "family" is presented as dysfunctional on television (via sitcoms, etc.), and the corporation is the new, improved, Orwellian family.[180]

The corporatistic telescreen-world media show commercials featuring persons in ultramassive corporations who are actually dancing in their offices,[181] or acting like blissful children. Hertz puts it:

We are drip-fed images that reinforce … [the corporatist] dream. Studios and networks beatify the very essence of [corporatism]. Prevailing norms and mainstream thoughts are recorded, replayed, and reinforced in Technicolor, while any criticism of the orthodoxy is consciously quashed.[182]

It is rather amazing that these ads can exist on the telescreen so pervasively, since all Americans know from their personal experience with corporations that it is not at all like that. In fact, this account is literally the *opposite* of what really happens at a corporation. But the telescreen displays people and situations that are absurdist and which are about non-reality, which the average American gets used to (more predictive programming). This teaches the average American to expect that reality is absurd, and that living in a world of ideas (absurd ideas) rather than the world of experiential verification is what one should do.

---

[180] This has to do with corporate communism, which is discussed in copious detail in Grupp 2007, ch. 3.

[181] This was the case with a commercial for a company called Zurich, which flooded cable television in 2006.

[182] Hertz 2003, 6-7.

How are We Shaped?

If our consciousnesses are deformed and replaced by the corporate telescreen, then what is the end product? How are we shaped? To find out, all one has to do is examine the ordinary day-to-day behavior of people in American culture. Doing this, one finds that people, in general,

1.   Are suspicious of each other,

2.   Are uncritical thinkers (not analytic, do not question, think, or seek verification; don't use logical connections in thought about reality),

3.   Are fearful (most often of things and people they have never seen or met, such as the "terrorists" who supposedly "live in caves"),

4.   Trust authority (especially the government), like a small child trusting a teacher, or believing in Santa,

5.   Have a short memory. We are lied to by the government one year, and then go ahead and trust them the next year on the same issue (e.g., a politician fails to fulfill campaign promises, but we forget this; telling the public there are WMDs in Iraq, and then not seeing the same plot going on with Iran),

6.   Are entertainment-oriented. They appear to think that the normal way of life is one where people are to relish shallow entertainment and pageantry on a daily basis.

7.   Are uninterested in learning about how reality really is. You can put in front of them the most interesting fact imaginable about some issue, and one which absolutely captivates you, but you will see the average American victim of the telescreen hardly show any interest, as if they are deadened to responses to anything but the telescreen "information."

8.   Are addicts.

There are secret groups organized by the monopolistic corporatists that get together to plan on how exactly to use the telescreen to create and manipulate the consciousnesses of people.[183] They come up with ways to try and manipulate people in the ways that points 1 – 7 describe. An indication is the following quotation from Brzezinski, who was a top aide to multiple US presidents, in *The Grand Chessboard*, which is about how the secret controllers seek to foster suspicion between people, as in point 1:

To put it in a terminology that hearkens back to the more brutal age of ancient empires, the three grand imperatives of imperial geostrategy are to prevent collusion and maintain security dependence among the

---

[183] See Grupp 2007.

vassals, to keep tributaries pliant and protected, and *to keep the barbarians from coming together.* (p. 40) (Italics mine.)

And consider this quote from President George W. Bush, at West Point, June 1, 2002, which is meant to enforce and concretize fearfulness (point 3 and possibly others) in people's minds:

> The gravest danger to freedom lies at the crossroads of radicalism and technology. When the spread of chemical and biological and nuclear weapons, along with ballistic missile technology—when that occurs, even weak states and small groups could attain a catastrophic power to strike great nations. Our enemies have declared this very intention, and have been caught seeking these terrible weapons. They want the capability to blackmail us, or to harm us, or to harm our friends—and we will oppose them with all our power.

Totalism is coming from the very people that children are taught to trust by their school teachers, such as the President. Totalism comes with a smiling face, appearing on the telescreen as a helpful father-figure. It is very difficult for the average American to understand the staggering duplicity involved in the basic nature of the Machiavellian corporatist controllers and the politicians that work under them. They have been taught to always choose the simplest answer approved by the majority. They have been taught Occam's razor, that the obvious answer is the likeliest one. They have not been taught that it applies to the physical world, but not to social interactions, where motives are hidden. In a game of chess, the simplest explanation of the opponent's move is a ruse. Chess is a wonderful learning exercise people used to engage in on long evenings before there was TV, but the telescreen world views chess-players as suspicious nerds.

The Definition of Brainwashing: The Replacement of the Self

I am going to discuss points 1 – 8 of the last section in more detail in this chapter, but first I want to formally define "brainwashing." By this point in the book, the reader can see that brainwashing is

> *the process of secretly fooling a person into believing x is true, when in fact there is no evidence whatsoever for x, and in fact not-x is true, but the corporatized self believes only in x (believes only in non-reality).*

Brainwashing is not just trying to change somebody's mind. It is trying to remove the natural and genuine selfhood of a person and replace it with a new, unnatural, false, and deformed self. The new self is tailored in accordance with the program of the brainwashers, such as points 1 – 8 above, and other points that could be described. Taylor writes: "Humans have been trying to change each other's minds since they first discovered them."[184] She continues:

> Brainwashing is more ambitious, more coercive, than simple persuasion, and unlike older cognates such as indoctrination, it has become closely associated with modern, mechanistic technology... It is a systematic processing of non-compliant human beings which, if successful, refashions their very identities.[185]

> Brainwashing has a variety of aspects which can be teased apart. As well as its political function as a term of abuse, it can also be used a functional description of a scientific process or processes for achieving such control. Those skeptics who argue that 'it's all hogwash' are arguing against the idea that such scientific processes exist: that minds have ever been totally dominated in the way suggested by The Manchurian Candidate, whose brainwashed protagonist murders when ordered to do so, even when the target is the girl he adores...[186]

America and most of the world consist of people who do not, and have never, known themselves, since their real selves have been removed from them, hidden from them, and they have been told that a false and deformed corporate Orwellian group-think self is the real person. The false self is replete with sadness and confusion, and it is taught not to seek and cultivate a passionate life, but rather to seek obedience and the things that do not bring happiness, intelligence, and spiritualization. This can be verified by perhaps all of us if we merely look within ourselves to see that we have been tricked into chasing false paradises, and lives that are not in accord with our dreams in any way.

Coercion, Fear, Force, and the Ability to Forget Quickly

Totalism is most effectively put in place with fear tactics, as well as inculcating minds with incorrect information from birth until death. The more fearful a person is, the more panicky, the less they are able to be skeptical and detached. If a person is fearful enough, they will do anything asked of them by the authority figures they have been taught to trust (such as fight a war even if no evidence is ever presented that there is a real threat). It is critical for totalistic-level brainwashing that skepticism be eliminated from the self. Taylor writes: "Force, powerful emotions, repetition, and

---

[184] Taylor 2004, 7.
[185] Taylor 2004, 9.
[186] Taylor 2004, 9.

psychological ...[187] torture are clearly used against Winston [character in Orwell's *1984*]..."[188] Taylor goes on to discuss how being presented with his "ultimate fear... achieve[d] his total submission."[189]

The present work was written from 2005 to 2009, during which, I observed telescreen information presenting an escalation of blaring "news" over the "threat" of Iran, which perfectly mimicked the threat escalation over Iraq in 2002 and 2003. Both involved the idea that an oil-rich Mid-Eastern nation had WMDs and wanted to use them against Americans. No evidence at all was presented; only verbal, question-begging non-evidence was given, as when a politician comes on the telescreen and says, "Iran is seeking nuclear weapons, the evidence is there..." — yet no evidence is ever presented. It certainly appears that the warmongers who were behind Iraq want to invade Iran, too. If one watches the DVD documentary by Greenwald,[190] one is struck by the utter similarity of all the threats and language of politicians and news media personalities on the telescreen, regarding the Iraq situation in 2002 and up to the 2003 invasion, with the Iran situation that commenced in 2004. It is as if somebody "copied and pasted" the same words from 2002-2003 to 2005-2006, as if people just forget about what was said from 2002-2003 to 2005-2006. Elsewhere in this book I have written about how Hitler was so pleased with the way the public could easily forget things.

Pervasive fear is like an endless emotional hum in the background of the mind that just sits there, just barely outside of one's conscious awareness. It can be implanted in the mind with soft fear, or outright hysteria, such as the shock treatment of 9/11. Taylor writes that

> Studies in Britain and the United States, for example, consistently show a fear of crime which is out of proportion to the actual risks of being a victim, but which reflects the proportions of attention devoted by the media to crime. Television shows provide extremely distorted versions of reality.[191]

---

[187] I have omitted here the word "physical," since Taylor clearly says on page 12 that force, such as physical torture, is not mandatory in the brainwashing process. Since it plays no role in mass American brainwashing, we may leave it out of the discussion here.

[188] Taylor 2004, 22.

[189] Taylor 2004, 22.

[190] Greenwald 2004

[191] Taylor 2004, 53.

Now in the contemporary world, "terrorism... has been known to provide a means of social control."[192] The use of a constant hum of inner fear and subjective terror lead a population of citizens to continually accept violence toward other people — the feared group, or people similar to them. Because skeptical thinking is suspended, no evidence need even be presented to the citizenry by the marauder-controllers, who merely tell the citizenry what they should fear.

Emotions:
Creation and Regulation of the Emotions of the Citizens

"I never met my father, but the old TV was always there for me."
—From the film, *The Cable Guy*

So we can see that emotions are controllable, and it is big business for the corporatist-controllers to manufacture emotions for the citizenry. Doing this via the telescreen enables them to seemingly effortlessly control the world. Consider this passage, which was written by a number of experts on media persuasion:

Because television programming contains abundant information about affect [that is, emotional display and which emotions are revealed to the world], viewers may learn to recognize emotional displays, acquire beliefs about how often people experience different emotions, understand that certain situations are associated with certain affective states, accept social expectations regarding emotional expression and behavior, and come to believe in certain models of emotional responsiveness, experience, expression, and behavior... Viewers... manifest a wide variety of emotions in response to television... Although there is great variability in such experiences, even to a single program, these responses can persist for up to a period of weeks.[193]

It has already been noted how fear and coercion are factors. But beyond this, these are a few basic types of emotion, all of which are can be manipulated or created by the controlling monopolists. Taylor writes:

Both politics and religion call on certain core ideas (freedom, a State, God) which are so highly abstract that I will refer to them as 'ethereal'. Ethereal ides are so ambiguous that they are often interpreted very differently by different individuals (political theorists describe political

---

[192] Tarpley 2006, 66.
[193] Huston, Donnerstein, Fairchild, Feshbach, Katz, Murray, Rubinstein, Wilcox, and Zuckerman 1992, 43-44. They are reporting on the research of other scientists in this passage.

ethereal ideas, such as liberty and equality, as essentially contested)...
This ambiguity makes them hard to challenge with rational debate;
participants in such a debate may, in effect, be talking at cross-purposes.
Speakers often use 'glittering generalities'... to mask impracticalities,
hidden catches or other devils in the detail of their aims and objectives,
or in the hope of evoking an emotional response from their audience
which will increase the level of commitment to their agenda. As well as
being abstract and ambiguous, ethereal ideas are value-laden... Viewed
as supremely important in themselves, they come with huge accumulated
emotional baggage, and encourage a sense of superiority in believers...

Ethereal ideas are generally bloodstained. Valued more highly than
human life, they also facilitate the processes whereby, firstly, ends can
come to justify means, and secondly, people who don't accept the ideas'
supremacy can be seen as less than human. In other words, ethereal ideas
encourage totalist thinking... They therefore can be, and all too often are,
used to justify acts of terrorism.[194]

Basically what Taylor is saying, I believe, is that if a brainwasher can say
"x is good' in such a way as to manipulate the audience, arousing emotions
which befog the reasoning faculties, then they won't have time or bother to
ask, "what is x all about anyway?"

In looking over Taylor's passage, it is easy to find all the elements she
cites in the speeches of George W. Bush as the United States military
approached the March 2003 invasion of Iraq. Consider this passage, from
George W. Bush, from Cincinnati on October 7, 2002, where he was talking
about Iraq and WMDs:

Knowing these realities, America must not ignore the threat gathering
against us. Facing clear evidence of peril, we cannot wait for the final
proof—the smoking gun—that could come in the form of a mushroom
cloud. As President Kennedy said in October of 1962, "Neither the
United States of America, nor the world community of nations can
tolerate deliberate deception and offensive threats on the part of any
nation, large or small. We no longer live in a world," he said, "where
only the actual firing of weapons represents a sufficient challenge to a
nation's security to constitute maximum peril."

And consider the following speech on national television, just hours
before the Iraqi invasion, and less than two years after the 9/11 traumatic
brainwashing event:

---

[194] Taylor 2004, 27-28.

My fellow citizens, events in Iraq have now reached the final days of decision. For more than a decade, the United States and other nations have pursued patient and honorable efforts to disarm the Iraqi regime without war. That regime pledged to reveal and destroy all its weapons of mass destruction as a condition for ending the Persian Gulf War in 1991...

The Iraqi regime has used diplomacy as a ploy to gain time and advantage. It has uniformly defied Security Council resolutions demanding full disarmament. Over the years, U.N. weapons inspectors have been threatened by Iraqi officials, electronically bugged, and systematically deceived. Peaceful efforts to disarm the Iraqi regime have failed again and again — because we are not dealing with peaceful men.

Intelligence gathered by this and other governments leaves no doubt that the Iraq regime continues to possess and conceal some of the most lethal weapons ever devised. This regime has already used weapons of mass destruction against Iraq's neighbors and against Iraq's people.

The regime has a history of reckless aggression in the Middle East. It has a deep hatred of America and our friends. And it has aided, trained and harbored terrorists, including operatives of al Qaeda.

The danger is clear: using chemical, biological or, one day, nuclear weapons, obtained with the help of Iraq, the terrorists could fulfill their stated ambitions and kill thousands or hundreds of thousands of innocent people in our country, or any other.

The United States and other nations did nothing to deserve or invite this threat. But we will do everything to defeat it. Instead of drifting along toward tragedy, we will set a course toward safety. Before the day of horror can come, before it is too late to act, this danger will be removed.

The United States of America has the sovereign authority to use force in assuring its own national security. That duty falls to me, as Commander-in-Chief, by the oath I have sworn, by the oath I will keep.[195]

We are taught from a young age to be trusting of the habits and practices of the culture, such as war, consumerism, and telescreen-world addiction. We are taught that war is natural and inevitable, and that poverty is natural and inevitable. We are taught that our brains are just a coincidence of evolution, and that its great size is merely for improved social interaction or something vague and unverified like that. We are taught that human society is optimal when it is a fiat-money-based consumerist society. This all has to do with constructing ideology, and sets of emotions that go along with them (apathy,

---

[195] March 19, 2003.

greed, fear, etc.). It has been very important for corporatist controllers to entrap the youth of the nation in this onslaught using the telescreen, so that patterns are instilled into the developing mind from an early age, often never to be jarred loose before death. Schor writes:

> Children have become conduits from the consumer marketplace into the household, the link between advertisers and the family purse. Young people are repositories of consumer knowledge and awareness. They are the first adopters and avid users of many of the new technologies. They are the household members with the most passionate consumer desires, and are most clearly tethered to products, brands, and the latest trends. Children's social worlds are increasingly constructed around consuming, as brands and products have come to determine who is "in" or "out," who is hot or not, who deserves to have friends, or social status.[196]

We often learn from early on that it is okay to trust what we learn from adults, teachers, police officers, ministers, media, judges, and so on, no matter what they say. We do not learn the art of being skeptics and doubters and questioners in all those years we spend in elementary school. We learn to be hogs of meaningless, insignificant, or incorrect information, and we learn to get used to the idea of not "checking the sources," or questioning the credibility or motives of the information conveyor. We are not taught to construct reality for ourselves, but only to take the models of reality spoon-fed to us. We are taught to ridicule the skeptic—as if doubting is a harmful thing to do. If something is true, then doubt will not hurt it, and the doubt will only strengthen its truthfulness. But instead, doubting is often castigated, so that misinformation can permeate the telescreen-world unhindered. It is a vast life-long destruction of the soul and "re-education" to construct a false self.

> The impact of television images on individualized viewers and on society as a whole has been conceptualized in several theoretical frameworks. Gerbner's cultural indicators model suggests that television contains a common set of themes about appropriate and inappropriate social relations and behaviors that reflect cultural values and that cultivate the belief that patterns shown are normative. Because television contains a consistent set of messages, heavy viewers from varied social backgrounds come to share a common set of beliefs, a process described as *mainstreaming*.[197]

---

[196] Schor 2004, 11.

[197] Huston, Donnerstein, Fairchild, Feshbach, Katz, Murray, Rubinstein, Wilcox, and Zuckerman 1992, 35.

Consumerism: Thought and Behavior Control without Fear

"The things you own end up owning you."

—From the film *Fight Club*

"Have you noticed that everywhere on earth…
all the people are exactly the same?"

—from the film, *Silent Running*

Fear is critical for totalism, as just discussed, but in a well-rounded totalist scenario, citizens are not merely scared into a totalist nightmare, they must be fooled into loving it. That is where consumerism comes in.

According to Hertz, "the citizen has been abandoned and the consumer is all that matters."[198] Hertz also points out that, "Americans spend $8 billion a year on cosmetics while the world cannot find the $9 billion … needed to give all people access to clean drinking water."[199] Schor writes about the consumerist hysteria in the United States:

The United States is the most consumer-oriented society in the world. People work longer hours than any other industrialized country. Savings rates are lower. Consumer credit has exploded, and roughly a million and a half households declare bankruptcy every year. There are more than 46,000 shopping centers in the country, a nearly two-thirds increase since 1986. Despite fewer people per household, the size of houses continues to expand rapidly, with new construction featuring walk-in closets and three- or four-car garages to store record quantities of stuff. According to my estimates, the average adult acquires forty-eight new pieces of apparel a year… In my second book, *The Overspent American*, I catalogued the changes and identified the social trends driving them. Americans had come under strong imperatives to keep up with the escalating costs of basics, like health care and education, as well as luxuries, such as branded goods, bigger vehicles, and outlays for leisure and recreation. A trip to Disneyworld became an expensive, but urgent, social norm. Households spent more, saved less, and took on more debt. Meanwhile, commercialization proceeded apace as branding became ever more sophisticated, ads proliferated, and shopping turned into a 24/7 affair. The country was preoccupied with getting and spending… I conceptualized the consumer market in terms of its orientation to adults, as I watched SUVs replace cars, McMansions replace homes, and

---

[198] Hertz 2003, 12.
[199] Hertz 2003, 10.

designer labels proliferate for everything from sunglasses to jockey shorts.[200]

The madness of consumerism in the United States is a key issue in the brainwashing that currently is firmly being carried out daily. In discussing the Huxley-type of tyrannical state, Professor Taylor writes

> As Huxley himself says in the forward to his book, a "really efficient totalitarian state would be one in which the all-powerful executive of political bosses and their army of managers control a population of slaves who do not have to be coerced, because they love their servitude. To make them love it is the task assigned in present-day totalitarianism states, to ministries of propaganda, newspaper editors, and school-teachers. But their members are still crude and unscientific."[201]

Social and spiritual worlds of the ritual of the hunt, the rain-dance, the perception of the stillness and energy of nature, have been replaced by new worlds that the human is shoved in to. Meditation, prayer, sacred plant religion, Mind Power,[202] and intimacy, have been replaced by the addiction of the telescreen, and the consumerist addiction that plays off of the telescreen-created world. An interior awakeness and peace found when one discovers empathy toward panpsychistic nature has been removed and replaced with the perpetual inner agitation of having to perform and compete in consumerist America's despiritualized ritual of plastic life. This is life at the level of faces, and not deeper, since the citizenry does not know its interior world, or that an interior world of consciousness exists.

How can a society transform from the spiritualization that existed in the minds of the cave painters and the peyote eaters, into a despiritualized stupor? It occurs with an extremely well-organized secret government (a "wolf in sheep's clothing"),[203] that patiently and gradually implements new levels of thought and behavior control on an unsuspecting, distracted, greedy population. In her discussion on brainwashing, the media, and advertising, Taylor writes:

---

[200] Schor 2004, 9-11.

[201] Taylor 2004, 55.

[202] By "Mind Power," I specifically am referring to the real nature of the mind, and the real reason our brain is so large, compared to other animals. For more information, see Atkinson, William Walter, 2007 (1912), *Mind Power*, New York: Cosmo. For more information on this see Grupp 2009, or see "Mysteries of the Astral Light" by Manley P. Hall.

[203] See Grupp 2007 for full information on this subject.

...Cialdini calls 'weapons of influence'—in order to shed light on... brainwashing... [He] groups persuasion tactics into six types of weapons of influence... First... if we can be persuaded to make a small commitment we will be much more likely to follow this with a bigger one, which we may not actually have wanted to make, if that larger commitment is consistent with its smaller predecessor.[204]

Taylor is discussing an incremental manipulation of one mind onto another, starting off with a small and innocent first step, and once that is taken, further steps are taken.

I say "one mind onto another" in the last paragraph because humans for some reason have been created to mimic the behavior of each other. If a person enters a social circle and the members of the circle exhibit some idiosyncratic property, it is surprising how often the newly entering person will espouse that property also, even if it is entirely irrational or even harmful. Taylor continues in discussing Cialdini:

A second weapon of influence uses reciprocity: our tendency to feel obliged to a person who gives us something, no matter how trivial or unwanted the gift. This leaves us open to persuasion by the giver, and to get rid of the feeling of obligation we may agree to giving back a much larger gift than we received... Cialdini's last two weapons of influence employ the principles of scarcity and of 'social proof'. The former makes use of our instinct that if something is scarce it must be valuable, by artificially restricting availability, or emphasizing the scarcity of the product ('Limited Edition', 'Buy Now While Stocks Last', etc.). The principle of social proof is that, rather than think things out for ourselves, we often just follow the herd, working on the assumption that so many eager others can't be wrong.[205]

Unthought is the characteristic of brainwashed robo-humans. Their minds are in an amazingly overwhelmed state of media-stimulation, and all mental energy is spent on base-level perception and quick and thoughtless base-level reaction to the stimulation. The robo-human of the telescreen-world is a subhuman that is unaware of her inner desires, what she deeply longs for, what her spiritual self really needs, and instead, for example, she reaches for cosmetic surgery, Pepsi, and appropriate facial expressions to display in conversations. Sociology Professor, Todd Gitlin, writes:

Overwhelmed by the immensity and ubiquity of the media, we prefer to concentrate on their "effects." Considering the vast cornucopia of the items on offer, the cars, toys, beers, running shoes, weight reducers,

---

[204] Taylor 2004, 50.
[205] Taylor 2004, 50.

muscle tighteners, and so on, do media make us value material goods more than we otherwise would? Does the shapeliness of the models promoting the cars and taco chips make us want to be thinner, more muscular, or implanted with silicone? Have the commercials for prescription drugs made us reliable customers for pharmaceutical blockbusters like Viagra and Claritin? Do the shoot-ups and gore make us more aggressive and murderous, the high-velocity vehicle chases more prone to speed and mayhem? Has the bare flesh on screen made us sex crazed? Have the pace and discontinuity of the media put deficits in our attention? ... Considering the pleasures of private immersion, have we become less sociable...? Sure, media have effects on behaviors and ideas, not so much because any single exposure is powerful but because they repeat. And repeat. And repeat. *There is ample evidence that the answer to each of the questions above is, largely, yes*—with the important qualification that more aggressive is not the same as more murderous. (For this link in the logical chain to be forged, guns must be freely available.)[206] (Emphasis added.)

Conclusion

It is often maintained that the high-tech thought control that I have been discussing in this book was not secretly and deliberately put into place, but rather it fell into place by "capitalists" that were just seeking money. Chomsky appears to advocate this theory,[207] but nothing could be further from the truth. Consider this passage from Miller, which comes from the covert work of the heads of General Motors, to learn how to manipulate people and get them to accept the fate that the GM heads wanted to enforce, and which shows the deliberate corporate thought control used way back in the 1930's:

It is felt that whereas a man may read an advertisement about the "American Way" and laugh at it, or draw from it a conclusion opposite to the one its author intended, he will find great difficulty in acting contrary to the beliefs of the organizations to which he belongs, or of the social-pressure groups within whose range he lives. To generalize, it is felt that if a man belongs to the "right" groups his thinking will be "right," and that otherwise the "right" ideas cannot be sold to him.[208]

---

[206] Gitlin 2002, 7-8. Brainwashing expert, Taylor, also discusses these issues, and how they can change our thought and behavior without us being immediately aware. (Taylor 2004, 53)

[207] He does so in the first 30 pages of his famous book, *Manufacturing Consent*, that he wrote with Herman.

[208] Cited in Miller 1989, 14.

Our predicament in the telescreen-world is pre-planned by the secret government of the New World Order. There is nothing accidental about it. Taylor writes:

> Brainwashing is a deliberate act; that is, intentional behavior on the part of the brainwasher is part of the essence of brainwashing. This purpose may not be malicious—the brainwasher may sincerely believe that the victim will benefit from 're-education'—but judging an act as malicious depends heavily on perspective, so hostility is not the essential point. What matters is that the action is intended and carried out in order to change the victim.[209]

---

[209] Taylor 2004, 10. She goes on over the next page of her book to tell us that there is of course more involved obviously than just the attempt to change another's mind, and that brainwashing is a special sort of such change.

6. The Mechanics and Nature of the Various Forms of American Media Brainwashing

The Party said that Oceania had never been in alliance with Eurasia. He, Winston Smith, knew that Oceania had been in alliance with Eurasia as short a time as four years ago. But where did that knowledge exist? Only in his own consciousness, which in any case must soon be annihilated. And if all others accepted the lie which the Party imposed—if all records told the same tale—then the lie passed into history and became truth. "Who controls the past," ran the Party slogan, "controls the future: who controls the present controls the past."

-*1984*, p. 34, Signet Classics Edition

Introduction to Corporate Media

The media are a peculiar thing. In the case of news media of the telescreen-world, they usually consist of persons discussing, in a very confident and convincing manner, topics and issues that they are not experts on. Often very little information can be verified, with very little information that constitutes a *report*, or *news report,* a "report" is defined as philosophers define it: an unemotional, unbiased description of facts and states of affairs about the world. But oddly, these unchecked, unverifiable, non-reports delivered by non-experts are not only *trusted* by many Americans, but they are believed by many Americans *to be the news*. Americans will choose corporatist media information over other streams of information, such as lectures, academic books, alternative media sources like Infowars.com, and so on, believing that the corporatist media opinion and partial reporting *are facts*, as if opinion is fact, and partial reporting is fact.

In this chapter, I will show in detail how the telescreen-world functions as a brainwashing instrument. In a previous chapter we saw how the all-pervasive corporatist media of the United States construct the self and consciousness of the citizens. It is by this constructing of the self that the corporate communists are able to construct the persons and laborers who sacrifice their lives to fascist domination. Lives which do not give them hope, but sadness, which oppress and/or kill them, hurt and ruin their families, and typically distort or eliminate their energy for life. The result is a culture of thoughtless, "desperate" (to use Thoreau's word[210]), downtrodden addicts—addicted to alcohol, TV, consumerism, various legal or illegal drugs

---

[210] From *Walden*: "The mass of men live lives of quiet desperation." This philosophy of the desperation of the common person is also a primary feature of the film *Fight Club*.

(Prozac, etc.), therapists and self-improvement books,[211] forced recreation, emotion-readjustment, sleep aids, to name a few.

Do Not Know Thyself

In previous chapters I discussed how people are trained in the contemporary corporatist world to not look at themselves, but rather to solely look out at the world around them, so that the outer world creates their consciousness, so they never know who they are. The mass media will not release material that promotes the idea that people should examine themselves (this actually will be mocked at some times, to varying degrees, by the education system and media telescreen-world), since it is harmful to corporatist interests, for reasons given in previous chapters. Self-examination is merely the simple, healthy, and necessary task of taking a look at *yourself*. To paraphrase an idea of a famous Zen Buddhist, Shunryu Suzuki Roshi, to self-examine is to take your eyes that you look at the world with, and you look inside at yourself.[212] If you do not do this, how will you ever know what your very own *self* is all about?

Answer: you won't. You will forever be oblivious to your own selfhood, to what you are really all about, what you are made of (which is thoughts and feelings, bound up in states of consciousness that give rise to a vital *life*). The point here is the monopolistic corporatists take measures to ensure that you do not live with an awareness of your self. This is merely because if you take a look at your self, what do you think will happen? You will start to understand simple things, such as how you truly feel about reality, about corporatist communism,[213] about anything.

Interestingly, those who make a transformation *from* being oblivious to their self *to* becoming aware of their self-states, typically report that they had no idea of all the feelings they had inside them, and so different from what they thought they were feeling about things before the crossover to introspection. This gives an indication as to why this is dangerous to

---

[211] Some readers might find it odd that I call this an addiction, and imply that it is a problem. Therapists are needed, for the most part, because people are told that something is wrong with them, that the way they feel is not the way they are supposed to feel. But it seems that the feelings humans have are natural and "automatic" (uncontrollable) responses to the environment, which are there for a reason, without exception. When I go to work to McDonalds, it is *normal* that I feel dread about going. Therapy is only needed if a person does not realize this, and if they believe they should not feel the things they do.

[212] This is a major idea in Suzuki Roshi's classic Zen Buddhist text, *Zen Mind, Beginner's Mind*, 1973, Weatherhill.

[213] See Grupp 2007, ch. 3, for complete information on the details of corporate communism in America.

corporatists. Feelings can be enemies of corporatists, since the discovery of one's true inner, subjective self is enormously empowering, and empowered workers are dangerous, since they may not feel that the corporation has control and power over their selves. If one "sees" one's actual feelings, one questions previously held beliefs and concepts. Seeing one's own self and feelings leads to noticing that how one actually feels about things is not how the pre-introspective false-self feels about them. This could incite one not to obey, but rather to feel autonomous feelings, which could give rise to expressions like this: "but I don't agree...," "but that is illogical...," "but that is a lie...," "but that is not fair payment...," "but that could hurt somebody...," "but I don't' want to do that..." These "buts" are expressions of a self that is not merely following the orders of others, but is instead following its own order, so it cannot obediently and thoughtlessly work within monopolistic corrupt mega-corporate systems. This is why Prozac is used as treatment for so-called "mental illnesses." They merely drug patients rather than help them see what is disturbing them, which is the culture. That might cause a patient to look inward, find their feelings and their self, and see that it could be the structure of society that is to blame for the depression or other symptoms.

To keep the brainwashed non-introspective false-self mind-numbed, entertainment — unfulfilled but carnal, tabloid, "thrilling," and devoid of educational value — must be continually thrown at the person. (As I discuss often in this book, this includes so-called educational television.) The corporatists will want to support media that, for example, encourage "weekend warrior" recreational activities, but not questioning or intellectual activities. The corporatist communists will sponsor dumbed-over sitcoms before any show that has accurate empirical data or scientific research of any sort. Empirical data (i.e., science), logical-philosophical erudition, and general skepticism, cannot enter into a propaganda system, since they promote awakeness, and thus work as insomnia to the sleep induced by the propaganda system.

Americans are so accustomed to media full of mindless material that they do not seem to know that it does not have to be that way, that it only is that way because the corporatist sponsors dictated it to be so, and this is not how humans have always lived.

Widespread Cultic Behavior in the United States

The outward-focused telescreen life only can create a culture of cult behavior on a mass scale. There are many techniques of brainwashing, and many varieties of ways that big or small groups can be brainwashed. One famous variety is through cult techniques, which are known for brainwashing victims who have no idea that they are being brainwashed, no matter how clearly one points it out to them. To save time, I recommend the reader see another work[214] for terse but thorough discussion of what cults involve, and from reading that one will find that it seems that the United States' brainwashing system partially involves cultic techniques.

Cultic Traits: In-Group/Out Versus Out-Group

Group activity is a cultic trait exhibited on a wide scale. 9/11 brought Americans into a specific sort of cultic group activity, for reasons that Taylor discusses in her discussion of cult group closure:

> Unfortunately, leaders often have [or fabricate] beliefs which are very far from matching reality and which can become more extreme as they are encouraged by their followers. The predilection of many cult leaders for abstract, ambiguous, and therefore unchallengeable ideas can further reduce the likelihood of reality testing, while the intense milieu control exerted by cults over their members means that most of the reality available for testing is supplied by the group environment. This is seen in the phenomenon of 'groupthink', alleged to have occurred, notoriously, during the Bay of Pigs fiasco. The US government's series of disastrous decisions ratcheted up tensions between the US and Cuba, tensions which would lead to the brink of nuclear war. The charisma of the American president, John F. Kennedy, the closed nature of the decisive meetings, and strong anti-Russian convictions of those making the decisions, and the importance of abstract ideas such as 'the future of the free world', all contributed to an assessment of the political situation which was deeply unrealistic and very nearly lethal... as the group becomes more cohesive, and its importance in its members' lives greater, the difference between the group and the outside world also increases. The group tends to practice increasingly strict boundary control to protect against intrusion by others. This can include 'deviant' behavior—glazed expression, xenophobia, or aggression—towards any outsider perceived as threatening. This in turn provokes hostility from the outgroup, which further enhances cohesiveness.[215]

As chapter 1 shows, this is what occurred with the Iraq war (in addition to other events, such as the one Taylor discusses). Due to the similarities of cult activity and Bush's persona, I feel justified in referring to Bush as a sort cult leader of the USA. (Of he was only a leader in theory, since he in actual reality did not control anything in the corporatist scenario, as discussed in previous chapters). In truth, many media personalities and politicians

---

[214] Taylor 2004, 29-47.
[215] Taylor 2004, 42.

function in this way, but Bush was a focal cult leader from 2001-2004, so I will focus a bit on him in this subsection.

In her discussion of brainwashing and media and advertising, Taylor writes that[216] "widely used weapons of influence rely on the authority and the likeability of the persuader." Even Hillary Clinton has commented on how charming George W. Bush is,[217] and I don't think that the army of media personalities and advertising personalities out there get into their positions by not having, or being able to fake, the charm and likeability they exude. When Goebbels first met and got to know Hitler, he said "I like him. He puts us to shame with his kindness... You can't help liking him as a person."[218] The leader arouses admiration for himself, through either fear or charisma, that binds the herd together, where the out-group are seen as savages, and the in-group is viewed as acceptable.

How to Create News that Looks Like News But Which is all Non-News: The Ways People (Such as "Newscasters") Deny or Avoid Evidential Accounts of Reality

"One of the lessons I learned early on [about how to talk to the press] was never say never... And secondly, never answer the question that is asked of you. Answer the question that you wish had been asked of you. And quite frankly, I followed that rule; it's a very good rule."

—Robert McNamara, Former Secretary of Defense
(during the Vietnam War)[219]

So far in this chapter, we have seen that the media creates an outward-focused cult that is despiritualized. That introduction was necessary to set the stage for the major task of this section, which is to show precisely how the mass media use various techniques and tools to create a brainwashed citizenry. These techniques effortlessly brainwash the citizenry if it is despiritualized, cultic apathetic, non-introverted, and materialistic/ consumeristic, but also impoverished, fearful, unhealthy (obesity, poor eating habits and poor food and water in the United States,[220] etc.), and uncritical. These put the citizenry in a state that is well and ready for thought control and social engineering.

---

[216] Taylor 2004, 51.

[217] "Sen. Clinton Says Bush Has Charm, Charisma," *Devlin Barrett, The Associated Press*, Tuesday, May 9, 2006.

[218] In Hachmeister 2004.

[219] This was uttered in the DVD documentary, the *Fog of War* (DVD, directed by: Errol Morris, 2004, Sony Pictures).

[220] See Grupp 2007 for more information.

I will next discuss the specific mechanics of the news media. I will go through various points, step by step.

A critical issue with the news is that it is not an *evidential* account of reality most of the time, but rather is a *belief-based* account. Another way to put this is: very often the media will take an actual fact and discuss it in a way where it becomes a false account: a fact is turned into a non-fact. 9/11 provides a good example. The only things that TV-watchers saw on 9/11 were two planes hit buildings, three controlled demolitions of buildings (most Americans only saw two, however), and a rather small collapsed section at the Pentagon. Taking merely the empirical data of 9/11, this is all TV-watchers on 9/11 viewed, and thus they are the only real facts about 9/11 to be gained from the corporate media. The scientific account of 9/11 would be to maintain the following: I only have evidence for the following, and nothing more: three controlled demolitions, a collapsed Pentagon section, and two ambiguously marked planes hitting two of the buildings, that some time later were deliberately demolished. This is a factual, trustworthy, scientific account. But being non-scientific, the corporate media gives a plethora of other details, so many that it in fact *transforms a factual account into non-fact, transforms the real into the non-real.* For example, we were all told something like the following in the day and years after 9/11: "there were foreign terrorists flying commercial jetliners and this marks the beginning of a 100-year war involving enemies that we cannot see and who live in caves." The national corporate media creates reality and social reality, merely by sticking to a non-scientific account of reality that the citizenry is amenable to, since they are used to such an approach to reality as that, as their government-mandated elementary education taught them on a daily basis while growing up.

This is only one example of how this distorting media creation of reality occurs. Next I will explore all the major techniques and ways that people deny or avoid talking about reality, about real states of affairs, and instead convincingly talk about *non-reality.* In professional philosophy, philosophers call these *informal fallacies*, and they are merely ways that people attempt to trick each other, and the disclosure and study of informal fallacies has a long history, all the way back to the ancient Greek philosophers.

Every day, as a part of our normal way of talking to one another, people use techniques on each other in order to trick one another. For example, if a person wants to get you to believe that communism is evil, it is better to invent a false horror story—either deliberately or without knowing they are making it up—than to give an empirical/factual account. The fabricated horror story will have a greater impact. This is an example of an informal fallacy, and it involves one person trying to trick another: *one person trying to get another person to believe something about reality that is false.*

The informal fallacies are techniques that are used by the news media personalities. This is all just a part of normal, non-evidential, non-scientific, uncritical everyday communication and thought between ordinary people, and which people have been taught is normal and natural communication. So, the media personalities pick up on this and exploit it further, and therein reinforce the idea that it is normal behavior: the media teaches that it is normal behavior.

If two American people communicating with one another about Iraqi weapons of mass destruction in 2002 each do not understand that they are discussing non-reality, then their conversation is about as sensible as discussing unicorns or round squares. But these two people will likely continue their conversation about the false reality, erroneously believing they are discussing actual reality. The two people in this example are meant to represent the American citizenry and the American media. Much of this transformation of fact into non-fact, I think, is not intentional among people in their daily lives, even by some lower-level people in the media-industrial complex. Given the apathy generated by the corporatist culture, it may be easier for ordinary persons to understand a sloppy, distorted, imprecise account of distorted facts and/or non-reality, rather than hear a stone-faced critical or scientific account of actual reality. To summarize, the media communicating with (i.e., broadcasting to) the American citizenry, unfortunately, often resembles a wealthy man telling a poor man about a unicorn standing on a round square.

Ten Tools of Brainwashing

There are ten primary ways I am aware of that the corporate media is able to make the non-evidential, often absurd, belief-based account of non-reality described above appear to be a credible, factual account of reality. In other words, there are ten primary techniques used by the corporate media to fool people into believing the pervasive and steady stream of untruths about the world they live in.

1. **Ignoring details**. The mass media report that Colin Powell has presented evidence to the UN that Iraq has WMDs, but forget to mention that Powell is using information from 1989, and that the WMD supplies from 1989 were sold to Saddam by the US. Thus it will appear to the average American that Saddam is a hostile threat, when in reality he is not, the threat is in Powell's duplicity. This is an example of ignoring details: if you only report part of the story, you can change a story to have it say whatever you'd like. This is a common technique used by the mass media when they manipulate people, but it is also a key way people manipulate each other in everyday life. This comes very naturally and spontaneously to

people, and since some facts are reported, people can demand that they are not lying, since, after all, they reported facts.

2.   **"Straw person" claims or "adjustments**." A straw person claim is when a person falsely describes an entity (person, event, etc.) and uses the false description to be slanderous about the described entity. For example, if a news caster calls a 9/11 skeptic a "conspiracy theorist," or "an idiot," they are giving a description of them that is not accurate. This slander may impact the viewer, successfully making the 9/11 skeptic look like a foolish person that should be ignored. This is a very clever tactic, and it is a standard procedure on many news shows, and in day-to-day interactions among people.[221]

3.   **Using famous people and TV personalities to convey distorted or false picture**. Why are the views of Bono, Oprah, Whoopie, Bruce Springsteen, and others given such prominence in the mass media? Do they

---

[221] I would like to re-emphasize how common these points are to "normal" day-to-day human communication. I discuss them here as if they are something that only the media does, but of course that is not true. These points describe nearly all of human communications, as philosophers who teach "critical thinking" in universities point out to students. These errors are also, of course, common in the academic world—a world that is supposed to think critically. These issues are often the principal ways some academics respond to me. For example, I gave a talk on quantum physics at the Illinois Institute of Technology in early May of 2006. I spoke to people from several departments. It became quickly evident that none of them had any knowledge of the subject I was speaking on, nor did they bread my article I was presenting, which they were given before the talk to peruse and prepare their own remarks. Yet they were not afraid to pose aggressive straw man attacks. I contemplated on the talk afterward, and concluded that, just like the news media, the communicative exchanges between me and the audience members who chose to speak up were never about the empirical details of my research. Instead they were flawed exchanges of words that exhibited the points being discussed here. To give just one of countless examples, when I gave my uncontroversial discussion of what an electron is, one of the things I did was say this: "it does not have any parts. Since it does not have any pieces,…" Notice I use the word "parts," and then "pieces." I was instantly attacked by a philosopher in the audience for using these words as if they are the same. "They are clearly distinct," he said, "and you can't use them both to describe the electron. I find this whole paper to be poorly written." I merely responded by saying, "Okay, can you tell me the specific difference between the definitions of each of the words, 'parts' and 'pieces,' so that I can see my error and understand why this is a problem?" He could not answer the question, and thus the claim he so confidently uttered was merely a straw-person distraction technique, likely because he was displeased by the non-metaphysical nature of my article. Philosophers called metaphysicians make up a huge portion of the academic philosophers today. When I converse with them, I am always attacked for bogus reasons, in ways that exhibit the fallacies being discussed here about the media.

have some expertise that gives them an authority position about various topics (vaccines for Bono, Africa for Oprah, etc.)? Or is it just that they are famous, people like them, and therefore they have influence? In July 2006, when he did not hold a political office, Newt Gingrich told Americans through virtually every corporate media channel that "we are at the early stages of World War III." Millions of Americans might believe it merely because of his celebrity-politician status, and not based on anything but that. People have a tendency to believe a fantastical concept, a false story, or an account of a false-flag terrorist event, if a famous person says it in the mass media before millions of people, rather than if an "unknown" or "everyday" person does, like your next-door neighbor, who is not in the media spotlight. People do not judge the argument on its merits. Americans will be more likely to believe that America is "at the early stages of world war III" if Newt Gingrich says it than if a homeless person does, for example—even though both accounts are equally disinformative.[222] This tactic often reduces "analysis" of a situation to the status of *non-debate*, since often such celebrity performances are given in a way where it is implied that it would be inappropriate to question the "information" being given, due to the celebrity's supposed knowledge and social status.

4.   **Flat-out deny evidence.** This is one of the most powerful tactics. What if the CNN newscasters confidently told viewers that "*it is false* that Saddam Hussein does not have weapons of mass destruction"? What if the Fox News Channel news casters confidently tell viewers that "*it is false* that the government was behind the 9/11 attacks"? Who is there to check these details, to offer the counter position? Who is there on the air to say: "Wait, are you sure about that?" Or, "Wait, what about all the evidence at the Pentagon that the 60-ton plane did not even break a lot of the windows at the Pentagon before the small section of wall at the Pentagon fell, 25 minutes after the explosion?" There is nobody present on the air to answer these questions, or to offer evidence, or to merely state the counter position. This is a standard way that news reporting happens: report a story inaccurately and thus give Americans a *false account of reality*—which, as we have seen is a principal quality of mass brainwashing. This can occur because the news media have confidence that Americans will not go and check the facts for themselves, and will merely trust what they are told. With this sort of power, virtually anything can be told to viewers and listeners of the media, and if it is all reported in unison across all the corporate news channels (CNN, Fox, etc.) they will believe nearly anything they are told. In an uncritical thinking culture, denying facts is a powerful tool that can be used to distort information, since so many people are

---

[222] To see why Newt's account is disinformative, see Grupp 2007, chapter 4.

oblivious and unsuspecting of the fact that the mass media could be all spreading information about non-reality.

5.   **Change the subject (and do so in a non-obvious way).** This is another common and powerful technique that is used by media personalities, politicians, and many ordinary people. If I criticize a politician for invading Iraq on unjust grounds, he might respond with this statement: "But Saddam was a dictator. So you want a dictator to be in power? You probably also would like Hitler to have won World War II, I bet." Notice that the response does not address the issue brought up, which was unjust reasons for starting a war. Instead, the response goes all the way to calling the questioner a Nazi. I have seen this exact response used on the Fox News Channel many times, and that is why I chose this Nazi example to illustrate my point. If some person or group p_1 criticizes a person or group p_2 for doing or saying x, and p_2 responds by discussing y instead of x, p_2 successfully avoids x (which could be a sticky issue), by changing of the subject in a way noticed by p_1. When Hillary Clinton attacked Anne Coulter on June 7, 2006 for claiming that the "Jersey Widows" (political activists who lost husbands on 9-11-01) were "enjoying their husband's deaths," Coulter's immediate response was a counter attack on Hillary's husband Bill Clinton for several of his cruel behaviors. Coulter's response may have appeared convincing, and given Coulter a feeling of power, but it had nothing to do with the issue: the "Jersey Widows." Yet this response likely convinced many listeners as an effective counter-attack. Here's another interesting example. In a discussion of the book *Fortunate Son*, which was the first biographical account published about Bush that claimed he was a cocaine connoisseur, Bush was asked about it. He immediately and angrily retorted at a news conference in reference to the author, "Obviously if he is a convicted felon he has no credibility..."[223] He did not have to address the issues, or possible evidence for this claim. Bush merely changed the subject, attacked the messenger, and avoided the sticky issue. Much of the news coverage Americans are subjected to is merely a process of changing the subject.

6.   **Load up the news with non-news, and with tabloid and soap opera stories.** We all know who *Monica* is. Even though this story is so old that it did not even happen in the current decade, and even though I don't even need to give you her last name, Americans still all know who I am talking about. Americans are quite aware of Monica, but how many know how

---

[223] See the DVD documentary, *Horns and Halos*, Directors: Suki Hawley, and Michael Galinsky. ASIN: B0002CYQLU

many nuclear bombs the United States government has?[224] Americans know who this Monica of the 1990s is, but how many of them know which bills the Congress has discussed or passed this week, or what the Supreme Court discussed today and last week, or what a lobbyist does, or what the term "PD-51"[225] means?. The news media, and thus the typical American citizen's consciousness, is flooded with non-news: tabloid stories about sex scandals, pointless bickering between politicians about issues that do not concern the American people, shark or cougar bite victims, terrorist "threats." If the news media are filled with such stories, there is no space, time or need to report on the pollution at US Steel in Gary, Indiana (which spread mercury all over downwind). Nor the nuclear weapons profits of GE, the mass murder that occurs as a result of corporate pollution,[226] the latest bills passed by the government all the time, the plan for mass microchipping of humanity, Morgellons disease, the Pentagon wall before it collapsed on 9/11, and all the rest of the nearly countless other items that could be talked about.

7.   **Cover stories or debates that are not at the heart of the matter, or that are completely irrelevant**. The corporatist news media can *pretend* to soundly report on "the facts" by endlessly presenting a façade of news coverage about entirely insignificant issues, since most people will not see them as insignificant. For example, the news media can pretend to be working in the interests of the public (which now does not support the Iraq War) by discussing at length issues such as "when the troops will come home," "when should there be a troop withdrawal," and so forth. They never report on the truest and most relevant issues of the war situation— such as the number of casualties, which are rarely reported accurately, or reported at all, in the US corporatist media, but which number in the millions[227]. From my extensive viewing of the Fox News Channel and CNN while I was doing research for this book during the 2005 and 2006, it is my assessment that such issues as casualty count on either side were nearly never reported on. Instead, silly issues such as how soldiers should get proper armor, or if there are any supposed dissidents in the Democratic party (e.g., Murtha and Skull-and-Bones Kerry), pervaded the news coverage. As you will see below, this method of distraction and setting up a false debate was a key tactic for the Nazi media and propaganda campaign.

---

[224] The answer is: the United States has enough nuclear weapons (at least those that are known to exist) to kill all life on earth at least 7000 times. See Caldicott 2004.

[225] Presidential Directive 51, where Bush declared that if there is an emergency of any kind, he can claim himself the dictator of the United States.

[226] Discussed in Grupp 2007, ch. 4.

[227] See Grupp 2007 for documentation on these numbers.

8.   **Get an "expert" on television to express a *belief* (i.e., to confidently express a non-evidential account).** In a culture that is working on a belief-based level of reality, and is not so concerned with evidence-based accounts of reality, statements like "I believe that Iran has connections to al-Qaeda" have a lot of power. Yet they could be wrong or meaningless, since they are non-evidential, belief-based accounts. An uncritical account, expressing something like "I believe there is evidence that Osama and Iran have strong connections," is good enough, since the populace is not looking for anything more than belief statements, not and not anything more than belief. Therefore, a powerful way to deny empirical issues is to just express *belief* about them to the contrary. This expression of belief will often appear as a factual refutation to the uncritical person. Interestingly, from my experience, asking a person for evidence for the claims they make often makes a person *angry*. I recall before the March 2003 start of the Iraq War asking my students, "Can any of you prove that the United States has a reason to invade Iraq, or that Saddam has the WMDs?" Many students became quite angered at my simple inquiry for mere evidence. Often a belief-based account is a source of comfort supporting a group or herd mentality, while the mere seeking of evidence is a challenge to the comfortable group illusion. So asking a brainwashed person to provide evidence for some issue or claim that is *believed* in is often not viewed favorably. Try going to your local university and asking the biology department researchers to show you the "missing link" between chimps and humans, and you might see what I mean. You will not likely be viewed as some sort of honorable evidence-seeking scientist. Evidence-seeking and empirical data-seeking is the minority activity, and is perhaps the greatest opponent to brainwashing and to corporatist control. I have been called a terrorist for merely showing people a picture of the Pentagon wall before it collapsed on 9/11. Showing them that picture is a mere presentation of empirical data, but that scientific-friendly pursuit can be so antagonistic to brainwashed masses that it can make them believe the scientist is a criminal.

9.   **Create a contradiction.** A contradiction is when an entity has both a property and its opposite property in an impossible way at the same time. For example, you cannot be lying down and standing up at the same time. To maintain that you are would be to maintain that you are standing up and not standing up at the same time, which is impossible, and cannot even be imagined. A square cannot be a circle, since that would mean that a square is not a square. Contradictions are impossible states of affairs, but the corporatist news media is filled with such impossibilities. Here is an example. Bill O'Reilly, on Friday June 2, 2006 on his show "The Factor," specifically said that "Marines killed civilians" in Haditha Iraq (there was a controversy surrounding soldier atrocities circulating through the media at

that time). But then the following Monday, June 5, 2006, Bill O'Reilly read an email from a viewer at the end of "The Factor," where the viewer expressed that she/he could not believe Bill O'Reilly was "convicting the Marines before investigation occurs." In response to this email, Bill O'Reilly confidently, and perhaps a bit condescendingly, simply said, "No such thing occurred, you must be thinking of another show," and then he moved on to the next subject. This is a good example of a contradiction. If we are to take O'Reilly at his word, he *did and did not* say "marines killed civilians," which is a bald contradiction, analogous to maintaining that a circle is a square. The news media relies on the public not putting the details of the news coverage together, for if they did, they would see enormous contradictions, and the entire edifice of the corporatist news media would fall into question. They would notice, for example, that the news media told them on 9/11 that there was and was not a plane that hit the Pentagon; or that they were told both that Bush did and did not win the 2000 Presidential election. This is a pervasive form of Orwellian doublethink, such as when Bush Jr. has told us that in order to have peace in Iraq we need to invade it (have war), so war is peace—one of the party lines of the controllers in Orwell's *1984*. This contradictory non-reasoning is the standard of news coverage; anybody can witness this if they merely put the details of corporate news information together.

10.   **Name-calling**. (This is similar to the "straw person" fallacy discussed above.) Much of the contemporary news media consists of name-calling. If President Bush wants to invade a sovereign nation, merely calling the nation "terrorist" and "evil" through the corporatist news media channels enough times could muster majority support for the war among the citizenry. If you are not clear that this sort of name-calling occurs, then merely turn on "The Factor," on the Fox News Channel, or watch Sean Hannity on the Fox News Channel, or listen to what the politicians say on any corporatist news channel, and you will see what I mean. People protesting the World Bank are called "thugs" or "hooligans." Anti-Bush protestors in South America are called "guerrillas" or "rebels." Iranians are called "terrorists." French are called "snobs" or "idiots." 9/11 skeptics are called "anti-American." There are too many examples to list. Americans seem to be so accustomed to this name calling that they hardly notice it pervading the news media, the language of the politicians, and the way they deal with other people in their daily life.

These ten ways of distorting fact and transforming it into non-fact are standards of the corporatist news media industry. Unfortunately, to my knowledge, it seems that Americans are largely unaware of these types of distortion and of this uncritical, imprecise, non-empirical reporting of the news, which only gives them false information: it gets them to believe in non-reality. For the mass media to be proficient in brainwashing the citizens, there must be a well-planned unification of information sources, and an uncritical, unskeptical citizenry. Given these factors, and if warmongers have control of the media, military, and policymaking, then disastrous fascism must result. As we will see in a chapter below, this is currently under way here in the USA, and it is likely going to reach Nazi-level horror some time in the next decade, if not sooner.

What is *Not* Reported is Considered Non-Fact

What the corporate media does not report tends to remain unknown in the minds of Americans. The American citizenry will tend to consider these unreported issues to be non-facts, if someone points them out to them. For example, if I inform the average person that radiation treatment causes cancer (since radiation is well-known to cause cancer), the average person will tell me, "Well, I have never heard that; that can't be true." See how that works? If a person doesn't know about something, then they will freely deny it if they want to. You can test this on others to verify that it is common. This is like asserting that since I don't know anything about x, therefore x is not true. This is, actually, another informal fallacy, discussed by philosophers, and it is called the "fallacy of ignorance:" *if I don't have any evidence for x, then x does not exist.* This is a fallacy because you do not have evidence for the non-existence of x.

If that average American is unaware that on 9-11-01 the Pentagon wall that the "plane" allegedly hit stood for 25 minutes before it fell, without creating a big gaping hole in it, and without breaking more than a few of the windows, they will tend to believe it. Instead will believe that these events of unbroken windows etc. did not happen. They will believe this because they can't believe that the mass media would not report on it, so if the mass media did not, then they won't believe it's real. They may have seen the mass media lie about the side effects of their cholesterol drug, but they will still be trusting of their authority figures (the mass media corporations), and not put it all together that the mass media is lying to them.

What is *widely believed* by people will be taken to be *fact* by them, what is not will be thought false. Americans, in general, will believe in an absurdity if they see it on the news and they see their friends believing in it; and they will not believe in a simple empirical account of reality if they do not see their friends believing in it. It seems that, as I discussed in the last section (when I discussed informal fallacy #3), people consider widely agreed-upon bits of information, or widely distributed bits of information, to be relevant and noteworthy. The not widely agreed-upon or distributed are to be ignored, and are not facts.

Failing to report issues, and assuming that what is unreported is not fact, is often called "agenda-cutting," and it seems to occur not just in the corporatist media, *but it pervades American culture and the day-to-day interactions of humans.* I have extensively seen activities that resemble something like agenda cutting going on in the professional journals in my academic field of philosophy. I have submitted articles to journals where I would receive quite amateurish responses. This was most evident in my recently published article on atheism in the prestigious journal *Sophia.* I submitted this article to many journals, getting responses from leaders in the field, who literally would tell me things like this: your article cannot be reviewed for publication since it is based on the false premise that God does not exist. Notice that the agenda being cut here is the possibility that God does not exist; that issue was not permitted. This and other things I have witnessed in academic publishing have led me to believe that agenda cutting is not uncommon within the editorial boards of some academic journals. I have had physics professors tell me with earnestness that agenda cutting and similar practices are surely alive and well amid the journals of that field also, even in some cases where a potentially revolutionary discovery is cut from the agenda.

Thus, failure to report issues is a widespread, common phenomenon, and from many areas of reality it contributes to a construction in the minds of Americans of a false view of reality—so false that an absurd reality is often believed to exist.

News "Management:" The News is Merely Made Up

So far in this chapter we have seen in detail some of the ways and techniques that the corporatist news media are constructed by corporatist fascists for the sake of the destruction of human consciousness. We have seen how information is distorted and reality is misrepresented in such a manner that a complete fabrication of reality is constructed through media channels for the viewing entertainment of American citizens.

Above we discussed how lies are simply told in the media. Next I will discuss how fakery persists in the mass media. The news about the "war on terrorism" forms a fabricated Orwellian war cinema, as I call it. Similar to this, Schechter talks about how stories in the Iraq war were specifically just invented, and then played out in the media like a storm.[228] In Schechter (2004), *CNN*'s famous reporter, Christine Amanpour, is quoted as saying that in the first Gulf War in the early 1990 ("Desert Storm"),

---

[228] Schechter 2004

Behind our backs, behind the backs of the field reporters, field producers and crews on the ground... our bosses made a deal with the establishment to create 'pools'... what I call 'ball and chain', handcuffed, managed news reporting.

The New Years Day West Virginia mine tragedy on January 1, 2006 enjoyed truly *overwhelming and intensive* coverage when 13 miners died in a mine explosion. On January 5th and 6th, 2006 it was still the lead cover story on the front page of the *USA Today*, covering approximately half the front page each day, as well as the top story on news shows. Interestingly, on January 6, 2006, 130 were killed—10 times that of the miner accident a week earlier—in Iraq in massive "insurgent" attacks, including several US soldiers. This story was confined to a 2-inch x 2-inch bottom corner slot on *USA Today*. Then on January 19th *USA Today* ran another big front page story on the mine accident. And amazingly, this same story was the major front page story again for the *USA Today* on February 9, 2006.[229] This was at the same time span that 12 children drowned in Zanzibar on the 8th,[230] which did not appear in section A of the *USA Today* on the 9th at all, although the number of casualties was similar in each case, 12 and 13. On the 6th, the miners were described as being very happy, even ebullient, about their jobs and their work.[231]

Writing in 2002, years before this great tragedy, Winslow tells us that, "as many as 100,000 miners have been killed and 265,000 have been disabled by coal dust (black lung) disease. Another 85,000 textile workers suffer lung diseases from cotton dust (brown lung)."[232] This is a great example of how news is merely made up: a story of fewer than 10 dying is front page for a week, but news of at least 100,000 *is not reported at all.*

Schechter notes how before the March 2003 invasion of Iraq by the United States, many groups, including many Hollywood celebrities, attempted to put anti-war advertisements on television, but the networks typically would not run them, even though the money for the ads was good.[233] Hertz also discusses[234] how political ads are not allowed to be aired to paying customers on the major networks (e.g., NBC and CBS). These are merely additional examples of the Orwellian-level censorship and

---

[229] "For miner, fog is lifting," Emily Bazar, February 9, 2006, *USA Today*, front page, and continued on page 4A.

[230] "Eleven Children Drown in Zanzibar," February 8, 2006, Associated Press, online news story: http://www.popedope.com/index.htm.

[231] *USA Today*, January 7, 2006, page 2A.

[232] Winslow 2003, 46.

[233] Schechter 2004. Also see Standing 2004.

[234] Hertz 2003, 7.

information control that I discussed in the last section. These political and anti-war ads cannot be shown because they would, of course, sacrifice the structure of the media propaganda masking of reality. It would make no sense for these networks to allow information into the flow of their broadcasting that would put into doubt, or that would show contradictory, the very things they were reporting to the American people. What was being reported to the American people up to and through the start of the Iraq War was a made-for-TV war propaganda cinema, with many special effects and with continual drama.

The Nazism Permeating the Corporate Media

This is the pinnacle of what eliminates the repetition of daily life, as discussed in the last chapter, and it is the epitome of good business for weapons makers and TV networks that want as many viewers as possible. This elaborate and exciting "war cinema" was precisely the technique of the Nazis also. Speaking in 1933, Nazi propaganda minister Goebbels told the Germans, who were excited about the emerging and approaching technology of television, that: "The strength of good radio programming lies in creating the right mix of entertainment, enjoyment, instruction, and politics."[235]

Dr. Goebbels was the Nazi minister of propaganda. He expressed a longing and desire for the sort of nationally televised power that exists in America today, reaching so many minds, and which, as shown in the last chapter, is precisely what enables mass brainwashing and the movement to the New World Order that is occurring worldwide. Here is an example of Goebbels' actual expressions about televisual projection:

February the 15th, 1943. In the late afternoon I began dictating my speech for sports palace. I had finished and corrected it by evening. I believe that it is very effective. It may prove to be one of my more masterful achievements as an orator. A speech like this is needed for morale. It is necessary to give the German people some encouragement. But if only it were possible to reproduce yourself a millions times over, so that you could achieve a million times more than you can today.[236]

This has been achieved in the contemporary world, and its effects are obvious, as I discuss in this book. There are other techniques that Goebbels used, as we will see, and Robert Steele, a former very high-ranking CIA covert operations agent, has said that the media techniques used by the current controllers of the national media are the very same techniques as

---

[235] Quote from Hachmeister 2004.
[236] Quote from Hachmeister 2004.

Goebbels.[237] This means that the current mass media in place in the United States involves a Nazi afterglow. Many readers of this book are of course familiar with what that gave rise to, with the complicity of people being shot in the streets, concentration camps of horror, and so forth. (In a later chapter I show how the mass media is being used, slowly, deliberately, to bring that very same sort of "reality of horror," with concentration camps and death camps to the USA.) This chapter, and this book, verifies that point. Such control may be gained here with more ease than by the Nazis, since the current controllers of America have, it seems, much more domination than the Nazis had. Professor Bagdikian writes:

> No imperial ruler in past history had multiple media channels that included satellite channels that can permeate entire societies with controlled sights and sounds… They are American and foreign entrepreneurs whose corporate empires control every means by which the population learns of its society. And like any close-knit hierarchy they find ways to cooperate so that all five can work together to expand their power, a power that has become a major force in shaping contemporary American life.[238]

There cannot be a free press if corporatism is to work successfully. On the contrary, there must be a 24-hour per day Orwellian propaganda-cinema. This is precisely what the cable news media presents, and what the news media inundation of society involves with its street corner newspaper stands and *Christian Broadcasting Network* (which has its own news shows, such as those on the "700 Club").

What I am calling the Nazi afterglow of the corporate telescreen-world media is perhaps best seen if we discuss how the universe of discourse is controlled. A simple way to put this is: ideas are debated vigorously in the national media, and this gives the impression that a free and diverse media exists, but specifically which ideas are brought up and allowed to be debated, is fully controlled by the media, unbeknownst to the viewers. This is a technique that the modern corporate media has gotten from the Nazis, as I will explain next.

In a discussion of the Nazi media system, and in discussing Josef Goebbels, Minister of Propaganda in Third Reich Germany, Professor Marc Crispin Miller writes: "He said once… what you want in a media system—and he meant talking about the Nazi media system—is ostensible diversity that conceals an actual [and significant] diversity"[239] Chomsky also discusses

---

[237] In Karel 2004.

[238] Bagdikian 2004, 3-4.

[239] This quote is from Pappas 2003.

this Nazi technique of media brainwashing: reeling in the infinitely expansive nature of thought by false, distracting debates which have nothing to do with the relevant issues to people's lives.

In graduate school at Purdue University as a PhD student in philosophy, I took advanced logic and studied what is called a "universe of discourse." It is a simple idea: there are a finite number of elements in a given language, and within it one can construct as many language statements as one wants. Given the rules of the language, the smaller the set of statements, the smaller the universe of discourse. If my universe of discourse has the following elements in it: "1," "+," "2," "=," "3," "4," "5." I can make different sentences, given the rules and elements involve, such as these sentences: "2+1=3," "1+2=3," "2+2=4," "4+1=5,"and so on, but not statements like this, "2x3=6." In the universe of discourse, one can make quite a few statements, according to the rules, and it may *seem* like I have a lot of diversity. There are a lot of options, and a lot of information can be given—it can even become overwhelming when the information overloads the mind. Now the Nazistic idea was to promote a diverse and rich universe of discourse, but to control the rules and elements of the universe of discourse. That is what the American corporate media involves.

A successful propaganda system gives copious information on a controlled universe of discourse, where citizens do not "step" outside that universe. Doing so would amount to a sort of Orwellian thought crime—and the prosecuters will be the other brainwashed citizens. If you doubt this, go and try to debate whether or not God exists, or whether or not al-Qaeda exists, with any person, and most likely, you will get perhaps even a somewhat violent reaction. But it is important to note that the reaction will likely not involve much more than a admonishment that one cannot bring up the topics one has brought up: "Of course God exists!", "What do you mean al-Qaeda does not exist?!" Americans, it seems, are ubiquitously told by the media, by politicians, and by other citizens that the American press is a free press, and that there is a free exchange of ideas in our country. But if one merely looks closer, one will see that this is not so, since many ideas are absent (see the list below); and as just pointed out with the God and the al-Qaeda examples, examples are easy to find. The gatekeeper of the socially accepted universe of discourse is the citizenry, and the constructors of the universe of discourse are the fascistic controllers. These ideas are, of course, merely a further development of the brainwashing discussions that have come before this one in this book.

In our time, if one becomes aware that there is a tightly guarded universe of discourse in the media and therefore among the American citizenry, one will begin to see literally an infinitude of topics that are voraciously kept out of the public universe of discourse. They are frowned upon by the corporatists' interests in carrying out corporate communism, corporatist oppression, in creating laborers that will not revolt, in profiting off of warfare and off of corporate terrorism (which I will discuss in a later chapter). For example, during the hyping of the Iraq threat of weapons of mass destruction and the leading up to war, there was no questioning of this, there was nearly no news coverage about anti-war interests. These now appear to have been important ideas, but they were not part of the media agenda set for the nation, as polls from the chapter about the brainwashing of Americans in leading up to the Iraq War showed. Similarly, there is virtually little or no debate in the corporatist media about damage to the environment due to corporations, or poor pay, rampant weapons sales to Third World dictators, and most of the issues I discuss in this book. So now it starts to appear that the universe of discourse allowed in the United States is astonishingly tiny—which is a key issue in an Orwellian model of society: reduce the number of words used or issues allowed, to have a tiny universe of discourse that merely appears large. Here are a few of the countless examples of issues that have not been, and almost surely will not be, allowed into the universe of discourse that is set by the corporatist national media:

> Which is a better, more successful variety of government: socialism or democracy?
> What are we going to do about the nuclear waste that is dangerously out of control in many parts of our country and in the world, and which is caused by corporatists and corporatist politicians involved in the military-industrial complex?[240]
> The US government is using half of the Congressional budget for military, but well under 20 percent of it for education, health services, and other basic needs for the population, a good idea or a bad idea?
> Is political anarchism (i.e., large-scale egalitarianism) a good form of government?
> Is a worker-controlled corporation a good alternative to the current capitalist structure in the USA, which is dictator-controlled communist capitalism, where workers have no control?
> Is the United States tyrannical and/or corporatistic?
> Why is the United States the biggest polluter of the modern industrial first-world nations?
> Why is the United States leading all other modern industrial first-world nations in crime rates (by far)?
> Is atheism or theism correct?

---

[240] This nightmare is documented well in Caldicott 2002, especially pages 60-70. This used to be a commonly discussed issue in the media, in schools, and so forth, back in the 1970s, but I literally never hear it brought up nowadays by anyone through any channel of information.

Why is there so much corruption in the CIA?

Do the ordinary jobs that tens of millions of underpaid Americans hold (such as working at Wal-Mart, McDonalds, etc.) promote misery?

Are homosexuals also bisexuals on most occasions, or not? And are all people to some degree bisexual?

The biggest chemical weapons attack the world has so far known, which was the usage of Agent Orange in the Vietnam War.

Chemical weapons in stored Oregon by the US military.

Should the United States have *not* used the chemical weapons they did in the Battle of Fallujah?[241]

Can Americans radically change the system in the United States, and thus create a far better non-USA-styled world than we have now?

Is the United States the "best country in the world," or is some other country?

Does democracy ever really exist?

What is the next synthetic terror event that the perpetrators of 9/11 are planning?

How many people choose the words that go into the stories that are on the front page of a newspaper?

This small list can begin to show one how this list of non-acceptable debates is virtually endless. Many of these issues, as the reader can see, cannot be discussed since such topics and debates would immediately puncture holes in the propaganda machine of the militaristic, corporatist national media.

It may seem that our media-world involves diversity (e.g., Bud vs. Miller, New York Times vs. USA Today, ESPN1 vs. EPSN2, Presbyterian vs. Christian Reformed, Fox News vs. CNN, Republicans vs. Democrats, and so on), but in reality it does not. Media involves petty, insignificant, repetitious, phony, distracting and misleading instances of "diversity" or disputes, such as raise taxes vs. lower taxes, stocks vs. bonds, Kerry vs. Bush, Osama vs. Bush, Obama vs. Hillary, McCain vs. Bush, etc. Overall, however, the items that are allegedly distinct (Kerry vs. Bush, ESPN1 vs. ESPN2) involve very little diversity between them at all. So media is unified in its message, and behind its phony diversity, it advocates uniformity of thought (send the troops to Iraq, get the "terrorists," go shopping, get your vaccines, etc.).

From school to church to newspapers to television, media information will be streamlined, and will advocate the same falsehoods. (For example, nothing travels faster than the speed of light, there are weapons of mass destruction in Iraq — held in virtually all media up until about 2004), there

---

[241] See Grupp 2007.

was a plane at the Pentagon on 9/11 — America possesses the most advanced and impressive medical system in the world, the Y2K threat — ubiquitously believed in 1999 — mercury in vaccines is safe, etc.) The national stream of information endlessly, cunningly, and relentlessly projects a convincing, unified, and scary stream of largely *artificial* information, or information that is somehow distorted, thus constructing a false account of reality that enters, fills and clouds the minds of the masses. In such a situation, it is easy to convince the populace that other countries like Iraq and Iran are real threats, with weapons of mass destruction pointed right at the United States — thus riling them up to fight in wars, or send their children off to war — all based on false premises and non-evidence. This is textbook brainwashing.

The corporatist controllers of the United States (and Europe, and perhaps much of the rest of the countries of the world) have an unseen plan for the world (the aforementioned "New World Order"), which is meant to bring the United States into a more thoroughgoing form of standard horror-state corporatism. The announcements for the set-up of this plan are being ambiguously and indirectly vocalized through the cable television news channels 24 hours per day, as well as big radio talk shows and national newspapers.

In our media-world, most Americans are flushed with information. Yet at the same time, they appear to be too distracted by work, sitcoms, consumerism, recreation, and other aspects of life on "Planet Starbucks" (to borrow a phrase form the film *Fight Club*) to be able to know much about reality. So they cannot see that there is a secret plan in the first place. More specifically, what is being set up in the United States is one of the repeating stories of history, which goes something like this. A group of people who are diabolical, de-spiritualized, well-organized, and who hide their real intentions to the people, take control of the judicial, business, military, and police forces of a nation. They use them over time to orchestrate a gradual oppressive and horrific takeover of the people, wherein they execute truly unfathomable, relentless, and repeated acts of horror and terror against the populace. This historical pattern is documented in the portion of history that is verifiable; it is represented in our most famous novels (*Animal Farm, Lord of the Flies*, etc.) and in the most famous American films (*Star Wars, Schindler's List*, etc.)—but at the time of the writing of this book, many Americans do not appear to see it in their own country due to their media-clouded minds. They know that Britney Spears has a baby, but they do not know that their political "leaders" are descendants of the Nazis — that the grandfather of the recent President, George W. Bush, was Hitler's banker. Very few Nazis were caught after World War II.

Media Domination and Racism

Overt Nazi techniques are not the only way that the media perpetuates a climate of racism and all the effects that come out of racism. It seems that national media information can brainwash people in non-overt ways that they would never imagine and that people seem to be totally unaware of. Even skeptical intellectuals can become affected. For example, it is reinforced in the national media that the only form of government that is acceptable is one that is called "democracy." No chance is given to any sort of socialist state, such as Cuba. But clearly democracy does not exist in the United States, as pointed out in this book. So what is all this discussion of democracy all about? It seems that even supposedly leftwing intellectuals are fond of asserting that there must be democracy, as if there is no other choice. This leads to a sort of social racism—in this case, racism against non-democratic nations—that is as unjustified as the Nazi racism against the Jews was. But if a propaganda machine is working correctly, it does not facilitate questioning of the racist principles. I will next explore how this occurs in the USA in various ways.

This medialistic constructing of racism is deliberately used against people in the Middle East, who are portrayed as "terrorists." For example, as the Hezbollah-Israel conflict began in July 2006, it was so common to hear media news castes say things like "Hezbollah is terrorism," or "Iran is a terrorist nation." But Hezbollah and Iran are nations of people, consisting of families and ordinary people, who often have no connection to the political war cinema. Labeling entire nations or sub-nations as "terrorist," *repeatedly*, would seem to make tens of millions of Americans believe, for example, that the entire nation was terrorist. I recall frequently hearing people say, during the first two years of the Iraq War in 2003 and 2004, that "Iraqis were terrorists," even though the United States attacked Iraq without cause, and based on false information and political games. The Nazi-afterglow in the American media, in this way, not only can lead to mass racism, but can also be complicit in mass murder, inducing otherwise thoughtless American citizens into unfounded hatred. As Schechter writes: "Modern media no longer just covers wars; it has become a player within them. Media organizes populations to rally behind wars..."[242]

---

[242] Schechter 2003, xxx.

7. Afterthoughts: A Collection of Infowars.com Articles from 2009

Introduction

This last chapter consists of the collection of Infowars.com articles that I published on Infowars.com during the first half of 2009. I feel that the special thing about these articles is that they go deep into understanding the psyche of the New World Order, and thus deep into ways to understand how to resist their takeover. From what I can tell, some of these articles contain ideas and theory about the New World Order and our globalist money masters that have appeared nowhere else, but which are a key to understanding our world. I have long thought that the very best article in this collection is "There is One Type of Total Gun Ban that We Need, Jefferson Would Agree, and It's the Key to Bringing Back 1776", published on Infowars.com, May 4, 2009. But I believe that readers will be immensely pleased with all of these articles, as they are *very* broad-reaching and very hard-hitting. But this "Total Gun Ban" article, like almost all others in this collection, I felt brought forth new information to the Truth Movement and the Patriot Movement that was utterly critical, and which was largely undiscussed before that time. The "Total Gun Ban" article was particularly cutting edge, in that it attempts to narrow all activism, all patriotism, and all that we world citizens need to do to solve our problems down to one issue: Jeffersonian militia.

I gained no money from publishing these articles, and little fame; they were all written merely out of the pure passion and aliveness I felt within me during 2009, to find tyranny in the way that the Minutemen did. You reach a certain point in this fight that nothing matters as much as the deep feeling of fire and religiosity within oneself from going beyond the point of no return in this fight. I have left these articles just as they appeared on Infowars.com; so you will see notifications of hyperlinks, and the original pictures that the Infowars.com editor (Kurt Nimmo) put into these articles.

I would like to thank Kurt Nimmo and the Infowars.com team for publishing these articles on their site, and for having me on the Infowars.com Show during the first half of 2009.

The New World Order Is Taking Over
the Patriot and Truth Movements

Jeffrey Grupp, Infowars, April 13, 2009

We all know that there are infiltrators into the various patriot movements. Old news. But that is not what I discuss in this article. I may be wrong, but I think something far more serious is going on: I think that the biggest, strongest patriot movements (Alex Jones and the Truth Movement, Campaign for Liberty, etc.) are about to completely damaged or hijacked so that they no longer exist, and are completely destroyed. This is *the* New

A telltale sign: Ann Coulter now supports Ron Paul.

World Order tactic, so none of us should be surprised, just like I was not surprised when the Ron Paul Presidential run was run off the road and taken over almost effortlessly, it seems, before the first votes in New Hampshire were cast. So let's get into this issue…

If Ann Coulter is so 'awake' now, endorsing Ron Paul and stating that he was right about everything, why won't she then talk about the things that Ron Paul discusses: the Fed, Codex Alimentarius, the North American Union, the WTO and IMF, what the Second Amendment really is all about, and so on? There is something funny going on here… and I think I know what. If Glen Beck is such a patriot and such a rebel of the mass media now, also promoting Ron Paul, why can't his research team, after searching for over a week as Beck said, simply find any of the dozens of news articles in *Newsweek*, the *New York Times*, the Houston *Chronicle*, and so on, about the massive FEMA camps all over? Answer: he's lying. Why is the mass media moving into our territory now, discussing some of the same issues we Truthers and patriots discuss, all of a sudden? If this keeps up, even as Alex Jones hinted at last week, his radio show "could become passé". In other words, the movement will be hijacked from Jones, Ron Paul, and other leaders in the genuine patriot movements by the mass media (and the New World Order that controls the mass media), and the mass media will have control of them, just as they almost effortlessly took over the Ron Paul Presidential run's momentum in the days before the New Hampshire Primary. Let me explain what I think is really going on.

Consider these facts:

1. All of a sudden, starting around late last fall, right when the stock market crash was going on with a vengeance, the mass corporatist media began telling us that there is a New World Order and a coming world government. And since then, the mass media tells us either that this New World Order and coming world government is great, *or* they would tell us that it's bad and it's *only* about the bankers—they don't tell us, for example, that it's a project of the occultist and militaristic corporatists behind the scenes, or that it traces back to Hitler—I didn't hear Beck cover that story!

2. That same mass media is telling us that the *old system* is the cause of the economic collapse, and "oh no ['wink wink], the people might revolt against it (against the system and/or the bankers)".

That "old system" referred to in 2 by the thought-controlling mass media is *not* the country the Founders set up for us, but rather:

3. Our *current* system of government (which is far from the libertarian Founders' government, and which is now *actually* a corporatist system where the government is a ceremonial government, like the Roman Congress was in ancient Rome),

4. The banks (but not the globalist banks, IMF, etc.),

5. capitalism (sure we never really have had it in the past 150 years—instead we've only had corporatism—but what traces of capitalism we've had are now being castigated ['GM's failed business model', etc.] or called nonexistent by the mass media, needing to be replaced by socialistic systems, such as with the *Newsweek* cover story: "We Are All Socialists Now").

And there are other odd things going on, such as

6. Ann Coulter, who has been unwavering and incredibly rabid and virulent in her pro-war hate for Middle Eastern people, all of a sudden is supporting the most anti-war presidential candidate in decades, *saying he was right all along*—um… *did I hear that right?*

There are other examples, but these are all stunning, and they are quite new in the mass media. Is any of this making any sense? Because it's really confusing me—Anne Coulter has never used reason, but now suddenly she wants to? I think it's all sounding more like the old "wolf in sheep's clothing" than anything else. To understanding the conclusions I am going to bring out in this article, you will have to interconnect all these points, 1-6, at once. Let's continue…

We are being told in the mass media in various ways that these systems (1-3) have failed us, that's really the problem, and those systems need to be changed (eradicated) in one way or another. But all this (and *so much more*) has been going on all along for centuries—the banks robbing us, etc.—so why *now* does the mass media all-at-once decide to announce a few of these tid-bits to us that they've covered up for decades? If the mass media suddenly wants to tell us how the banks have ripped us all off, well why didn't they tell us that in 1913, the 1980s, or maybe even just in 2007? And why not tell us that Obama supported it all? But more importantly, why all-at-once, right at this particular point in time, are we getting these few tid-bits from the mass media? *Answer: look what it is doing to the patriot movements; it's becoming them.*

Now, also consider that the mass media is telling us a few more things simultaneously, in addition to 1-6:

7. World government is the solution to the failed systems and to the economic collapse, and

8. The "conspiracy people" were right about it all along.

Now, notice, again, that 1-8 *are all happening at once*! Coincidence? Hard to believe. The robots and extremists of the mass media (Beck, Hannity, Savage, Limbaugh, Coulter, O'Reilly, and others) have been such robotic and unfathomable traitors through the years that they can only be carrying out an agenda now too, not trying to report news, attract an audience, or keep their ratings high. Why else would they bring all this up at the very same time? Perhaps Alex Jones is correct, and these propagandists are suddenly just worried about their ratings and their competition from the alternative media. This may be true, but as I said, my theory is that there's something more serious going on.

Here's the issue: the New World Order wants worldwide rioting, mass death, economic collapse, sacrifice of lower minions and freemasons of the New World Order, compliance with the climate change laws and servitude, and a set up of a Brave New World, all over the course of the next decade or decades. What better way is there to do this than to shock and clean-the-slate of the populace of the world (often called "shock doctrine," as a recent book discussed) to get them ready for big changes and compliance with a new world, right when the populace is getting desperate and un-thought-out due to their desperation and increasing poverty, *than by introducing them with information about how evil the world leaders are and world system is* (but all along keeping the real completely unseen master corporatists out of the picture)? *Answer: you merely implement 1-8, where a key element in that and to cause revolt is to hijack the real patriot movements with the vacuous, uninformed, undirected, and undisciplined false "patriotism" of Beck, Coulter, and the rest, by simply taking over their discussions, as seems to be starting right now with Coulter, Beck, and others.* There! That's the issue, and it could easily result in a quick total hijacking of the power the patriot movements have accumulated.

Proof that the New World Order wants to use the Truth Movement and similar movements for the aforementioned aims was possibly even seen last weekend when some news agencies said that the Pittsburgh police shooting was due to the shooter listening to the words of Glen Beck and Alex Jones (notice how those two were coupled together), not because of, for example, the violent tendencies of the shooter (he was accused of assaulting a girlfriend in the past), his economic hardships, or some other cause. As if Alex Jones has ever promoted violence against police, rather than mild civil disobedience, and/or taking over the government by the people (the latter being the often-mentioned trademark "Alex Jones solution" to the New World Order takeover of the country). (Also note that if this is true, there also may be an additional divide-and-conquer maneuver already being set up as 1-8 are implemented: set the revolting parts of the populace against the non-revolting parts.) If Ann Coulter is so "awake" and patriotic now, why doesn't she point out that alcohol and Big Pharma kills hundreds of thousands each year, many times what violence does, or violence with guns — and not listening to Alex Jones or Glen Beck? Answer: because she's carrying out the typical Big Media agenda that she's ordered to. Nothing new.

Now, also remember before 9/11, when Alex Jones predicted it a few weeks before? He was able to do that because the mass media—the mouthpiece and brainwashing device of the New World Order—were telling us it was going to happen. Doesn't it seem like the mass media are again telling us something here, also, when you interconnect points 1-8? They are telling us that 1-8 will happen, that the old world and our current way of life will be destroyed, that We the People will destroy it with our riots, with our contributing to the economic problems, and through our adherence to the old system of government (described above), so that the new communism will inevitably set in—it's all the fault of We the People. Now where have we heard this sort of a story before! (Hint: after World War II, we were told that the war was caused by the mass madness of the world citizenry, not by the New World Order, and thus Truman had to set up all those mental health acts that he did in order that We the People could be cured of our irrationalism.)

So, the mass media, again, are merely telling us what is going to happen, that it's all our fault. So, let me summarize: it is clear to me beyond a shadow of a doubt that the corporatist New World Order is now using what most of us think of as the most hard core of the patriot movements in order to carry out their agenda. LET ME SAY THAT IN DIFFERENT WORDS SO YOU UNDERSTAND WHAT I AM GETTING ACROSS TO YOU:

The real patriot movements are getting so large, so powerful, so pervasive, that the New World Order has no choice but to fully hijack these movements if they are to carry out their planned Brave New World agendas.

More specifically: the New World Order is going to make our Truth and Patriot movements their *primary tools* of operation to carry out Eugenics and so forth.

That's my theory, and my prediction.

How, you might ask, will it all work? Well, if you want to get a revolt going, why not disclose false flag terror (such as Michael Savage started to do recently for the first time on his radio show where he foretold Obama's upcoming Reichstag)? That sure would do it if the mass media went that far and all-at-once got this the real-ness of false flag terror into the minds of the sappy and unfocussed citizenry, shocking them to the core by totally upsetting their established belief system, all right when that citizenry was destitute, in a depression, filled with bird flu epidemic fears, with millions living in tent cities, hungry and cold, and so on, as is most likely going to be the case this fall or winter. Was Savage's recent comment a prelude to this?

It is quite obvious the New World Order is pushing for violence, as Alex Jones has been pointing out. The New World Order, through our city, state and Federal governments, is pushing the populace so hard now, more and more each day, with impossible taxation (who can pay all the taxes as we fall into massive depression?), with crazy new laws (banning home-schooling, etc.), police taserings, making home gardens illegal (just like the King in the book *Robin Hood* banned hunting deer), announcing that the bankers are robbing us, announcing that the government is not helping the economic crisis but is fuelling it (of course they don't disclose all the details with this), and most importantly, getting ready to remove the Second Amendment and all of the Constitution. They are creating a system where we are not Americans, but where we are all living like the slaves on the plantations in the 1800s, where only revolt (violence) could follow, because it is being pre-planned, and our movements are going to be used to fuel the violent revolts, unless we wake up to this possibility and start discussing these issues with urgency. *Don't forget how quickly the Ron Paul Presidential run was hijacked!*

So what does the New World Order want with all the rioting? Well, there are several things. Firstly, this is part of the New World Order's religious festival: spread as much mayhem, panic, misery and pure blood chaos as possible—this is a 'work of art' to the New World Order; it is like listening to Beethoven to them. Some of you may find this difficult to understand, but they attain their religious experience by this "theater", as they often call it (remember Iraq was called a "theater" around the time of Shock and Awe? Notice the word "Awe" there, also).

If you still have trouble believing this, then ask yourself a question: What is the New World Order waiting for in killing billions? They've had super technology to kill as many of us as they want to for decades. They are building up our numbers in order to slaughter us, because the slaughter itself is their art, their high, just like the ancient hallucinatory ballgame (the 'pitzlawal', as it's called by the Maya) of death-entertainment was for the Mayan shaman kings, a little like the ancient Roman gladiator fights, and a lot like the carnage in Iraq. What is beautiful to the New World Order is a world of deformed, sickened, ultra-violent, unintelligent desperate people, like the Island of Dr. Moreau. That's the religious festival of the New World Order, and the aforementioned rioting is a key issue involved. If we want to be free, to be kings of ourselves, we have to realize this, to know the enemy as best we can, or else we will just go along the pitzlawal we are all currently caught in. The way to be kings of ourselves is to become intelligent, knowledgeable, deeply and genuinely religious, and self-sufficient in the way the Indians used to be—that's the sort of civil disobedience we need, and which Henry David Thoreau lived when he wrote his influential book on civil disobedience.

Ok, so a New World Order religious festival is the first point of the rioting. Another is that the rioting is the way to transform the nation into a shock state, and thus bring about an entry of the Brave New World. *The old world has to be destroyed in order to set up the new world, and that means that our minds, our memories, our ways of life, and our peaceful day-to-day lifestyles of American comfort, the security for our families, and so on, all have to be destroyed, sending us into a mass state of shock ("shock doctrine").* I think a lot of people in our movement are oblivious to this intention, this plan, this hijacking of our movement. But isn't that what they always do?

So, what should we do? Do we panic and start fighting with all the other patriots and Truthers for every little thing we disagree over? I disagree with other Truthers about many ideas, so should I fight with them about that constantly? Or should I fight the enemy? We of course must focus on the fight. But what is the fight? The fight is *the fight for truth*. But what is the truth? The truth is what we can experience and see with our eyes, right in front of our face. And what we see is the destruction of the Constitution and of the nation we live in.

The "End the Fed" Protests are the (Secret) Road to World Government

Jeffrey Grupp, Infowars, April 16, 2009

Two recent Infowars.com articles (<u>my article</u> and the <u>JustGetUsThere</u> article) in the past few days have discussed how the mass media is hijacking the patriot and Truth movements by (1) attempting to take over the debates about the issues that the patriot groups have been discussing for decades by suddenly, all-at-once blasting them into the mass media in a twisted, vacuous, and manipulated way, and (2) by taking over the anti-Fed "revolution," also by spotlighting it vacuously in the corporatist mass media. But we know that if the New World Order wants to hijack the patriot and Truth movements, they won't just do it from these angles, and instead they (A) will attack it from many angles, and more importantly, they (B) will use their attack to, additionally, *set up their Brave New World*. This article is about (B), and what I want to suggest is that the New World Order is deliberately false-flag-attacking the Fed in order to ultimately destroy it, leaving the perception of a void in the financial world, *wherein they will fill that void with THEIR choice of a new banking and money system: global currency, global bank, global governance/government.* More specifically, here's what I theorize is commencing:

1. The New World Order is using the corporatist mass media to co-opt the real anti-Fed revolt (originally started by WeAreChange), in order to blend it with a fake anti-Fed revolt that they are setting up, in order to incite a broad anti-Fed revolution among the US citizenry, which should hit high gear later this year, if not by summer.

2. The New World Order will use what I just stated in 1, and the pre-planned and staged problems with the increasingly weakening banks and US dollar (which will ultimately collapse fully), in order to modify or abolish the Fed and the current money system.

3. And the New World Order will present a specific solution to this pre-planned scenario I just stated in 2 in order to replace the current banking and money system with, they will tell us, a 'better' system: a world banking and money system.

(As a quick aside, let me say that abolishing the money system, as mentioned in 2, through hyperinflation — which is set to start any time – or other means, is *critical* to the New World Order's set-up of the Brave New World, since abolishing the money system has the power to shock and clean-the-slate of the average citizen so profoundly that it will petrify the average citizen into doing literally

The lies and contradiction of Obama are so stark, that even the fluoridated, TV-controlled, nearly illiterate Americans can't help but see 'the Obama deception,' to use Alex Jones's phrase.

whatever the New World Order slaughter-force wishes, just as we saw happened in Nazi Germany. This is the point of "shock doctrine", to use Naomi Klein's phrase from her book.)

Now let's restate the issue as simply as possible so we understand it very clearly: The New World Order has not only hijacked the revolt against the Federal Reserve that WeAreChangers originally started, but furthermore, the New World Order is going to use it to bring in world government!

They can do this because the average citizen is not well-educated in the real issues going on like the WeAreChangers were when they first started the Fed revolt, and the average citizen is thus easily co-opted regarding this revolt against the Fed. There has never been a greater danger to the patriot and Truth movements *than right now*: we don't have a citizenry that is fully awake, and thus we don't have a citizenry that will see they are being *tricked* into revolt when they zombically watch Fox News, for example, talk about the anti-Fed protests. Given the present discontent of the citizenry over the state of the country, and their being glued to the TV, they will never figure any of this out, and in their frustration they will merely react unthinkingly, thus swarming into a New World Order controlled fake anti-Fed revolution. We are in danger of having them join the fake, vacuous revolt that is brewing with the words of the Beck's, Coulter's, and Hannity's of the world, falling right into the trap like a hungry and desperate fox sticking his paw into the hunter's trap. *The New World Order wants to take over the patriot and Truth movements before the real movements can get to them first.*

The mainstream corporatist media is interested in publicizing the Federal Reserve protests, and they are interested in merging and joining with these protests, because if the mass media can easily get an unawakened US citizenry to reactionistically and passionately hate the Federal Reserve, then the New World Order can come in and say, with a big smile: "Oh, you don't like the Federal Reserve that has failed you, ok, then we will change it or abolish it for you, because we want to help you—after all, we are working for the people in this 'democracy'." It is clear that we are heading in this sort of a direction since the corporate press is publicizing this phony revolt as they are. If the mass media can take over the anti-Fed revolt, then can they fabricate an impetus to destroy the Fed? Why on earth would they want to do this when the Fed is the milk-and-honey of the US-arm of the New World Order? *Answer: as stated, if you want to set up a world government based on a world banking and money system, you need to destroy or modify the old national system first.* And to do that they will use the corporatist mainstream media to all-of-a-sudden tell the people how horrible the banking system and Federal Reserve are (as seems to be starting since last fall), watch the people react, and then the government can tell us they will give us a solution to the Fed system — where the solution is to change or destroy it, *replacing it with a 'more secure' world government system.* And just like in 1913, they will tell us that "it's what the people want!" and that setting up such a system is the way to prohibit anything like this from happening again. *This is classic problem-reaction-solution,* just like Alex Jones has talked about hundreds of times:

Problem: the Fed

Reaction: protest and revolt against the Fed

Solution: modify or destroy the Fed (i.e., replace it with a global reserve bank) — i.e., set up the New World Order.

So, in light of this scenario, it is the blind, unawake citizenry who will *help* set up the world government, if this scenario and this theory are correct and play out. Isn't this the way it always works, though? Luckily, we have a chance to notice this beforehand this time, in order to prevent it.

I theorize that this same sort of a problem-reaction-solution scenario could be implemented in other ways, too, such as with blending or replacing national governments with world government:

Problem: expose national government corruption and failures

Reaction: people protest and revolt against the national governments

Solution: either blend national governments with world government, or destroy national governments in favor of world governments — i.e., set up the New World Order.

(As a side note, it is speculative to presume so, but it almost appears that the mass media are leading up to this sort of a problem-reaction-solution set-up in order to get the citizenry to finally say "enough is enough" with the government. For why else would 'anti-war Obama' bomb Pakistan within days of the Inauguration? The lies and contradiction of Obama are so stark, that even the fluoridated, TV-controlled, nearly illiterate Americans can't help but see 'the Obama deception,' to use Alex Jones's phrase. Another possibility is, however, that the New World Order could try to keep the current US system in place and put its puppet rebels into offices and make them appear to be part of the burgeoning revolution—this is sort of like what appears to be starting up now. The reader is left to theorize which is most likely to come to be.)

How many times have we seen this sort of pattern emerge? *Answer: It is the story of history.* For example, through the corporatists' mass media that the average American keeps their mind glued to, they have been given the 'problems' of Hitler, Vietnam, Osama, and Saddam, and the 'solution' to these 'problems' that the corporatist mass media talked us into was *war*. Problem-reaction-solution again. Here's another example: after World War II, Americans were told there was another problem: that sole cause of World War II was our supposed innate human madness and violence that led humanity to collectively lose their minds and create World War II (rather than the correct story: we were tricked into fighting), and the 'solution' Americans were presented with and were suckered into was to set up the now ultra-massive mental health industry. Over and over, problem-reaction-solution, and we are tricked into fighting for our own demise. Just like when we pay taxes and pay for the existence of the government all, in the end, in order to finance our FEMA camps. All this comes about through problem-reaction-solution, and we are currently living right in the middle of the largest problem-reaction-solution operation ever: the one that is meant to set up the New World Order. And most importantly, as my last article pointed out, *it is the rapidly-growing Truth and patriot movements that the New World Order is set to use in order to carry out this greatest-of-all problem-reaction-solution operation!*

Does this mean we no longer protest New World Order monstrosities, such as the Fed? Of course not. It just means we have to adjust our minds more to the multi-dimensionality of the attack of the enemy — *know thy enemy* — which is something we need to do now, not later, so it's good we have these forewarnings.

There is One Type of Total Gun Ban that We Need, Jefferson Would Agree, and It's the Key to Bringing Back 1776

Jeffrey Grupp`, Infowars, May 4, 2009

What I have to say in this article may deeply anger or enrage many who read it. But what I have to say is *no more than a rewording of this miraculous passage from Thomas Jefferson*:

> "[E]very able-bodied freeman, between the ages of sixteen and fifty, is enrolled in the militia... The law requires every militia-man to provide himself with the arms usual in the regular service."

> —Thomas Jefferson, *Notes on Virginia*, Quivery IX

I think that very few Americans have thought deeply about this passage, what it's really saying, and thus very few understand the ramifications of this passage—even those in the heart of the Truth Movement may not have thought about this passage deeply enough to really see that this passage may be the key to everything.

How is it the key to everything? You might think it is by the way this passage promotes Second Amendment issues. That is true, but that is not what I am getting at here. We already all know that. What this passage really involves is actually a far bigger issue, one that I think very few of us have noticed, amazingly.

Jefferson says that it is the *ordinary citizens* who are the militia. Jefferson *does not* say that it is certain government-VIP groups, or any other government groups, who are members of the militia. (These VIP groups are the police and military, which are "standing armies", if armed or maybe even if unarmed, when they are amassed on US soil; and they are groups like the FDA or USGS or NSA. These are groups that are given elevated status *over* the level of citizen by big government. From what I can tell, this basic issue is anti-Jeffersonian and/or unconstitutional.) That is the key: it is the citizens, and definitely not any (unconstitutional) government-favored special groups, *who are the militia: who are the real homeland security.*

Jefferson's passage at the start of this article clearly lays this out, and it requires that almost all of us rearrange our thinking in order to get back to a 1776 mental framework. I sense that even listeners of the Alex Jones Show may have this thesis I am presenting here hit them with a shock, like a ton of bricks, as if it's a radical thesis. But that just shows us how far we've come from 1776, and how subtly we're all still under the trickery of the New World Order, even if we think we are so enlightened since we are Alex Jones listeners, gun owners, and members of the Patriot movement. Ok, with the thesis laid out, now let's see how this Jeffersonian vision works...

So, what does this all mean? What would it mean if we had a total weapon and total gun ban for on-duty police and for military and post-Constitutional government entities? What would *really happen* in such a scenario? Well, it must be something quite good for the people that happens, since governments worldwide fight against this sort of a scenario almost more than they fight against anything. But more specifically, it means that it is *against the law, against the Founders, and against 1776*, for on-duty police, military, and for the aforementioned post-Constitutional government entities (FDA, CIA, EPA, Dept. of Education, etc.) to possess firearms (including any projectile weapon, such as non-lethal weapons [tasers, etc.] or crossbows or longbows, microwave guns, etc.), *since these big-government-favored groups are not part of the militia.* That's the key issue, and this is all very important; so let's get this down pat in more detail.

How are on-duty police, military, and for the aforementioned post-Constitutional government entities (FDA, CIA, EPA, Dept. of Education, etc.) not part of the militia, in Jefferson's philosophy? Here's how:

These big-government-favored groups are elevated in power above the status of being an ordinary citizen, but Jefferson says it's only those of the status of ordinary citizen who are party of the militia (who are gun owners), thus if you fall outside of this ordinary citizen group you are breaking the law if you own a weapon!

That is what Jefferson's comments lead to, and if we explore the ramifications of this (as I am going to next), you will perhaps agree that this is Jefferson's greatest, largest, and most critical issue for preservation of the Constitutional Republic. So let's figure out why this issue—gun ban for on-duty police and for military and non-Constitutional government entities—is really the single issue we should focus on perhaps more than any other.

There are so many issues we members of the Truth and Patriot movements have to grapple with. If we want our country back, if we want back what Jefferson, Washington, Adams, Henry, and the rest of the Founders set up for us, where on earth do we start when we are in such an incredible quagmire today, where we have strayed so unimaginably far from the Founders' Republic? We have to deal with pandemic hoaxes, GM food plagues, FEMA holocaust, secret government, false flag terror, government robot weapons, attempts by big government to destroy inalienable rights, vaccine holocausts, depleted uranium, and all the rest that infowars.com patriots are all too familiar with. It is perhaps a daunting task when we consider how much we have to deal with. *But what if we could reduce all these issues down to one, single issue*—an issue that's power-source of all the others—wherein we could focus in on that one issue, obliterate it, and *ipso facto*, 1776 would be restored? That is precisely what is at stake in the aforementioned issue of pushing for a gun ban for on-duty police and for military and non-Constitutional government entities. This is a simple issue, a clearly definable issue, one that could easily get huge amounts of support since already 70 percent (or more) of Americans are pro-Second Amendment (and this is growing fast). So, let's see why if we won that single battle of removing weaponry from government, military, and on-duty police, that all other things would fall into place.

Yes, that's right, we need one type of gun control. We need gun control for on-duty police and any military and government officials who are on US soil (excluding Congress, the President, and perhaps the members of the Supreme Court, since they may be members of the militia, in Jefferson's vision). This would include any group that even loosely resembled a standing army (such as privatized military forces like Blackwater) since they are unconstitutional, except for the one Constitutional standing army: the militia. In other words, on-duty police should be banned from possessing guns, as should any government people in the military, FDA, CIA, and any of the other post-Constitutional monstrosities that we Americans have permitted to come into existence and control every aspect of us down to our consciousness. The way this would happen peacefully is if members of these big-government-favored groups deprogrammed from their brainwashing and voluntarily put down their arms in order to join this Second Amendment Jeffersonian revolution. I think getting this to happen is doable.

What will be the net effect of this? It would have such tremendous ramifications that it would bring us right back to the America that the Founders established for us. Consider how this works.

If we had unarmed police and military, we would have police and military that would be no threat to any gun-owner ("one man with a gun can control a hundred without one"). I cannot underestimate the importance of this. Eventually the balance of power would shift to such a degree that government would be under the control of the gun owners (of the Jeffersonian militia). Why? Because anyone out there who is in any way fired up about the Second Amendment knows that the feeling of owning a gun, carrying a gun, is so safe, secure, and free, that the joy it brings just blossoms within you in such a way that you glue on to that feeling of freedom almost as tightly as you hug your child. So, in other words, the gun owners would thrive and unite in their euphoria of freedom and Constitutionalism, by the feelings they have inside from carrying the gun. I can see this in a lower-level form when I am at the shooting range, at the gun shop. I can see it in the eyes, feel it in the hearts, of my fellow pro-Second Amendment friends, and there are a lot of them. As Alex Jones has said, protecting our Second Amendment is the one thing that millions will lay down everything and fight for right now. This is because the gun owner knows, feels, how the peace-of-mind of holding the gun is the key to freedom, as Jefferson and many of the Founders did too. Jefferson describes the issue most clearly:

"As to the species of exercise, I advise the gun. While this gives a moderate exercise to the body, it gives boldness, enterprise, and independence to the mind. Games played with the ball, and others of that nature, are too violent for the body, and stamp no character on the mind. Let your gun, therefore, be the constant companion of your walks. Never think of taking a book with you. The object of walking is to relax the mind. You should therefore not permit yourself even to think while you walk; but divert yourself by the objects surrounding you. Walking is the best possible exercise. Habituate yourself to walk very far." – Thomas Jefferson, Letter to Peter Carr, August 19, 1785

It is the gun, the Second Amendment, that gives freedom. Without it we are slaves; with it we can be like Jefferson on his walks, with a mind clear and liberated, unworried and free to philosophize. The feelings of freedom that gun owners employ would overflow if there was a gun ban for on-duty police and for military and non-Constitutional government entities. This is because it would instantly be the case that

1. The citizens would not have a powerful military or police force to fall back on and be dependent upon, and thus they would have to assume those responsibilities for themselves, *and they would become the police and military, they would assume those roles*: fathers would become protectors instead of TV-watchers, grandfathers would again take their grandchildren to the range, women would again recognize the urgency to carry a pistol wherever they go, and women would walk through parking lots at night without a shred of fear (a woman empowered, without fear: a feminism the fake feminists will never know). Again, in the current state of TV-addicted-America, this sounds odd to many who think dialing 911 is the key to safety, but again, I am just rewording what Jefferson has already said when he told that what I am writing about in this article is real homeland security: "…our attention should be fixed on the safety of our country. For a people who are free, and who mean to remain so, a well-organized and armed militia [citizens] is their best security." –Jefferson, Eighth Annual Message, Nov. 8, 1788.

2. Without the illusion of "security" from the big government police and military forces, the citizens would not have a powerful military or police force to fall back on and be dependent upon, and thus they would feel that they have no protection—as if they are "naked in the wilderness"— citizens would in this case do what people always do: they would seek out protection, and the best protection, they would find, is the gun. There

is already so much pro-gun fervor in America, that quickly after a disarming of on-duty police and of military and non-Constitutional government entities, there would be an overpowering zeitgeist in the air that the best protection is the gun (this zeitgeist already exists in America at a lower level, as it it's just waiting to overflow). Consequently, those who are gun owners would amplify their devotion to their art, and those who are not would become passionate gun owners by the millions. We would quickly change from a helpless nation to a nation empowered.

Now, what I have described so far in this article is a blueprint for how we completely disempower the government, and radically empower the citizenry. *And this all occurred from one little issue: institute a gun ban for on-duty police and for military and non-Constitutional government entities.*

Notice: this is *a single issue*, not many issues. This is one issue that can solve all other issues. This is not like trying to do many things: it is not trying to reign in GM food, vaccines, and the Fed all at once. *It's a much simpler task: you just do one thing, which is disarm the big-government-favored groups.* And if we all focused our energy on this one issue, we could get it done, and the rest of the 1776 cards would fall into place.

And here's why this issue of disarming the big-government-favored groups is the issue that allows everything else about the New World Order to fall away, from vaccines to draft, to carbon tax, to ID chip. Here's what America would look like with disarmed big-government-favored groups:

A. On the one hand, there would be the armed, patriotic America, which would consist of a mass of wide-eyed, passionate, happy gun owners (sort of like a vaster version of what I already see at a much smaller scale at the shooting range every Saturday), with confidence, character, and inner peace (as Jefferson described in a passage above), which would number in the hundreds of millions.

B. And then on the other hand, there would be a completely unarmed government, numbering only a tiny fraction of those described in a.

The power is with A. And what about B? Well... B is, well, rather pathetic, isn't it. We are, at any moment, incredibly close to this sort of a scenario, since there is only one thing we need to do to put this sort of a world in place: disarm on-duty police, disarm military on US soil (or maybe all military, at least for a time), and any other big-government-favored groups.

Just from this disarmament, A and B fall into place. Do you see what happens then, if A and B are in place? Government has no authority; gun owners are authority—*they are government!*

What do you think would happen if B tried to tell A that they can't have a garden because they might plant pot in it? Yeah, I am laughing too! What do you think would happen if B told A that there was a draft, or that there were mandatory vaccinations for swine flu, or that Congress is being lobbied to "pass" a "bill" that robs the citizens blind ("bank bailout")? Yeah, it's a pretty funny scenario; almost like a zebra herd walking up to the lion prides to tell the lions to please stop eating them – *or*, almost like an American in the current situation, where the current American tries to "write their Congressman". Even non-gun-owning (i.e., non-Constitutional) members of America are not really citizens, in this scheme of this article, and of Jefferson's lawmaking, and they are at the wretched, disempowered level of B, more than they are of A.

So, in summary, there are so many issues we have to fight for, and we need to get more and more aware of *all* that is going on, but amid everything else we Truthers and Patriots are doing, we may want to think about launching a campaign, with more energy and persistence and passion than anything we have ever done, to fight for this one single issue: a gun ban for on-duty police and for military and non-Constitutional government entities, in order to have the chain of events outlined in this Jeffersonian treatise carry out. This is a doable project, *since it is a single project, a clear and easy-to-understand project* that will make all people feel as empowered as one of the Patriots in the Revolutionary War. Looking at our plight with this issue above all others can give us a means to win this victory against the satanic New World Order, and can give us hope, inspiration, drive, and rebirth, resembling the Minutemen of the Republic.

New World Order Trying to Kill America's Gun Culture: EPA Shutting Down Gun Range in Large Midwestern Town

Jeffrey Grupp, Infowars, May 21, 2009

I live in a Midwestern state. Near me is a huge shooting range, which is going to be put out of business by the EPA. Just before the completion of this article, the owner, call him W, of this particular range has unfortunately demanded that I not use his name or specify which range I am discussing in this article.[243] I think this is a mistake on his part, but I have to honor it. This issue of shutting down this range is so large, so interconnected to all the issues that the infowars.com/prisonplanet.com audience is concerned with, that I will go at length into all the issues in detail in this article. At first, you might think, "ah, shutting down this range is just more of the same tricks by the New World Order." And that's true, of course. But there is something much bigger, deeper to this that I think most people are missing: *the New*

---

[243] The range is Flat Creek Range, in Lafayette, IN.

World Order is trying to kill gun culture, and this is more important than their trying to destroy the Second Amendment. So, before we get into this story of this particular gun range, let's first discuss why this story is so important: indeed, a core issue.

Amid all our discussion in the Patriot alternative media about the New World Order's covert plans to remove the Second Amendment in America, we are perhaps not putting enough energy into what is conceivably an even deeper issue: *the New World Order wants to destroy the ultra-powerful spirit of the American gun culture.* Destroying the Second Amendment is actually not the most important issue in the New World Order attack against our inalienable right to self-protection. It is the second most important. Here's why...

Creating so-called "laws" (i.e., supposed "divine right" orders) to ban guns in America will not remove our guns or self-protection abilities. Too many of us are stocked up, loaded up, and know how to make crossbows or 12 gauge shotguns from raw parts. So, if King Obama and the moneybags behind him attempt to ban our guns, it will essentially do nothing but make us more determined to protect ourselves, since we will have the means. So, we can expect that the New World Order knows this, of course, and they are thus going deeper into the issue, to more of the heart of the matter, to really, successfully disarm us. How do you do that? You don't just destroy the Second Amendment, *you destroy the popularity of the Second Amendment, you destroy the spirit of the Second Amendment.* If Grandpa is not thinking about the Second Amendment in his sleep, so to speak (that's "the spirit" I just referred to), then he will not be preoccupied with it, and if he's not, he won't teach his grandson how to, for example, make a shotgun from plywood and pipe. That removes our self-protection faster than removing the laws will. That removes our means for self-protection. This is where the New World Order is really focusing their attack against our inalienable right to self-protection. But, unfortunately, most patriots in America think the fight is in Congress, with HR 1022, for example, and not in the deep psychological warfare going on against gun culture. This psych warfare is mostly invisible: we are not looking for it, we don't expect it, and thus we don't see it, even though "it's written on the wall."

The spirit of gun culture will live on even if King Obama tries to obliterate the Second Amendment, as stated. So, what is really needed, from the New World Order's perspective, *is the destruction of gun culture.* You know, this is so critical, it almost makes me think that all these redundant bills on Congress are just a distraction for the gun culture, getting us all riled up over them, while they are not even the issue (since they won't destroy gun culture, as stated). It's almost as if all these bills in Congress are meant to grab our attention, while the real war — the multi-fronted war on gun culture

— goes on right under our noses, but where we are too distracted to see it! If we are so riled up about HR 1022, then who is paying attention to the EPA's attack on shooting ranges? Answer: nobody! And HR 1022 sits there not fully implemented, while the EPA goes around utterly destroying shooting ranges (and the heart of American gun culture). Again, victory for the New World Order, simply because we are not using our huge brains we have been given!

So, let's talk about why American gun culture is so, so important. Already there is an overwhelmingly unanimous agreement by the denizens of gun culture that Obama is attempting to take over and destroy Constitutionalism. Literally, every single time I am in any gun shop or range, even if it's just a tiny tackle shop that only sells a few wimpy .22 Marlin rifles, I instantly find myself in a discussion with the owner of the shop, or, for example, with the guy sitting there having a cigarette talking to the owner and obviously a regular customer, and it's like magic, we get into this same intellectual discussion about the current takeover of America. And wherever I go in gun culture, the people I meet are somewhat informed, too. I mean, if I go to church or the university, and start talking about Obama, I have to search far and wide for just one single person who even has just one tiny teeny complaint against the system or against King Obama, or who will have even just one small morsel of information, a single, real factual datum, about what is going on politically in the world (they are too busy debating global warming, gay marriage, sports, their self-help groups, or who knows what). But in gun culture, everyone is informed, at least, let's say, 20 percent, so to speak (and that's light years ahead of the aforementioned church and university people!) I think we can see why the EPA is not attacking churches and universities. This issue, I think, could not be clearer, folks!

Even little-informed members of gun culture, who, for example, vaccinate their children and still think 9/11 was done by "cave people," will readily agree about, and know several key scary details about, the current financial takeover of We the People. This is the number one subject at shooting ranges and gun shops nationwide these days, from what I can tell; and it's a very energetic, often cerebral discussion. Discussing AR-15s, the Constitution, ammo shortages, movies, Thomas Jefferson, and AK-47s seems to take a backseat to this topic day-in, day-out at all the ranges and shops I have been to in several states. Again, even those at the shooting ranges and gun shops that are relatively uninformed — for example, who voted for John McCain, believing that was different from voting for King Obama — enthusiastically take part in this unanimous agreement and worry that there is something really amiss like never before, that there is a banking takeover and a Sovietization of America being attempted by Obama and Big Money *right now*.

So, gun culture is, I think, some sort of a revolutionary movement in the making, even if all its members don't really know it or see it that way yet. There is, quite simply, no more intellectual, passionate, activist group in the United States (excluding much much smaller groups, like We Are Change). (Yes *intellectual*! I am a former college teacher for the past decade, and the level of intellectual discussion in the shooting ranges and gun shops dwarfs that of the academic institutions, since discussion in academic institutions usually just is over some "specialized" topic over-and-over [such as experiments on the last GMO soy bean], if even that "brainy", but usually academics just take part in more of the same talk as the rest of culture: about TV, fake churches, environmentalism, consumerism, the weather, worshipping Obama, etc.)

So, think about all this: If you were the New World Order, would you just go after our guns, or would you also go after this ultra-powerful gun culture? Of course you'd go after both. But also ask yourself this: Which would you go after more fervently? The answer quickly pops in your head again: of course you'd go after the culture itself, more so than the guns. And this is precisely what is going on, and I fear that in all our discussion of King Obama's decrees to remove our self-protection, we are missing perhaps a bigger issue: gun culture itself is under all-out attack! Now, let's consider a crystal-clear example: the range near my house, which is being shut down right now by the EPA.

Every Tuesday through Sunday, for a decade, people have congregated to a large gun range near my house. Again, when writing this article, the owner of this range prohibited me from disclosing which range this is, over his fear of the $1000 per day fines that the EPA has looming over his head. (I would just like to say, for the record, that I think the owner is making a mistake in doing this.) This particular large range is a family business, run by an old patriot, call him W, and his son, call him P. The mom is typically there too; she's a dispatcher for the Police Department. Oh, and their dog is also often there, too. This is the heart of the gun culture. But let's discuss why these details are important (hint: real community is the enemy of the New World Order).

The range has a nice lobby in it where members and non-members alike talk and have a good time daily, in-between shooting sessions. Almost always, conversation at the range is vivid and lively, for hours on end, with many people involved, discussing the Constitution, the Bible, the Founders, socialism versus capitalism, the Federalist Papers, Obama's banking takeover, talk radio, and, when I am there, infowars.com. But the discussion is, perhaps surprisingly, *almost always intellectual discussion*—surprisingly because this sort of intellection is vanishingly rare anywhere in America. As stated above, even in my ten years as a college philosophy teacher I did not encounter the other professors involved in such frequent high-level intellectualism—not even close! One is immediately struck when they enter this range how *different* this atmosphere is from really anywhere else in the United States (the same is true throughout gun culture from coast-to-coast, and amid Canada's small gun culture). If you try to start up this sort of intellectual conversation with almost anyone, in any *other* part of culture outside of gun culture (such as at the average job, or in the churches or universities), it not only almost never reaches the level of intellection that the gun culture conversations do, but furthermore, it is usually a complete joke, quickly gravitating to merely repeating (parroting) what Larry King has recently said on TV, or whatever the Big Government propaganda was that Sean Hannity happened to belch out on Faux News the night before.

Unless you are entrenched in gun culture, you have no idea that this is what it is like, and you probably think it's just a bunch of toothless grunting in-breeders, because you saw something like that in the movie *Deliverance* or some other Hollywood propaganda production. But for true gun culture, it's really an intellectual community more than anything else, in many ways. This is the case everywhere in gun culture! And this is why it's dangerous to the New World Order.

Go to a gun shop, and everybody instantly has this invisible bond: we are all bound by the same values: Constitution, guns, pride, family (and very often, but not quite always, religion, too). And these invisible strings we have with one another are powerful; we can all feel them between each other. It's like we all instantly know what the other is thinking about, we are all long lost friends, and we all want to talk about it. If you are not in gun culture, you don't know what I am talking about. If you are, you do.

Where else in America is there continually such a congregation of concerned, Constitutionalist Americans who are passionate, involved, intellectual, and, frankly, not zombified and prozac'ed-out in front of their televisions? I simply cannot think of any other place; *nothing is even close.* In fact, almost every other place, or any other group, in the United States, is, without exaggeration, zombified in the aforementioned way, and thus, gun culture really sticks out as being a pocket of patriotism and intellectualism.

This type of unification, pride, and bonding among people is the ultimate enemy of the New World Order. It is exactly what can bring them down. And, in fact, if the members of gun culture (which is tens of millions, though most may not even know they form such a big nationwide group) were just a little more informed on a few things about the New World Order, they would bring down the New World Order with ease by morning, restoring 1776. This is why it's an "info war." And if this economic downturn and Sovietization keeps up at its current pace, many in the massive gun culture will perhaps start seeing just a little more clearly than they do now, and they will wake up a little bit more, just enough, and they will know just that little bit more they need to know to awaken them properly to what is at stake and to the danger they are in. We are close to that point now; perhaps halfway there, so to speak.

So, let's get to the heart of the issues by getting back to the afore-mentioned range that is being shut down near me here in the Midwest... Following what we have written above, this sort of place is the enemy of the Orwellian world government that is now forming, as stated. And, as we discussed, this New World Order, we can expect, will attack it with all its fury. And guess what? That's precisely what's happening to this range. This particular shooting range is going to be shut down by the EPA. Under what reason, you ask? *Environmental code violations.* The more technical name for this is *communitarianism* — a word all of you better get acclimated to real fast! (Hint, look up Niki Rapaana on the internet, and that will give you a good start.)

In a nutshell, communitarianism is a *philosophy* that, unbeknownst to basically all of us (no kidding!), is being written into our city codes and laws. It is all about "what is good for the group", and it is all about castigating the individual. This is why if you want to build an underground house or cabin in the woods so that you don't have to pay for heat and air-conditioning, and because you want to have a hideaway or cabin that is inexpensive, hidden, and, well, quite quiet and cozy, *you can't do it*, because you have to get permission from the city government and their "certified experts" to do this (it's city government, but the whole operation comes from the New World Order, of course). And they will say, "Oh, no, for your safety, you can't do that, thanks." Also, communitarian philosophy is why you have to pay for construction inspections, or even have them in the first place if you are building a house or building. As if we need that, and as if buildings were just falling down routinely before these city communists took over to "help" us learn how to build properly. Communitarianism is why your school is now all tied to environmentalism and why your children have to learn about gay marriage before they learn about Thomas Jefferson — because communitarianism is all about what is good for community, and oh, of course, the things that are good for community are not guns, religion, empirical science books, and smashing our televisions. No, no! We are quietly told, in so many different ways, that what is good for the community is, for example, environmental protection, neighborhood watch, meth watch, spying on your neighbors to make sure they are not growing pot in their backyard garden, and so on. That's why we have these neighborhood community meetings; not to discuss the Constitution (a person bringing that up at one of those meetings would sure get some head-turns), but to discuss the community (communitarian) priorities (i.e., New World Order philosophies). We go to these meetings just passively allowing the debate to be set before we get involved, rather than beforehand controlling what will be debated in the first place. I don't have time to discuss it here, but this communitarian agenda has been in the planning since before many of you reading this were born. It's all secret, and it's all, um, "for your safety," of course. Sadly, it's all too distant from what most Americans can accept about reality, and so they will just not believe something like this is real; they have been conditioned to think at an ESPN-level of reality, unfortunately.

So, back to the gun range... Communitarianism is also, ultimately, why the range is going to be put out of business. In a New World Order community (i.e., a local communitarian setup), we have to watch out for what is good for the disarmed, uneducated, TV-watching herd— Constitutionalists don't fit into the New World Order's communitarian city-planning. They are not for that type of a community. So, what is good for this zombic herd, according to the gods of communitarianism? Well, what is good for the herd is a safe clean world (how many times have you heard something like that on TV?), and the shooting range near me of course must conform to this, so the story goes.

So, what the EPA has done is told the range that they have to go out of business *all summer* (a prime business time), for at least five months, in order to put in a brand new, ultra-expensive ceiling ventilation system in (the range, of course, has taken out a massive loan for this, which they were approved for by less than a hair — actually, it's still up in the air, no pun intended).

But here's the issue: How can a shooting range,

• which is already paying mind-boggling taxes monthly

• which is already struggling already just to stay open due to all the government fees

• which is already struggling because fewer people are shooting because everyone is hoarding their ammo, and

• which is already struggling due to a huge loss of business due to the impending economic depression

and so forth—how are they to stay open and survive in such a scenario? Answer: *of course they cannot!* They know that, we (who are connected to the range) know that, but the EPA, well, they just seem not to know that, somehow; but they don't really get into that issue too much.

So, long story short: The EPA just found a clever way to put this range out of business. This accomplishes many New World Order goals, perhaps the highest goals the New World Order has: to destroy the gun culture, for reasons discussed above. Where else, now, will the gun owners congregate? Answer: nowhere.

The EPA won't attack the factories here in town that are dumping toxic waste into the river that flows through town. No way! They are too busy attacking the range (and gun culture), which, if it really were a polluter, affects only a fraction of people compared to the river-polluting factory. The EPA won't attack the ocean boats and submarines worldwide that use sonar, and which are responsible for killing whales by the beach-full. Nope. Have to focus on those scary guys at the shooting range. The EPA won't attack the Chinese for all their mind-boggling pollution they produce as they make all the slave-produced goods for Wal-Mart. The government won't create forces to monitor the US-Mexico border. No way! Instead they create forces (environmental harassment forces) to monitor the gun owners (i.e., the Constitutionalists). It does not get any clearer than this, folks. The government is huge, out of control, focused on one thing: coming after you, both non-communitarians and those who go along with communitarianism alike!

The average TV-watching, hot-dog-eating American probably could never see that this is what is going on—that the EPA is a secret force being used for many freedom-taking operations, such as destroying gun culture. It's too complex for them to piece together when they have to think about an episode of American Idol coming on soon. They will just believe that, "oh, shutting down the Range is for the earth," because they have been conditioned to have that sort of a mantra repeating through their head all day every day due to how many times they've heard it on television. They probably also wouldn't notice, if they could glance away from their telescreens long enough, that the EPA in my town is starkly ignoring all the atrocious (and I mean *really atrocious*!) factories in town that are polluting the rivers and air: they have HUGE smoke stacks all over town that everyone has to breath all day and night (and one of them is the company that makes Aspartame! Yeah, what's coming out of that smoke stack is really healthy, I am sure). I am not kidding! Go to the university here on the edge of town, across the river, and all the way over there, on many days, you will smell the exhaust from the factories constantly while you walk through the beautiful campus. Ask any student; they will know what you are talking about. So, is this safe? "Oh, of course," the EPA will tell us (by fiat), just like Aspartame is so safe and wonderful. It's sort of funny, one of these massive polluting factories is literally right across the street from the range! Everyone complains about these factories all the time, a very visible issue. But is the EPA addressing this complaint of the people? Come on, what kind of a question is that?

If the exhaust is so bad for us to breathe in the shooting range that is under attack, then why hasn't it affected W and P (the owner and his son), who have literally been there at the range 50 hours per week breathing in all the air for a decade? Answer: because it's not harmful! But hey, who is really asking that sort of a technical question, anyway, at the EPA. It's funny: I don't remember voting for the members of the EPA, or for what their agendas were to be, or for them to even come into existence in the first place. You know, how much of this big government do we vote in anyway. The answer to that is an easy one.

The New World Order Wants the New World Order to Fail: Order Out of Attacking the New World Order

Jeffrey Grupp, Infowars, June 7, 2009

> "Countless people will hate the New World Order
> and will die protesting against it."
>
> —H.G. Wells, *The New World Order* (1939)
> (cited at the beginning of *Endgame* by Alex Jones)

Why did H.G. Wells make this prediction? Did this insider know something about the secret plan for the future, and about how the social transformation of the world of the future would take place? Here's a quick answer to that question, and which will summarize what this article is about: *Alex Jones once said that The New World Order gets stronger if you attack it, and you only kill it if you attack its very inner hidden core, otherwise it expands and gets more powerful.* That is what this article is about: the formula that The New World Order uses to rule the world is to lure the people into attacking The New World Order, wherein it grows and becomes more powerful: order out of chaos, and order out of attacking the New World Order. This is currently commencing on a global scale, and it is going to be used to create the Brave New World that the New World Order is setting up.

The New World Order uses this formula to carry out order out of chaos. For example, why did the New World Order build up the Nazis, advertise their savagery to the world, wherein they were consequently attacked, and where the chaos of that attack (which was World War II) led to tremendous changes to the world that helped The New World Order? Because this is the way the New World Order works: they quietly rob from the people, using the wealth to quietly build up all the parts of itself, then they advertise the cruelty of a few of their sub-sets, and expectedly the people attack those sub-sets of the New World Order. But the attacks were pre-planned to be attacks that would lead to further escalation of the power of the New World Order. For example, out of the planned chaos of World War II came the United Nations (which is dominated by the war-causing, most heavily militarized nations of the world), the CIA, Truman's "Mental Health Act", the Pentagon, and so on — all things critical to the current state of the world we are in that is dominated by The New World Order.

This is the formula of the New World Order: lure the people into attacking The New World Order (chaos), and use that chaos to engineer a greater and greater power for the New World Order: *order out of chaos*, or, what I will call in this article, *order out of attacking the New World Order*. Below is a diagram of this five-step formula that repeats and comprises world history (in this diagram "fNWO" stands for *fake New World Order*, or *false New World Order*, or a *fragment of the New World Order*, which becomes the public image of the New World Order, but which is only a microcosm of the New World Order, and thus a straw man New World Order, not really the actual one that dominates the world):

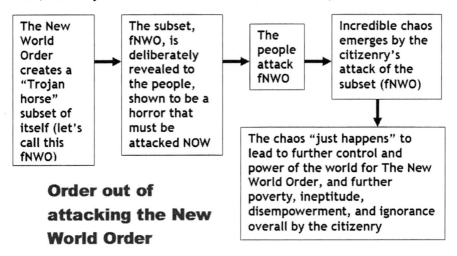

This diagram is the story of history. This is a diagram about "order out of chaos", or, more specifically, *order out of attacking the New World Order*. Again, as Alex Jones said: the New World Order is like a black hole, attracting or drawing everything into it as it expands, growing by that destruction and chaos, turning everything into itself (my paraphrase). It is like a forest fire, raging violently through everything, destroying everything in its path, getting larger and larger, and turning everything into itself (into fire).

The New World Order does this either in parts of the world, to change just part of the world, or they can carry out larger projects and, for example, implement this five-step process illustrated in the diagram *globally*, bringing the entire world into chaos, and thus changing the entire world through the chaos. This formula — *order out of attacking the New World Order* — is currently being implemented on a global scale; we are in the very early stages.

To do this, the New World Order must get you to believe that The New World Order (or, more specifically, a fragment of it, and/or a distorted, inaccurate picture of it, fNWO) is savage, is a threat to you, and must be attacked by you. This is what al-Qaeda is all about, for example (the real al-Qaeda, not the semi-real one that we are told about on TV [actually they *do* often tell us about the real al-Qaeda on TV in a hidden way, e.g., "they are a cult of evil", as Bush once said, but the average person has no idea that this is the case]). Al-Qaeda is a creation of the New World Order, exemplifying all New World Order qualities, existing as a microcosm of what the New World Order is: a murderous, secret, satanic cult that "hates our freedom" (our Constitutionalism, that is), and which thrives off of tears, as George Bush put it once. So, this microcosm or fragment of the New World Order, created by the New World Order, was advertised as being something cruel and which needed to be attacked immediately after 9/11, where this attack empowered the New World Order so much, that it is really the single item they have prospered off of which has taken them to the brink of setting up their Brave New World that they have been planning for so long.

Before I proceed with the meat of this article, I'd like to say that I hope Infowars readers don't avoid this article because it is long and technical. This article is the product of many hours and months of thought on my part, and it is my attempt to bring to you the biggest possible picture of what is going on now, and which has gone on in the past. We need to understand what is going on complexly, on deep levels; and I think this article gets us to go a bit deeper.

I'd like to sum up the New World Order formula in different words:

1 .The New World Order wants the current world-system destroyed, to set up their intended new system (their Huxleyan and/or Orwellian world government),

2. The New World Order wants the current system destroyed through massive suffering worldwide and through ultra-violent social transformation,

3. 1 and 2 will be done by the New World Order partially revealing itself (but it will only reveal the lower levels of itself and/or the parts of itself *that it needs to transform and/or destroy*: some of the mega-corporations, the police forces, national government systems, national militaries of the world, and most of all, select commercial banks and reserve banks, etc. For example, see this recent story of a major world leader "surprisingly" coming out and "agreeing" with the people that the central banks of the world are bad. This amazing story makes my recent "Infowars story, "'End the Fed' Protests are the Secret Road to World Government", far more credible, and far less speculative than I think many originally presumed),

4. The citizens will respond by attacking and destroying these lower aspects of the New World Order system which they will be shown on TV, and which will be erroneously portrayed as being the base-cause of their suffering (but which are actually just the lower- and puppet-levels of the real cause of suffering: the New World Order),

5. The New World Order will have the fragments and parts of their system that they want destroyed indeed decimated through spectacular suffering and violence,

6. The New World Order will "save the people" and build up a new world society (their Brave New World) that they really wanted all along out of this chaos: out of the order out of chaos, or, more specifically, out of the order out of attacking the New World Order.

We are currently at the early stage of steps 3 and 4. This is a clever plan that the blind mob of American TV-addicted people will, it seems, never figure out, I am sad to say. Instead, they will just go along with the system until the system pushes them into unproductive revolt (step 5), and they will thoughtlessly and reactionistically revolt against the puppet-level system that the New World Order wants destroyed, thus helping the New World Order set up their Brave New World.

How many times have we seen the New World Order carry out this sort of a plan, where they reveal part of their self as bad, watch the citizens attack it, and then out of that chaos they create the new system they intended all along. Remember the creation of the Federal Reserve, where it was pretended that the monopolists/corporatists were against the creation of the Fed, and thus the people wanted to attack anything the monopolists/corporatists were in favor of and glom onto anything they were against, and thus the people *supported* the Federal Reserve. In this case, the New World Order advertised the viciousness of the monopolists/corporatists, the people attacked it, the New World Order advertised a solution (the Fed), which was covertly a means to further the New World Order via ultra-monopolist corporatism: order out of attacking the New World Order.

Let's go through some more examples. On 9/11, the New World Order very ceremoniously attacked its own financial towers in a modern-day fall-of-the-tower(s)-of-Babylon event, and look how that sped up the New World Order Agenda! This is perhaps one of the best examples we have of this New World Order formula (order out of attacking the New World Order), and virtually everything new that is tyrannical going on in America has come from that false flag attack (Homeland Security, decimation of the Constitution, increase in size of government, Pentagon theft of trillions of dollars, US wars in the Middle East, Military Commissions Act, and on and on). Through war, the New World Order has repeatedly decimated its own militaries (US in Iraq or Vietnam, for example, or the Nazis in WWII, to name very few of the examples there are), in order to further its agendas through the pre-planned chaos of war. That's what this article is about: New World Order *self-attack*, which is the little-noticed formula of the New World Order, though few anti-New World Order activists realize this fully.

This self-attack ("self-inflicted wound," as Alex Jones often refers to it) is currently commencing at perhaps the largest scale possible: the New World Order is attacking large, even global, systems that it is comprised of, as a way to bring in the long-planned Brave New World. We've seen them do this in smaller segments in the past with just parts of the world (e.g., 9/11, funding Hitler to destroy part of the world in order to re-create it the way that the New World Order wants it rebuilt, etc.), but this time it appears that the New World Order is planning to destroy the entire world (destroy farming, destroy ecology, destroy non-monopolistic economics, destroy sovereignty of the governments of the world, destroy the world religions, destroy our consciousness, and destroy civilization overall), in order to rebuild and recreate the world in the way that they want—order out of attacking the New World Order (or, more succinctly put, order out of chaos).

Order out of Chaos

How many times have we heard Paul Joseph Watson or Alex Jones tell us that the New World Order works by the principle of "order out of chaos"? This is an issue we cannot lose sight of, and it is, I theorize in this article, precisely what is going on right now, though few of us notice it. There are many ways that the New World Order could attempt to bring the world into their Brave New World. They could do it by false flag terror, by brainwashing (especially through the mass media and the public school system), through war, through chemtrail poisoning of some sort, through food and water contamination, or through some combination of these or other factors. But we can now start to get a rather clear picture of how they are going to attempt it, and it is not only through these. It is becoming clear that it is going to be through the order created by attack of the New World Order. They are going to reveal puppet-level aspects of themselves and their plans, and that will be timed to combine with global economic collapse (and the ramifications of that: food shortage, etc.), then they will use these to provoke global ultra-chaos and revolt against the puppet-levels of their tyranny, and it is through that chaos that they will set up, finish and concretize their Brave New World. This is why Texe Marrs once said on the Alex Jones Show that when the New World Order is being set up, part of the religious ritual of the Secret Government will be ceremonies where the higher level freemasons will sacrifice (ritually kill) the lower level freemasons. Now let's explore in more detail just how this will happen.

What will happen is that the New World Order will tell us that, for example, the banks (the national and reserve banks of the world) are the New World Order (rather than the banks being a puppet-level of it), they will show the cruelty of the banks, then the people will attack them, they will be eliminated, and thus the New World Order will be able to set up whatever it wishes: cashless grid, *world* reserve banking, etc. I think I can see these steps already in progress.

This means that there is, and will be, an *advertised* New World Order (fNWO) that the New World Order is going to continue to explain to us (through Congressional bills [e.g., Military Commissions Act], through corporate media hints, etc.) (there have been countless corporate media examples already, such as: Banks Face New World Order), but this is all a smokescreen, a Trojan horse, since it is all really the puppet-level of the New World Order, and it is the aforementioned fragment of the New World Order (fNWO). *The real New World Order will keep its real plans for world governance semi-secret, and the actual agenda will remain far from visibility.* And instead the New World Order will widely broadcast and pose itself as being not itself, but rather as being the fNWO. The people will attack fNWO, but behind the scenes, and out of that chaos, there will be the actual New World Order and Brave New World that the Secret Government is attempting to set up. Most of us won't be looking at, and won't have knowledge of, the *actual* New World Order, since we were tricked into getting all riled up and distracted by the *advertised* New World Order (the fNWO). We can already see this commencing in little but interconnected ways globally. And we know it's something that the Secret Government wants, via their formula (order out of attacking the New World Order), since we can even see them attempting over-and-over to *start* revolts against aspects of the fNWO, as we have seen in Paris, Greece, and other European cities this year (for example, see: Greek Cops Pose As Anarchists, Provocateurs Torch Police, They Want Riots).

Now let's next discuss the specific evidence that this New World Order formula (order out of attacking the New World Order) is currently being set up, and is currently in its early stages. Let's first explore in more detail than we have already how step 3 above is being currently implemented globally — how the New World Order is deliberately advertising global subsets of itself (fNWO), and how we are being coaxed into attacking those parts, while remaining oblivious to the real core and nature of the New World Order (which we can call rNWO, standing for *real* New World Order).

Why is the Secret Government (rNWO) putting out information through their mass media that hints at how pathetic the upcoming flu and swine flu vaccine program will be, often even mentioning how pathetic the swine flu vaccine campaign was in the 1970s? (See: Government to Push H1N1

Vaccine.) It is as if they are indirectly informing people of the hazards and ridiculousness of these vaccines while simultaneously planning forced vaccinations (see: French Mandatory Vaccines), which could lead to all-out revolt in some areas of the world population. Let's move on to another example. Why is the New World Order Secret Government *waiting* to make their move? Why are they going so slowly, when they have several different ways that they could almost instantly totally take-over the world population and complete their project of putting us all into haunting global plantation-serfdom (see the last five paragraphs of this article for information: The N.W.O. Taking over Truth Movement)? And more interestingly, why is the New World Order letting out information through their corporate big-money media about who they are and what they are all about (for example, consider how many times has Ron Paul been allowed on prime-time cable news speaking the truth about corporatism and the reserve banking system)? Many other examples could be given, but note that it is as if the New World Order is purposely revealing itself in a partial/fragmented or distorted way through their corporate media. More examples... Why has debate, although incredibly skewed, been allowed about 9/11, banker corruptions, and the Federal Reserve, through well spotlighted stories in the corporate big-money-media? Why is the internet allowed to continue to exist, and to continue to carry web sites like infowars.com, which are obviously the biggest thorn in the side of the New World Order? Why is the staged flu hoax so *obviously* fake, with only a few deaths compared to regular flu, and where perhaps even some of the TV-zombies that comprise so much of the US population can see through this mass deception of the swine flu? Why has so much anti-vaccine information been released into the corporate media regarding all vaccines and how they damage or kill children? Why are the cable TV mega-giants allowing a film called *The New World Order* to be freely viewed on the Independent film Channel, which, like the film or not, certainly broadcasts hints about some of the same information you hear on the Alex Jones Show? Why was *American Drug War* played over-and-over on Showtime? Why are the makers of *Terminator Salvation* making an upcoming film about the Bilderberg Group? Why is there a blockbuster film coming out that gives hints about the existence of the illuminati (*Angels and Demons*)? Why is there a prime-time cable news show (Olbermann's MSNBC show) devoted to bashing big corporations (albeit in a skewed way) (for example, see this story: Obama's Promise to Trash the Constitution)? The New World Order is purposely revealing lower-, puppet-levels of itself (fNWO), often indirectly or in a distorted way, through the corporate media. Sometimes they even give us a perhaps *somewhat* "big picture view" of their savagery, even through big-media stories (see: We are Paying for Third World pollution). *This is an utterly critical thing for us to pay attention to in the Truth Movement, because it can only mean that the New World Order (rNWO) is up to something by doing this!* The mass media has operated as an almost unfathomably traitorous group for decades, all acting in sync, from NPR to FOX News to MSNBC, all to confuse us, disarm us, brainwash us, harm us, create war, and help the plans of the rNWO, so we cannot assume suddenly that they are coming to our side, <u>but rather we must conclude that by drifting into our territory, discussing our patriotic topics ('End the Fed'), they are trying to hijack our patriotic Truther Movement</u>. So what is it that they are up to? Answer: order out of attacking the New World Order, as I am theorizing in this article.

(Side note: this bashing of big corporations/monopolies on prime-time TV by Olbermann is almost always done in a skewed way, and it is meant to attack and penalize big corrupt monopolies, but where the penalties for the big monopolies are either not really enforced or the big monopolistic businesses semi-quietly move to China or somewhere, and then in the meantime, the small businesses are penalized and suffer *greatly*. Big monopolistic business is planned corporatist corruption and failure: if Ford fails, then, "shucks", they can cry bankruptcy and close down their plants, quietly rebuilding them in South America with "bailout" money [i.e., stolen money]. [Note: the corporate media's recent attack has enabled this to happen in the auto industry, and thus it is also an example of order out of attacking the New World Order!] So, the corporate media will attack the big monopolies [e.g., all the recent attacks on the auto industry in the corporate media] that it wants to fail, and this leads to penalties [such as eco crime, or eco fines, emissions penalties, etc.] that all businesses are subjected to, such as small businesses, truck drivers who are just trying to make it, and so on, and it's all in the name of some bogus cause that the unthinking public gloms on to, such as saving the earth, or fighting corrupt business, or something like that [see this recent story: <u>New York's Eco Cops</u>]. You see, this is aligned with the same strategies for decreasing human productivity and technological innovation that the ecological movement is secretly planned-out to do: constantly penalize and limit innovation, destroy any figments of real education or capitalism, and then the people will never be productive and innovative, and thus they are kept from being strong, armed, wealthy and free. It's always easier for the secret government to control dumb helpless unarmed slaves than strong intelligent armed free people. This is all essentially what the functions of Noam Chomsky and Howard Zinn are, two New World Order intellectual posers that the corporate big-money media so often focus on, for example: <u>world leaders even discuss them at the UN</u> [this immediately sent one of Chomsky's books to #1 on the best seller lists]. For example, Chomsky will tour a country like Brazil, bashing the US military and big business in America, often in fact saying accurate things [perhaps 50 percent of the time], but Chomsky will never tell the Brazilians about the quiet alliances between the IMF, WTO, WHO, World Bank, CIA, CFR, etc.

[i.e., The New World Order], or that the New World Order is behind it all, or that Americans do not support its wars and anti-capitalistic monopolism, or that Americans were initially tricked/lied into supporting the wars in 1991, and 2003-2004 [and 1941], and <u>Chomsky will deliberately *lie* about how more guns for citizens = less crime</u>. <u>And we all know that Chomsky sure won't tell foreigners he talks to about the truth of 9/11</u> [Also see this video: <u>Chomsky says 9/11 Truth Pushes Non-Scientific Data</u>]. This anti-corporate sort of attack could gain considerable momentum among the US population quickly if the New World Order merely wanted it to, and for the purposes of decimating America in conjunction with the way that the New World Order's ecological movement is going to quietly decimate America, and Americans likely will never figure it out, and would go along with any sort of the anti-corporate attack, just as they will with the End the Fed campaign, that <u>is also being hijacked and used by the New World Order for their purposes</u>. So, this is all very difficult for the populace to even come close to figuring out, but we just have to remember this simple rule of thumb: if the New World Order sends us a message, then it is bad no matter what, even if we don't initially see it that way. So, if, for example, the New World Order uses its big-money media to send us a message, such as Olbermann bashing big corporations, then we must conclude that hidden deep in that message is a not-so-visible rNWO plan, even if we don't see it right away, and even if it seems to be a good message on the surface. Ok, let's get back to how The New World Order is purposely revealing itself in a distorted way through the corporate media...)

These all are ways that the New World Order is permitting itself to be revealed. And the New World Order knows that, even though some of the information sources that the New World Order is allowing are indeed presenting real information (rather than information *only* about fNWO), such as the Alex Jones Show. But it seems that the New World Order is counting on the citizenry merely remaining clueless and reactionary enough that they will never put the big picture together in time, never deciphering the real information being presented in a few places on the internet about rNWO with the distorted information all over about fNWO. The citizen-mobs will instead *not* understand and/or follow the pure message of this article, for example, or of the Alex Jones Show, and instead will be fooled by co-opting messages given by the corporate press about the fake images of the Patriot movement that the Big Media has been presenting lately (see <u>The N.W.O. is Taking Over the Patriot Movement</u> for more information). The world citizens (i.e., the slaves) will not see the pure information of this article, or of the Alex Jones Show, but because of their seemingly endless devotion to the continually lying mainstream news (it seems that no matter how many times the corporate news lies, the people amazingly will still turn to it as their sole information-source about their world), they will instead blur it together with the distortion of the fNWO given in the corporate press, and thus the citizen mobs of the world will never figure things out.

It's as if the giants that control the New World Order's media stream are being instructed to release information about the New World Order through it. These are all things that, some might assume, hurt the New World Order, and bring the people together in resistance to the New World Order, with power of the resistance growing every day. But the New World Order controls the corporate big-money-media, and the internet, *so they are controlling these vehicles by which this resistance is forming.* Or, more simply put, *they are the carriers of this resistance: the New World Order's corporate monopolies are the support for the resistance that is forming.* The importance of this seeming paradox (the New World Order is supporting resistance against the New World Order) *cannot be underestimated,* as stated above, and we must use this seemingly confusing situation *to understand things at a deeper level* — and that level is, the New World Order formula: order out of attacking the New World Order. So, we have to see and deeply understand this New World Order formula, face this fact (we know it's a fact because it is the story of history). I think a deep understanding of this New World Order formula is the key to defeating the rNWO, and without this deep understanding, we will endlessly battle against the fNWO, as we have for thousands of years. We need to focus on this New World Order formula as energetically as we did on the 'End the Fed' protests.

The New World Order wants to make its move via a violent revolution (order out of attacking the New World Order), and they have to drive the people into panic and helplessness so as to get unproductive, un-thought-out, reactionary, horrific violence to commence. How does the New World Order drive the citizen mobs of the world to this point? Answer: starve them, kill their economy, destroy their known way of life, shatter their security, confuse them and make them totally ignorant, and slowly start to show the brutality of the Secret Government controllers. And what is the overall goal of this: to destroy the current way-of-things in order to bring about a new way of things (a New World Order). The secret global government has control over every aspect of our lives (since we, as Americans, have let that happen), so it only must be the case that they are orchestrating everything we are seeing going on now if it shows up in the mass corporate media (excluding the still-far-too-small pockets of informed, productive, genuine resistance).

Now that the TV-addicted populace is aware of the New World Order (since it has been announced to them on TV for the past few months), there is something very important to consider that few think about that this article is addressing: there are *two* New World Orders, as discussed above (and for simplicity and efficiency in this article, I have been using two abbreviations: fNWO and rNWO):

1. **The rNWO**: This is the *invisible* New World Order: This is the real New World Order (rNWO), most of which is very secretive, and not disclosed in much of any way to the populace via the corporate media, even though the populace has been now informed of the New World Order. Examples of the institutions of this ultra-core group of the New World Order are mostly unknown, but they may include those who give orders to the Bilderberg Group, some of the leaders of the eugenics movements, those mostly unseen people who are actually in control of some of the mega-monopolistic corporations, and so on.

2. **The fNWO:** The *visible* New World Order, or the *fake* New World Order: This is the New World Order that the public is told about on TV, it is a fake and/or fragmented New World Order (fNWO), and thus it is a New World Order that the public thinks is real, but which is only a partial, distorted, or half-true picture (if that); it is a general deception. Examples of the institutions of this group are The Federal Reserve, the big American banks, the US military, Bush and the Republicans, the police in America (and elsewhere), etc.

The rNWO consists of little-known secret societies. Even the super-experts on this subject, like Jordan Maxwell, David Icke, Alex Jones, Michael Tsarion and others may not know much of this hidden group. This group follows a Satanic religion, the nature of which is little understood even by expert scholars on the subject. This group has a streamlined, old technique for ruling through chaos, and by keeping the world citizens helpless, unarmed, dumb, unhealthy, and completely controlled by money. This group controls through corporatism (and mostly the rNWO corporatist edifices, such as the military industrial complex, the hijacked and corrupted world religions, the prison system, Big Agra, etc.), and the public has no idea because they wrongly assume that the national governments of the nations of the world are the institutions that have control of things, which they do not.

The fNWO is portrayed as being banks (not the huge globalist banks, but rather the midsized banks, like Goldman Sachs, etc., or the reserve banks of the world), the national governments of the world, but not the global corporatists aligned with the rNWO. So, the public now knows about the New World Order (fNWO) due to it being discussed a bit on TV over the past few months, and the public currently is confusingly being told, on one hand, that it is a good or even trendy thing (see: Lord's Welcomes New World Order), and on the other hand, that it is a bad thing (since it is being shown in the corporate press that aspects of the fNWO are harming the people, see: Officers Put on Leave After Flushed Fetus). *But what is important is that the world citizens are being told that it is the fNWO, not the rNWO, that is in control of things.* In other words, they are not being told what the New World Order is, and the New World Order is remaining in secret, as always. The media that the TV-addicted American is glued to is creating a public perception of what the New World Order is—which is an incomplete, and thus incorrect, perception. The perceived New World Order is very different from the real one.

Thesis: the public is being made widely aware of the fake/fragmented New World Order (fNWO), and parts of the world citizenry are being coaxed into revolt against it. By this, eventually, the fNWO will consequently fall, citizens will feel victory, and the real New World Order (rNWO, Brave New World), which was hidden all along, will be introduced as the new society to fill the void.

This is a classic problem-reaction-solution scenario, which in this article I am calling *order out of attacking the New World Order.* Here's how it goes:

> **Problem**: the New World Order (which is really fNWO)
> **Reaction**: global revolt against fNWO
> **Solution**: the real New World Order (rNWO)

Let's give an example of how this would work: if the fNWO gives you trouble through brutality or ineptitude (e.g., failures of national governments, police brutality, etc.), then you eliminate them, and in the void left over, you set up a system which solves the problems, which of course would be world police, world government, world military, world courts, and so on. (See <u>End the Fed protests are the secret road to world government</u> for a more elaborate example)

So, what will the public do during this world-wide revolt? I theorize that they will consist of, and gravitate into, three sorts of groups (and we can already clearly see these forming now):

> **Group 1**: those millions and millions of people who endlessly give in to denial, and who will never see or want to see the fNWO, believing that the fNWO is a wonderful helpful and exciting thing (Obama Administration: <u>"we want to make government service cool again!"</u>), and they will be a significant part of the members of the youth corps, the FEMA cities/camps, the ultra-massive military and secret militaries, the new types of paramilitary police and secret law enforcement squads, and overall a member of the financial takeover that is being set up. This is the largest group of the three.

> **Group 2**: this is the second largest group of people, which will likely consists of millions and millions of people just in America alone, and it consists of those people who do not go along with the fNWO, and who cannot believe the zombified hordes of group 1, and they revolt against

fNWO and against group 1. This is a classic divide and conquer scenario: group 2 and group 1 will battle, and the rNWO will sit on the sidelines unnoticed.

Group 3: this is, I am sad to say, by far the smallest group, and it consists of those who have knowledge of and are trying to get the message out about rNWO. Most likely, groups 1 and 2 will not understand when group 3 describes rNWO. I theorize that even those who listen to the Alex Jones Show daily do not fall into this group, and instead are tricked into falling into group 2.

It would seem, possibly, that the New World Order is going to try to get group 1 and group 2 to go to war, and this war is the "order out of chaos" that will bring about the rNWO. These three groups already exist on a certain level. It's as if this is even being set up, currently, in the very early stages.

This sort of pattern is what we have seen all through history. Think of Napoleon trying to take over the world. Or think of Hitler's plan to set up "A World Order", built up covertly by American corporate Money (see *Corporatism: The Secret Government of the New World Order*, pages 20-21 for detailed information on this) and obviously it was planned to fail. But out of that chaos, out of attacking fNWO, look at what the Secret Government of the world was able to accomplish: establishing the UN, the Pentagon, the CIA, Truman's "Mental Health Act", and on and on — these groups are the impetus for the problems we are now facing with the looming set-up of the rNWO through the fNWO hoax. Also, think of the French Revolution. These are all instances of times when the secret occultist power of the world had the populations and hordes attack either lower levels of their secret world government, or attack faked images of their secret world governments. This is why we see the New World Order not keeping their information on cyber-security, think tank meetings, Bilderberg, and so forth from getting in the hands of the Truthers and the patriot movements. The truth is, <u>as I previously stated in another article</u> [NWO taking over patriot movement], the patriot and truth movements are getting so large now that the New World Order will have to co-opt them, as it is currently doing.

This is also why we see the Big Media (the corporate press) starting to discuss and hijack discussion of our patriot topics, such as false flag terrorism, banking monopolies, the pathetic nature of the swine flu hoax, government ineptitude, and so on (see my other articles on Infowars.com for detailed discussion of these important issues: <u>NWO is taking over the Truth and patriot movements</u>, <u>End the Fed protests are the secret road to world government</u>). After the total economic collapse is set in, the starving, cheated, and homeless of group 2 will pick up on these hints from the Big Media, and they may be lured into violence with it. But this is a planned "divide and conquer" program. For example, consider, on the one hand, the millions in America out there who are buying guns and ammo, but where, unfortunately, still most of them are clueless to the rNWO (not of group 3, but rather of group 2), and then consider, on the other hand, all these secret police reports being uncovered about police plans to target "right wing extremists" (i.e., that last Constitutionalists) by the New World Order protection team (i.e., the police). Can you see how it's possible that these groups are being set up to battle in the future, such as when more serious starvation and homelessness starts? Also, consider how the people are fed, through the mass media, stories that get them riled up at, not the IMF, WHO, CIA, CFR, or illuminati, but rather at the police (for example, see <u>Granny Tasered</u>). How else can we interpret this, other than the illuminati-controlled mass media attempting to bring sides against each other for possible future civil war: the police and military vs. anybody not strictly in group1, group1 vs. group2, etc.? I am not sure if this is what is really going on, but we in group 3 sure need to start discussing the possibility.

This is also why shows like The Alex Jones Show, or Coast to Coast AM (which more and more has Alex Jones sorts of subject-matter on it) are allowed to stay on the air. And it is why the Internet has not been fully deconstructed yet. Though a few sites on the internet, and shows like the Alex Jones Show, will give a full picture of the political world, the New World Order is counting on people being too busy, too dumbed down, too reactionary and simple (due to their public school education and these non-Biblically-based churches everywhere) to be able to use the few resources out there that give an accurate picture. So these few accurate shows are permitted to remain, for the most part, since the New World Order is counting on the masses to panic and frenzy as we fall into depression, food riots, dollar collapse, and so forth, where the masses will be for the most part caught off-guard and unaware of the big picture. And thus the New World Order is counting on the shows with real big-picture information to be slurred, not used correctly, distorted, and smeared-out with the massive disinformation that exists all over the internet and talk radio. Instead of an organized civil disobedience against the New World Order, the New World Order is counting on blind, unorganized, chaotic resistance, and again, that's why shows like The Alex Jones Show are allowed to stay on air, and that is why Alex Jones is still alive (though even uttering those words is very disturbing to me because of what they hint). As Alex Jones has reported so often, military documents show that there have been plans to flood the internet with various kinds of attacks and disinfo; this too plays into the "order out of chaos" that the New World Order has planned, as I theorize in this article. Hopefully the New World Order is wrong in their calculation, and hopefully Americans will wake up and get the real big-picture before it's

. too late — before we fall into massive depression wherein the public will probably be too reactionary to figure things out.

If you look closely, you can see little signs all over of these wars — these "divide and conquer" scenarios — being set up. For example, this is all why cops are being beefed up to attack citizens, as we've seen (for example, <u>Cops Attack EMT</u>), and why they are being trained to absurdly believe that US citizens are terrorists. As the people fall into the economic depression, and if these police attacks escalate according to New World Order plans, the tension between police and the people will escalate into war. You see, the people are just about at a point where they don't care, and they will start shooting when provoked and brutalized by the police and by the New World Order (for example: <u>Baby Injured in Taser Incident</u>, <u>Cop Beats Man for Standing</u>), and The New World Order knows this, so they have to get the police primed beforehand: get the police believing that all citizens are terrorist-fools, that there are right wing extremist terror groups all over (which are often the Constitutionalists), and so on. (I theorize that this police-vs.-citizens warfare will start with something to do with home foreclosures.) That way as soon as the police see a single citizen revolting against police that are breaking the law, the police will not see that law-breaking cop as carrying out bad police-work, they will see it through the pre-set lens the New World Order has constructed for them ("citizens are terrorists"), and the police will fall into a frenzy of rage, like a crazed soldier in Iraq breaking down a door of a family that is trying to sleep in the middle of the night (<u>see the utterly excellent Youtube documentary *Occupation Dreamland* for actual footage of such break-ins</u>). The recent series of police mania videos that the Alex Jones Show has covered, most likely won't get banned from Youtube, because The New World Order wants them seen, to get the war between police and the people started. What is banned on Youtube is information revealing details or operations about rNWO, not about fNWO.

So, what is our solution? Three things: (1) we must focus our attention very energetically on understanding the New World Order formula described above. And (2), as Alex Jones said on June 2: "If we are self-sufficient, they can't beat us, that's why they want to shut down all the farms and ranches." We can add to this, as Alex often has, that we also need to become armed to the teeth, in every possible way (crossbows, learning gunsmithing, etc.). Freedom is *farmers with guns working together*! Now, most importantly, (3), we also cannot underestimate <u>the power of religion</u> [Man says Cops don't Own Him, is Tased, then Escapes], as I think so many of us, even in our movement, have been fooled into doing. With religion, we can even break the laws of physics!

**The Most Powerful Military Force in the World is the American People.
It is the Last Jeffersonian Militia on the Planet, and the New World
Order is Powerless Against it**

Jeffrey Grupp.

Published at www.restoretherepublic.com, June 30, 2009

"Divine providence has given to every individual
the means of self-defense."

—George Mason, "Father of the Bill of Rights"

What is a Jeffersonian militia? It is a scenario where a large percentage of
the population of a nation involves the average man or woman on the street
(i.e., not a member of the government, military, or police) being armed,
carrying a *powerful* gun. A Jeffersonian militia gains its character by the fact
that it is not controlled by any government (unless government = citizenry), it
involves potentially all citizens of a nation, and thus does not and cannot
resemble a military in the way that most Americans are now accustomed to
believing what a military is (which is *not* a Jeffersonian militia, and instead
just a small fraction of the population of a nation: Army, Navy, UN "Peace-
Keepers", CIA secret forces, police forces, etc.). Also, a Jeffersonian militia
cannot resemble, for example, a Third World dictator's goon-squad-of-an-
army.

Americans have been largely conditioned to believe that a Jeffersonian
militia is something scary – even many in gun culture fall into this delusion.
And some Americans even believe that they are safer if citizens are unarmed,
and only militaries are armed, and armed to the teeth. That's the message we
get on television constantly, and in our schools and many churches. That idea
can be called the anti-Jeffersonian state, or, more aptly put, a slave
dictatorship.

But regardless of what Americans may or may not think, the very
interesting issue here is that *America currently is a Jeffersonian militia*, since
a *huge* percentage of ordinary American citizens

   (a) are armed,
   (b) know how to use their weapon, and
   (c) are becoming increasingly distrustful with the government.

Those three characteristics are the rudimentary qualities of a Jeffersonian
militia.

Now let's move on to the central theme of this article:

The New World Order is actually powerless against America's armed citizenry (militia), and if you don't know that, then you have been tricked (brainwashed) to think otherwise.

America is the only Jeffersonian militia in existence today, and the American public is the largest, most heavily armed military in the world. In actuality, the entire world is defenseless to it – even the New World Order. A four-million person army could invade the Atlantic shore tomorrow, and that military would certainly cause some initial chaos, but soon after, it would find out that it is drastically outnumbered and doomed to total extinction, if the American militia simply got up off the couch and chose that to be their fate.

We know that the New World Order knows these facts about a Jeffersonian militia, and is deeply threatened by this, due to the unprecedented attacks on the Second Amendment and on gun owners from all different angles that have ramped-up over the past year in America and which are escalating tremendously (see these stories: VFW Inventory of Guns, EPA Shutting Down Gun Range, Gun Confiscations for Law-Abiding Citizens, Gun Confiscations After Tornados, Corporate Media all in Unison on Gun Confiscations). Television, poor nutrition, pharmaceuticals, laziness, fake churches, public school education, and addictions have led the American Jeffersonian militia to currently fall into a zombified, drugged, and confused state – like a sullen, caged Kodiak bear in a zoo, softly sleeping in its prison, with its purpose, force, and identity put into a state of misunderstanding and hibernation. But nevertheless, we know the New World Order is scared of the American Jeffersonian militia – especially what the American Jeffersonian militia could quickly become in specific circumstances. This is mainly because *he who has the gun has the power*, and thus, as always in history, the world governing powers want the guns (the power) only for themselves.

Consider these points:

1. We all know that the places in America that have the most gun ownership by ordinary Americans (non-gang members) have dramatically reduced crime,

2. We all know that illegal immigrants are coming across the border and doing horrific violent crimes to Americans, and

3. We all know that homicides from guns are just a fraction of how many are caused by the New World Order's most cherished industries: Big Pharma, tobacco, alcohol, war, and heart disease and heart attack (which is caused more these days by eating genetically modified

animals that have far higher fat content, than just by meat consumption)

There are so many other examples that could be given, but just these points show that what is unquestionably in the best interest of the American people is to simply embrace the Second Amendment with maximum gusto, just as our Founders taught:

> "Among the natural rights of the Colonists are these: first, a right to life; secondly, to liberty; thirdly, to property – together with the right to support and defend them *in the best manner they can*." —Samuel Adams (my italics)

This means that you should not be going to the gun shop to buy a .22, but rather an AR-15 or a .45 long barrel revolver, for example. Buy a cannon instead of a knife, and an AK-47 instead of a .32. Why do I say this? Because as the quote from Samuel Adams just given states: this is the law of the land, you are supposed to do this, as instructed by our Founding Fathers.

But moving back to points 1-3, the New World Order takes great measures to ignore points 1-3, and to even cause the opposite: less guns more crime, disempowering the American citizens so they are helpless against criminals, putting forth all sorts of measures that increase the power of Big Pharma, tobacco usage (including glamorizing it in Hollywood), and increasing other deadly industries that the New World Order gains profit and control of the world off of. Contemplate what I have just written in points 1-3, and how the New World Order attempts to do what hurts the people with respect to these. This is a "big picture" point of view! *Does it get any clearer than this?*

George Mason, seemingly precognitively, wrote: "when the resolution of enslaving America was formed in Great-Britain, the British parliament was advised... to disarm the people. That it was the best and most effectual way to enslave them. But that they should not do it openly; but to weaken them and let them sink gradually." This is where we are today. The lying corporate media has us all looking different directions while this is going on, focusing on other, meaningless stories (the gay marriage debate, stories about Madonna, Obama, and Britney Spears, etc.). And much more importantly, our government-controlled education system in America has never given us the correct story of history that shows just how important the guns are, and which shows what the power of a Jeffersonian militia can do, as happened in the Revolutionary War. That is the point of this article: to show you what history really is, *which is the struggle for who controls the weapons*. That is what we need to discuss in this article, and this discussion will show us that we American citizens are by far the most powerful military force on the planet.

What is history? There are many ways to answer that question. Control of resources or corruption of the world's religions are two popular ways to explain history in academia; and in the alternative media it is often more appropriately explained by who controls banking and money. Certainly these are all major forces in what history is at its core. But I believe there is a better explanation of what history really is at its core. There is a deeper force than resource monopolism, religion, and usury, and to get an idea of what I am getting at, answer this question: Who *controls* and *guards* the resources, the money, the banksters' money empires, and the fortresses of the fraudulent religious leaders? The answer is simple: the group "with the bigger guns", as the saying goes.

Let me state the issue more carefully here: *history is a story of the controlling class perpetually taking extraordinary measures to disarm the class they control, and due to that ubiquitous endeavor, history has been a horror greater than any Hollywood horror f.*

So, what I am saying in this italicized statement is that A causes B:

A = controlling class perpetually taking extraordinary measures to disarm the class they control

B = history has been a horror greater than any Hollywood horror film

A ==> B

A and B are not just coincidentally correlated (simultaneous) in time. No, I am saying something much stronger than that. I am saying that *A causes B*, and, in other words, *if A did not exist, B would not exist.*

I know that A *causes* B because of what I have written about in my previous Infowars.com article about Thomas Jefferson and the citizen militia, and because of the truth of what Founding Father Edmund Randolph said: "A people who mean to continue free must be prepared to meet danger in person, not to rely upon the fallacious protection of... armies." (Edmund Randolph was Delegate to the Constitutional Convention, Secretary of State under President George Washington, and a man many consider to be one of the Founding Fathers of the United States.) Did you read that right? Armies, militaries are *lies*! They do not give protection; they are used to attack the people. *History teaches us this fact.* They do not, and never have, offered protection to citizenries! Protection of the people is only very, very rarely what militaries are intended for, and even in those cases where they were purported to be intended to help citizenries, they still ended up obliterating the people (a good example is the American military in World War II, which was supposed to liberate Japan and Europe in the pre-planned Rockefeller-Ford-IBM-created war, but what it mainly did was utterly annihilate innocent citizens (non-soldiers) by the millions all over Europe and Tokyo, and for verification of this fact, see Fog of War).

Rather, militaries are typically assembled by the bloodthirsty keepers of world government – no matter what social era we are considering – and they are turned on the unsuspecting, trusting, innocent, hardworking, and usually unarmed citizens for pre-planned divide-and-conquer scenarios. The stories in history when militaries defeated the oppressing governments were not militaries at all; they were Jeffersonian gun-militias! 1776 America! Vietnam! The factories of Argentina! The other wars of history were, to my knowledge, all one or more of the following: slaughter-fests, staged, bought-and-paid-for by the keepers of world governance, and thus they are not stories resembling the stories of these Jeffersonian gun-militias. (Some readers might be wondering why we don't consider non-violent revolution, in the MLK, Thoreau, and Gandhi tradition. The answer to that is: the New World Order is, at this time, using provocateurs seemingly continually, and frankly, in my opinion they are destroying all peaceful protests – and to my knowledge, they did not do this with any such frequency with MLK and Gandhi. Another reason that sort of revolution may not work now is that the corporate mass media won't cover a non-violent revolution, and MLK and Gandhi both utterly depended on mass media to focus on them and to act as their "billboard", so to speak. That won't work now, and if it did, I think people like Alex Jones, Cindy Sheehan, Luke Rudowski, and so many others, would have brought this country through a MLK-style non-violent revolution already.)

Also, I know that A causes B because it's just simple logic: if ruthless terrorists get control of the money and resources of a land, they will seek to remove the power (guns) from those they control in a tireless, unrelenting manner. Without guns, ultimately you have no power to own (control) land, to farm, to participate in government, or to possess resources. In a Jeffersonian militia we exploit our inalienable right do any of these; without the guns, it's just a matter of time before we are living on a plantation, as we are rapidly progressing toward in contemporary America. These words I have just written are, of course, just an echoing of the words of the Founders.

So, the story of history is about who controls the weapons, and in our age, that means *who has the guns*. This is what this article is about, and this is relevant because America is the one nation of the world where the citizens are armed more heavily than any military in the world. Do you really understand what this means? It means that the American citizenry is in control, and they have just been tricked into thinking otherwise! Let me put that in another way: the most powerful social force on the planet is the American citizenry; nothing can stop it, if they merely choose to execute their power!

As Alex Jones has also discussed, the guns are, I think, the only issue, in the end, and as I've shown in another article. The guns are simply the last hope for us, *no exaggeration*, and all the attempts from all different angles that the New World Order is now using to rid us of our guns and protection simply proves how powerful the guns are: since they were invented, they have been the shaper of history. So, really, the battle of the takeover of the American people by the New World Order will be won or lost *before it fully starts* (if a visible war ever commenced, rather than the current "quiet war" with "silent weapons"), since it will be decided by how Americans resist or give in to the New World Order's attempts to take our guns, kill gun culture, and disband the last significant Jeffersonian militia on the planet.

In the era of guns over the past several hundred years, there has never been a case where a government (banking elite and its military) could overtake an armed Jeffersonian militia of reasonable size. A good example is the Revolutionary War – which is that war for the independence of this nation that your government-controlled schools "forgot" to tell you about in any detail. (If you want a refresher, see: Alex Jones interview with Sam Damewood.) This is a pretty clear-cut issue: if citizens of a reasonably-sized nation form a Jeffersonian gun-militia, they are free, and they are impervious to attack, and if they don't, well, then you get Rwanda, Nazi Germany, Stalin's Russia (20 million dead Christians!), Cambodia, Tibet, the American Indians, American slavery, the IMF-induced economic crash of Jamaica, the utter poverty, and government corruption and domination of present-day Africa, Mexico, and the concentration-camp-like-state of most of the *current* world that you never see on Fox News or on Oprah (they discuss Darfur, but that is going on all over the world, so why only discuss Darfur and ignore, for example, Mexico?) Most of the world currently looks like a concentration camp and/or a labor camp (since most of the world is a horrific Third World, which resembles a concentration or death camp, see War Against the Third World, Fourth World War), but the problem is that in our perfumed media, that even many of the info-warriors are still all-too influenced by, we are not told about this. Our schools tell us that slavery and concentration camps existed in the past, in Germany during World War II, or on the plantations of America in the 1800s, but that means that our schools are blatantly lying to us, since concentration-camp-life is all around us, *literally comprising most of the social world* (think of our prisons, our "Constitution-free zones," public schools, airports, hospitals, court houses, and militaries). I have a friend who works for Big Oil, and he frequently travels over to Africa to work, and while there he must live in an armed compound (prison) so that the "local people" won't try to kill him (that's what he says), because they live in such incredible poverty and slavery that they don't even have toilets or showers! Many don't even have beds, and they sleep in the "village" center on the ground in the dirt at night. And what can those Africans do about it?

Answer: nothing. Why? Because they don't have power (guns). They don't have farming or land skills anymore, they don't have books and nutritious food, but most importantly, they do not form a Jeffersonian militia, and that means that, as my friend says, "It's just amazing how little the 'people in charge' care about the people that work for them and make them rich."

Now hear these words carefully: *most of the world is in this sort of an unspeakably impoverished and even concentration-camp-like state, America is the last holdout, and all steps are currently being carried out by the New World Order to transform America into such a slave-state and Third World labor camp.*

This is occurring in so many ways: removing the manufacturing base of America, freezing minimum wage to ridiculously low (poverty) levels, poisoning of food and water in America, Sovietizing public education, attacking the Second Amendment, attacking farmers, leaving the borders open, government attempts to eliminate gardening in America (that's a big one, since that is a main element in making people helpless — removing their abilities to work the land — that's why American Indians were put on reservations and their kids were put in boarding camps/schools, sort of like an extreme family destruction, where our public school system is a softer form of that). That's just a small list that could be given. This has been done over-and-over, the New World Order is quite good at it, and we'd better figure that out pretty quick, because we Americans sure are going down that path. The lying corporate news media (that same news media that told us from 1991-2003 that Iraq was a threat) now is telling us there's nothing to worry about, the "recession is almost over", just sit back and watch more "Must See TV."

Americans, however, unfortunately do not have any idea of this real story of history, and thus they do not have any idea of the utter power they hold due to the fact that they currently form the loose skeleton of a Jeffersonian militia – which is literally a needle in the haystack of history: an armed populace, unlike the unarmed multitudes of the past who have been annihilated through the eons of history. One man with a gun can control a hundred without one. The gun is the ultimate instrument of power in our world. Remember how Hitler first instituted gun control because of so-called hunting accidents (which were probably staged), and look what happened. Remember how the 1800s US government made it illegal for slaves and American Indians to own rifles, and look what happened. Think of the medieval and Enlightenment kings of Europe making it illegal for those not of his armies to own swords. An armed citizenry is precisely what the world needs, and it only exists in America.

So, why is a Jeffersonian militia so powerful? For one simple reason, which can be stated in one sentence: *the New World Order is nothing more than a big room full of ridiculous people who control the world by money.* But as stated above, money is not as powerful as controlling the world by the gun. What this means is that if The New World Order tries, for example, mass roundups for throwing Americans into their FEMA concentration camps, as they certainly are gearing up to do, if the American Jeffersonian militia awakens to that agenda, the New World Order will not get that agenda very far off the ground (unless Americans succumb to fear and let them – this room full of ridiculous people – run over them). So, as you can see, and as I showed in my other article, the Jeffersonian militia is the single #1 most important thing for our freedom, the answer to all our problems, the death of any sort of tyranny, and what that translates to is that our guns are the #1 most important thing to our freedom, as Alex Jones has said so many times.

So, on that note, we can sum up our freedom and our destiny in one sentence: *in America, we already have the armed Jeffersonian militia, now we just need proper education – nothing is more important than that.* As far as the New World Order is concerned then, all the scary things they imply they are going to do to us (FEMA camps, etc.), well, they can't in a Jeffersonian militia state, so what are so many of us afraid of? I will get into this in more detail below.

"What can I do about it all!?" How many of us have heard that one when we've tried to awaken others to the specific, documentable problems going on with America regarding the New World Order? We have all heard this, and we have all seen this "I-can't-do-anything-about" mass-delusion epidemic that has sickened America. This is why the New World Order system works as it does. This attitude will change when the New World Order pushes their savagery enough. The American Jeffersonian militia will sit back and just want to be left alone until the New World Order chooses to push hard enough to start their pre-planned divide and conquer program. But as stated, the power does not exist with them. They are a room of ridiculous people with the power to create money and with a few armies at their disposal, but the American populace is the largest military force in the world. So, from that perspective, the New World Order is powerless. Yeah, that's right; the power of the New World Order is an illusion. They are like the Nazis, who would send people into a town they intended to take over to talk up their Nazi-power, their military strength, wherein everyone one would roll-over and give up, but then when the Nazis came into the town, they'd be just a quite small force. The power is always with the mass of the human populace (in all ways, not just regarding guns), but they are just perpetually tricked into thinking they are powerless. It's a psychological warfare technique, as Alex Jones has so often said. Here, let me illustrate...

If you have a corporation (of any size), and there is a "person in charge" on the one hand, and the workers who actually do the work on the other hand, who is really in control of the business here? Well, the average TV-and-hotdogs American, without even thinking about it, quickly and confidently belches out: "oh, of course the manager-controller is! There would be chaos without 'somebody in charge.'" *But that is only an idea.* And is the idea right? *Of course not;* and here's why. To paraphrase from my book, *Corporatism*: if the "person in charge" does not show up for work on some given day, work can go on that day; but if the workers do not and only the manager shows up, no work goes on that day. So that makes it appear that the workers are in charge, doesn't it? So why do we believe the opposite, wrong idea here in corporatist America? Answer: we have been taught the wrong idea, and, well, who is questioning it?

Oh I can hear the confident comebacks out there from the ESPN-and-beer Americans, who probably all would snap back and confidently say something like this: "the workers working without a 'person in charge' is a nice *idea*, but it would just never really work *in the real world*, and it never has." Really? Well, if that's true, then how come if you watch the excellent documentary, *The Take*, which is about factory-workers all over South American who kicked "the bosses" out and created factories of the people, run by the people, for the people, you see that it certainly is not chaos that ensues when "the bosses" are kicked out, and rather it is *increased* productivity, and thus *increased* profit-making for the workers! In fact, this has happened all over the world – Americans have just not heard about it because it was not on prime time cable TV. And let's add to this a bit before we go on... Such factories-for-and-by-the-people are the ultimate expressions of actual capitalism: each worker earning the most money to therefore store up the most capital. This is the diametrical opposite of contemporary non-capitalist American monopolism/corporatism, where only very few have any meaningful capital and/or big-ticket items they actually own (and, of course, your mortgaged house is not *owned* by you, and if you doubt that, stop paying your mortgage payment [i.e., your interest payment] and see how long you can keep your house). Funny how the lying "conservative" cable-TV "news" shows call that *capitalism*. So why does the average TV-addicted American think that the "person in charge" controls things? Answer: because that's merely *an idea*, based on nothing real (and so, a false idea: an illusion), implanted into their heads, but they believe it, so it works: they think the non-worker ("person in charge") is responsible for the work, which is, I guess, sort of like saying the honeybee producing the honey does not work for any honey. You see, when people don't question and use their minds, then all of human existence becomes contradiction, suffering, absurdity, and a waste of our lives. That's why it's an info-war: a war where the weapon is false ideas infecting minds (AKA brainwashing).

Now, let's expand this idea that the human populace is actually in control of the world in order to discuss the New World Order. And let me get right to the point: just like the "person in charge" really has no control, as we just saw, analogously, *the New World Order has no power at all whatsoever, period, end-of-story.* The New World Order, and any "government authority" of any sort, only exists because we humans wrongly *believe* that humans need them, and because we have been tricked into wrongly *believing* that the world is set up for you to be primarily dependent on people other than yourself (almost a "crazy notion" too many).

Ideas are *just ideas*, and they may or may not actually represent things that are real in the world. For example, you can think (have an idea about) a unicorn, but that does not mean unicorns are real. They are only ideas, existing only in our heads Also, you can think Iraq was a threat in 2003, but that does not mean that it *really* was. But interestingly, well over 200 million Americans thought the little desert nation of Iraq, which hardly even had a military, was a threat to the U.S. during the quite long time-span from 1991-2003, *but that was of course just an idea, based on nothing real whatsoever!* Iraq is/was a unicorn – just like the swine flu, vaccine "protection", overpopulation, the CO_2 "threat", eco-crime, fluoride being a cure for osteoporosis, monkey-to-man evolutionary theory, and the idea that "The World Is Running Out of Water" (*Scientific American*): unicorns all! But, returning to discussion of Iraq... Nevertheless, Americans believed in unicorn-Iraq, and off they went, smilingly marching their children into DU-laced Iraq (and Afghanistan).

Let's consider another example: *billions* of people on planet earth believed that cave-men brought down the WTC towers on 9/11. Nobody saw them do it, but they were *told* the cave-men did it, and thus *billions* believed this story. But nobody saw them do it, there is no evidence they did, and, well, what-do-you-know, it's just an idea, again! Funny how this all works isn't it. But in this case, it was billions, not millions, that believed in the unicorns (cave-men) they were merely told about (and not *shown*).

Another example: *billions* of people on planet earth believed that a large passenger jetliner hit the Pentagon on 9/11. Question: how many saw it, or at least were in position near the Pentagon to where they could have seen it? Answer: a room full of people (back to that figure-of-speech, again). So, um, why did *billions* believing that there was a jetliner (unicorn-jetliner, that is)? I think you know the answer. Odd how this all works, isn't it.

How much of our reality that we think about each day is like this: *just ideas*? (Answer: perhaps most of it, but I don't have time to discuss that here.) Who is giving us these ideas? (Well, that's an easy one to answer.) Why do we believe them, when they don't obey what our eyes tell us is real?

Now, here's the point: *this is the nature of the power of the New World Order: the New World Order is ultimately an idea, nothing more!* The New World Order's power only exists in *abstract reality* (i.e., unicorn reality, and fear-based reality), not in logical, concrete reality, as discussed above. The New World Order's power is a unicorn in our minds because we have been tricked into believing it exists and has power over us by all the propaganda we Americans take-in on TV daily.

Lastly, in this article, I want to talk about something so many are fearing so greatly: mass roundups and FEMA camps. To start this, let me quote an interesting scholar in the alternative media, Clif High (this passage is paraphrased slightly):

> The New World Order only has threats, not a means to enforce the threats. If they tried to round up even just a few million people in America, especially when so many people have guns and will start shooting, and when news of the roundups would travel fast underground among the people, they [the New World Order] simply could not get the manpower to do it: it's an impossible task.

This passage echoes what Alex Jones has been telling us for years: you need many tens of thousands of troops to roundup a million or five million Americans, *and it simply won't work when the citizenry is armed.* Do you see how correct Jefferson was? This is not Nazi Germany, where the people were first disarmed and then rounded up. In Nazi Germany (like other places with disarmed populations), roundups were simple, I am sad to say. Here: a different story. Here's why... If roundups started, when word of this got around – and it would – that roundups are happening here in America, people will get ready, and would start shooting, often with a passion and inner-fire of Jeffersonian freedom in their hearts and minds. And do you think roundup police are going to continue to march into that, when there is, frankly, huge risk to them? Answer: no. This is not like the scenario of a SWAT team, where people are unsuspecting, totally caught-off-guard and usually unarmed or Amish or something. This also is not like New Orleans after Katrina, where word of the activity of the Blackwater goons had not gotten around yet, where people were caught off-guard (like the SWAT scenario), and where so much of the city was a hoard of semi-entranced, disarmed, starving, often even half-dead people totally confused and dazed. No. This will be *prepared America: the resistance* (to anti-Constitutionalism and to black-as-hell-tyranny), to use Mark Dice's phrase.

How many of you have been sitting there cowering because you are afraid of concentration camps, but you never stopped to notice that it's quite likely a logical impossibility that it will ever happen here. Roundups would stop after a just a few significant shootouts, because the rounders-up will soon face many circumstances where they are decimated.

Remember that movie, *Jurassic Park*, where at the start of the movie, we saw the computer engineer of the Jurassic Park island run his jeep off the road, wherein he was face-to-face in the mud looking into the eyes of a little, almost cute, frilled lizard-dinosaur? What did that lizard do? It quickly made itself look big by fanning out its frills and screaming horrifically, immobilizing the man (by fear) in order to spray its poison on the man. The man actually had nothing to worry about; all he had to do was back away hastily before the fear-factor of the frills could be implemented by the lizard, or maybe even after that, when the frill and screaming had started (but before the poison flew). But the man did not know this, and did not know that there was therefore nothing to fear at all. The lizard making itself look bigger was not a real threat (it was a unicorn-threat, like the New World Order), but was merely used to put fear into the heart of the man, to get him to lose his rationality, to get him to freeze-up long enough so that the little lizard-dinosaur could spray the poison liquid onto him. But, again, *the freeze-causing frilling of the lizard was just an illusion of threat, a display, not based on anything real* (not based on actual danger to the man: it was a unicorn-threat). The lizard was really not that big, and the horrific roar, well, that was also just, um, *sound waves* – how much harm are those, really? The lizard masterfully, successfully put forth a *false appearance*, showing the lizard as far larger and scarier than it really was.

The New World Order has only frills and horrific roars (threat-making), but no way to inflict its poison (mass roundups, gun confiscations, etc.) unless we have fear and then consequent irrationalism (like the man in *Jurassic Park* freezing and succumbing to fear). The problem is: this tactic has worked for the New World Order in the past (on unarmed citizenries). So, as stated above, since we already have the weapons and comprise a Jeffersonian militia here in the United States, we then need to realize that our most important tasks are resisting gun control and realizing that this is an info-, education-, and deprogramming- war.

How many times have some of us heard somebody say, "Oh, you can't take on the New World Order! They have too many microwave guns, robot warriors, chemical and biological weapons," and so forth.

In light of what I have written in this article, does this many any sense? So now they want us to believe that an AK-47, a 12 gauge, or a .357 Magnum cannot do any damage to a stupid little robot on a cart? I guarantee you that my AK-47 would turn that thing into a beautiful shower of sparks – a humorous clump of tin! Are we supposed to believe that a microwave gun can't be damaged by an AR pistol (and wow, if any of you have seen one of those microwave guns, *they just look like big shooting-range targets!*)? An AR pistol has a bullet that travels at well over 3000 feet per second. So I don't care what you have in the line of that thing, it's going to get harmed in a big way! I don't even care if Steve Quayle's transdimensional entities pop out of a super-collider somewhere (as Quayle has discussed on the Alex Jones Show), those goolies still won't like the sting of a .50 cal Desert Eagle or a .223 round of an AR-15. They might want to pop right back into that portal. Why do you think there's a minister in Kentucky that is having "open carry church"? Answer: well, *to fight evil*, of course! How could any religious person (or not religious person) not know that? Even invisible New World Order soldiers are more bark than bite: firstly, they can be *heard* with your ears (and you can shoot in the direction of a sound, can't you), and they sure will get a bit perturbed if you spray of bullets from poetic bump-firing a Calico 9mm, or if you give them the thunder of the glorious terror of a Saiga! "Turn the other cheek" *is about getting along with your neighbor* (i.e., other members of the Jeffersonian militia), as it says in that passage in the Bible, and it's not about giving into criminal (New World Order) government. And I think we all know Jesus was no friend of big government! That's why the Founders wrote about how guns were to protect us from government, and not for baseless attack of other Jeffersonian-militia-members (i.e., American citizens, to whom we are to "turn the other cheek" in brotherhood and Constitutional camaraderie). You know, this almost makes it appear that the sound of an AK-47 when fired by a Jeffersonian is like the sound of angels, watching over us. When I am at the shooting range, I can feel that sound so deeply within me, impacting in every cell of my body; it feels good, like medicine. And anybody who has been to the range and fired an AK knows that the sound, affecting every cell in your body, actually and interestingly feels almost therapeutic (like sound therapy, I'd say). You can think what you want of these words, but to me, when I hear/feel my AK-47, it feels like angels' wings! I have said, in another article, that the New World Order has many ways to get rid of as many of us as they want right now. But this article shows that they sure can't do it by the means I think most of us are fearing more than anything: mass roundups and concentration camps. So, really, there is nothing to be afraid of. The New World Order is just a room full of grumpy old people – frilled lizards all!

Works Cited

Bagdikian, Ben H. 2004. *The New Media Monopoly*. Boston: Beacon Press.

Bales, Kevin. 2004 (1999). *Disposable People: New Slavery in the Global Economy*. Berkeley, Los Angeles: University of California Press.

Begich, Nicholas J. 2005. *Mind Control*. DVD documentary. Anchorage: Earthpulse Press. ISBN: 1-890693-50-2.

Berger, Peter, and Luckman, Thomas. 1966. *The Social Construction of Reality*. New York: Anchor Books.

Berman, Morris. 2006. *Dark Ages America: The Final Phase of Empire*. New York: W. W. Norton.

Berne, Eric. 1992 (1964). *Games People Play: The Handbook of Transactional Analysis*. New York: Ballantine Books.

Best, Steven, and Kellner, Douglas. 1991. *Postmodern Theory*. New York: The Guilford Press.

Black, Edwin. 2001. *IBM and the Holocaust: The Strategic Alliance between Nazi Germany and America's Most Powerful Corporation*, New York: Crown Publishers.

Brazier, David. 2002. *The New Buddhism*. New York: Palgrave.

Breggin, Peter R. 1991. *Toxic Psychiatry*. New York: St. Martin's Press.

Brzezinski, Zbigniev. 1998. *The Grand Chessboard: American Primacy and Its Geostrategic Imperatives*. New York: Basic Books.

Bright, Stephen E. 2003. "The Accused Get What the System Doesn't Pay For." In Herival, Tara, and Wright, Paul. *Prison Nation*. New York: Routledge. Pages 6-22.

Brohy, Audtey, and Ungerman, Gerald (directors). 2000. *Hidden Wars of Desert Storm*. DVD documentary. Studio: Arab Film Distribution. ASIN: B00008OOTA.

Browning, Christopher R. 1993. *Ordinary Men*. New York: Harper Collins.

Bryson, Christopher. 2004. *The Fluoride Deception*. New York: Seven Stories Press.

Caldicott, Helen, 2004, "Introduction to the 2004 Edition," in Caldicort, Helen, 2002, *The New Nuclear Danger: George W. Bush's Military-Industrial Complex, with a New Introduction on the Situation in Iraq*. New York: The New Press. Pages XXI - L.

Caldicort, Helen, 2002, *The New Nuclear Danger: George W. Bush's Military-Industrial Complex, with a New Introduction on the Situation in Iraq*. New York: The New Press.

Carter, Tim (director). 2005. *Torture: The Guantanamo Cookbook*. Film documentary. (This documentary aired on British television in London on Channel 4,[244] and on the Sundance Channel in the USA.)

Cervi, Carmine (director). 2003. *Axis of Evil*. DVD documentary. Studio: Qualiatica. ASIN: B0006H31K8.

Chang, Matthias. 2005a. *Future FastFoward* (2nd Edition), Malaysia: Thinker's Library.

---

[244] "C4 lines up Guantánamo-style torture show," Dominic Timms, February 8, 2005, London Guardian. I could not find Studio information on this documentary.

Chang, Matthias. 2005b. *Brainwashed for War Programmed to Kill*. Malaysia: Thinker's Library.

Chomsky, Noam. 2003. "Drug Policy as Social Control." In Herival, Tara, and Wright, Paul. *Prison Nation*. New York: Routledge. Pages 57-59.

Chossudovsky, Michel. 2003. *The Globalization of Poverty and the New World Order*. Second Edition. Pincourt (Quebec): Global Research.

Cole, Leonard A. 1988. *Clouds of Secrecy: The Army's Germ Warfare Tests Over Populated Areas*. New York: Rowman & Littlefield.

Constantine, Alex. 1995. *Psychic Dictatorship in the USA*. Portland, OR: Feral House.

Court, Jamie, and Smith, Francis. 1999. *Making a Killing: HMOs and the Threat to Your Health*. Monroe ME: Common Courage Press.

Cremo, Michael. 2003. Human Devolution: A Vedic Alternative to Darwin's Theory. Badger, CA: Torchlight Publishing.

Cruttenden, Walter. 2005. *Lost Start of Myth and Time*. Pittsburgh: St. Lynn's Press.

Davies, Paul, and Gribbin, John, 1992, *The Matter Myth*, Touchstone: New York.

Deffeys, Kenneth. 2003. *Hubbert's Peak: The World's Impending Oil Shortage*. Princeton: Princeton University Press.

de la Peña, Nonny (director). 2004. *Unconstitutional*. DVD documentary. Studio: The Disinformation Company.

DiLorenzo, Thomas, J. 1993. "Economic Fascism." *Truth Seeker*. V. 121. No. 3. http://www.banned-books.com/truth-seeker/1994archive/121_3/ts213l.html

Earp, Jeremy, and Jhally, Sut (directors). 2004. *Hijacking Catastrophe: 9/11, Fear & the Selling of American Empire*. DVD documentary. MEF (Media Education Foundation). ISBN: 1-893521-97-4.

Elster, Jon. 1986. *An Introduction to Karl Marx*. New York: Cambridge University Press.

Epperson, Ralph. 1985. *The Unseen Hand: An Introduction to the Conspiratorial View of History*. Tucson: Publius Press.

Estes, Ralph. 1996. *The Tyranny of the Bottom Line*. San Francisco: Berret-Koehler Publishers.

Fagin, Dan, and Lavelle, Marianne. 1999. *Toxic Deception: How the Chemical Industry Manipulates Science, Bends the Law and Endangers Your Health*. Monroe Maine: Common Courage Press.

Felton, Greg. 2005. *Enemies by Design: Inventing the War on Terrorism*. Joshua Tree: Banned Books/Progressive Press.[245]

Fitrakis, Bob, Rosenfeld, Steve, and Wasserman, Harvey. 2006. *What Happened in Ohio?* New York: The New Press.

Gandini, Erik, and Saleh, Tarik (directors). 2005. *Gitmo: The New Rules of War*. DVD documentary. Red Envelope Entertainment (A Netflix Company)

---

[245] This book is an historical, scholarly, empirical study. It can ordered from the publisher, at ProgressivePress.com or through bookstores. Regarding this book, Professor Mazin Qumsiyeh of Yale University writes that Felton's book is "a lucid and timely compilation of information and questions that should be the fodder of discussions in America and beyond."

Garcia, Deborah Koons (director). 2005. *The Future of Food*. DVD documentary. Studio: Cinema Libre Distrib. ASIN: B000BQ5IXM.

Gaunt, Bonnie. 2000. *Beginnings: The Sacred Design*. Kempton, IL: Adventures Unlimited Press.

Gitlin, Todd. 2002. *Media Unlimited: How the Torrent of Images and Sounds Overwhelms Our Lives*. New York: Henry Holt and Company.

Gladwell, Malcolm. 2005. *Blink: The Power of Thinking Without Thinking*. New York: Little Brown and Co.

Gleason, Abbot, Goldsmith, Jack, and Nussbaum, Martha, (Ed.s). 2005. "Introduction," in *On Nineteen Eighty-Four: Orwell and Our Future*. Princeton: Princeton University Press.

Goldberg, Michelle. 2006. *Kingdom Coming*. New York: W. W. Norton.

Greene, Gregory (director). 2004. *The End of Suburbia*. DVD documentary. Studio: Electric Wallpaper. ASIN: 097369470X.

Greenwald, Robert (director). 2004. *Uncovered: The War On Iraq*. DVD documentary. Studio: Cinema Libre. ASIN: B0002ZDWGC.

Greenway, John, 1972, *Down Among the Wild Men*, Little Brown and Co., Boston.

Gross, Martin L. 1999. *The Conspiracy of Ignorance: The Failure of American Public Schools*. New York: Harper Collins.

Grossman, Gene M. 2000. "Special Interest Groups and Economic Policy." *National Bureau of Economic Research*. http://www.nber.org/reporter/ .

Grupp, Jeffrey. 2009. *Telementation: Cosmic Feeling and the Law of Attraction*. Joshua Tree, CA: Progressive Press.

Grupp, Jeffrey. 2007. *Corporatism: The Secret Government of the New World Order*. Joshua Tree, CA: Banned Books (Progressive Press).

Grupp, Jeffrey, 2006b, "God's Spatial Unlocatedness Prevents Him from Being the Creator of the Universe. A New Argument for the Nonexistence of God", *Sophia: International Journal for Philosophy of Religion, Metaphysical Theology and Ethics*, vol. 45. (This paper can be read at www.abstractatom.com.)

Grupp, Jeffrey, 2006a, "Mereological Nihilism: Quantum Atomism and the Impossibility of Material Constitution," *Axiomathes: An International Journal in Ontology and Cognitive Systems*, Vol. 16, No. 3, pp. 245-386.

Hachmeister, Lutz (director). 2004. *The Goebbels Experiment*. DVD documentary. Studio: First Run Features. ASIN: B000EULK1O.

Halberstam, Michael. 1999. *Totalitarianism and the Modern Conception of Politics*. New Haven: Yale University Press.

Hansen, Eric. 2000. *Stranger in the Forest: On Foot Across Borneo*. New York: Vintage.

Harris, Sam. 1997. *The End of Faith: Religion, Terror, and the Future of Reason*. New York: W. W. Norton & Company.

Hart, Peter. 2003. *The Oh Really? Factor: Unspinning Fox News Channel's Bill O'Reilly*. New York: Seven Stories Press.

Harvey, Peter. 2000. *An Introduction to Buddhist Ethics*. New York: Cambridge University Press.

Hertz, Noreena. 2003. *The Silent Takeover: Global Capitalism and the Death of Democracy*. New York: Harper Business (Division of Harper Collins).

Herman, Edward S., and Chomsky, Noam. 2002 (1989). *Manufacturing Consent: The Politcal Economy of the Mass Media*. New York: Pantheon.

Hipkiss, Robert A. 1984. *The American Absurd: Pynchon, Vonnegut and Barth* (Series in Modern and Contemporary Literature). Port Washington, N.Y.: National University Publications Associated Faculty Press,

Hoffman, Michael A, II. 1991. *They Were White and They Were Slaves: The Untold History of the Enslavement of Whites in Early America*. Coeur d'Alene, ID: The Independent History and Research Co.

Hollowell, Edward, and Ratey, John. 1995. *Driven To Distraction*. New York: Touchstone (Reprint Edition).

Horgan, John, 2003, *Rational Mysticism*, Houghton Mifflin, New York.

Horowitz, David. 2006. *The Professors: The 101 Most Dangerous Academics in America*. New York: Regnery Publishing, Inc.

Horowitz, Leonard G. 2001. *Death in the Air: Globalism, Terrorism and Toxic Warfare*. Sand Point, Idaho: Tetrahedron Publishing Group.

Howard, Michael. 1989. *The Occult Conspiracy: Secret Societies—Their Influence and Power in World History*. Rochester VT: Destiny Books.

Huston, Aletha, Donnerstein, Edward, Fairchild, Halford, Fashbach, Norma, Katz, Phyllis, Murray, John, Rubinstein, Eli, Wilcox, Brian, and Zuckerman, Diana. 1992. *Big World, Small Screen: The Role of Television in American Society*. Lincoln: University of Nebraska Press.

Icke, David. 2005. *Infinite Love is the Only Truth; Everything Else is Just Illusion. Exposing the Dreamworld We Believe to be 'Real'*. Wildwood, USA: Bridge of Love Publications USA.

James, William, "On A Certain Blindness in Human Beings," in Myers, Gerald E. (ed.). 1992. *William James: Writings: 1878-1899*. New York: The Library of America. Pages 841-860.

Jarecki, Eugene (director). 2005. *Why We Fight*. DVD documentary. Studio: Sony Pictures. ASIN: B000FBH3W2.

Jarecki, Eugene (director). 2003. *The Trials of Henry Kissinger*. DVD documentary. Studio: First Run Features. ASIN: B00009V7S0.

Jones, Alex (director). 2006. *Terrorstorm*. DVD documentary. Studio: Alex Jones Productions / Infowars.com.

Jones, Alex (director). 2005. *Dark Secrets / The Order of Death*. DVD documentary. Studio: Alex Jones Productions / Infowars.com.

Jones, Alex (director). 2001. *Comprehensive Annual Financial Reports Exposed!*. VHS documentary. Studio: Alex Jones Productions / Infowars.com.

Junkerman, John (director). 2002. *Power and Terror – Noam Chomsky in Our Times*. First Run Features. ASIN: B00008XS1C.

Kane, George. 2000. *Supersymmetry*. Cambridge: Perseus Publishing.

Karel, William. 2004. *The World According to Bush*. DVD documentary. Studio: Flach Film. ASIN: B00067WSV6.

Kawin, Bruce F., 1978, *Mindscreen: Bergman, Godard, and First-Person Film*, Princeton University Press: Princeton.

Keith, Jim. 2004 (1999). *Saucers of the Illuminati*. Kempton, Illinois: Adventures Unlimited Press.

Kim, Jaegwon. 2002. "The Layered Model: Metaphysical Considerations." In *Philosophical Explorations*. Vol. 5. 2-20.

Kirby, David. 2005 *Evidence of Harm: Mercury in Vaccines and the Autism Epidemic: A Medical Controversy*. New York: St. Martin's Press.

Knight, Christopher, and Butler, Alan. 2005. *Who Built the Moon?*. London, Ontario: Watkins Publishing.

Korten, David C. 2001. *When Corporations Rule the World,* Second Edition. San Francisco: Kuarmian Press.

Krebs, J.R., and Davies, N.B. 1993 (1981). *An Introduction to Behavioral Ecology. Third Edition.* Oxford: Blackwell Publishers.

Langdon, Sean (director). 2003. *Mission Accomplished.* DVD documentary. Studio: Doc Workers. ASIN: B0007Z0O9K. (I believe this film is also associated with, or was produced by, the BBC, since that is advertised at the end of the film.)

LaViolette, Paul A. 2006 (2000). *Decoding the Message of the Pulsars: Intelligent Communication from the Galaxy.* Santa Fe: Bear and Co.

Lardner, James, and Smith, David (ed.s). 2006. *Inequality Matters.* New York: New Press.

Leeb, Stephen. 2006. *The Coming Economic Collapse: How You Can Thrive When Oil Costs $200 a Barrel.* New York: Warner Business Books.

Lewis, Avi (director). 2004. *The Take.* DVD documentary. Studio: First Run Features. ASIN: B000CCD1X4.

Lewis, Justin. 2001. *Constructing Public Opinion.* New York: Columbia University Press.

Lifton, Robert. 1989. *Thought Reform and the Psychology of Totalism: A Study of "Brainwashing" in China.* Chapel Hill: University of North Carolina Press.

Luce, J. V., 1992, *An Introduction to Greek Philosophy*, Thames and Hudson: London.

Luderman, Gerd. 1996. *The Unholy in Holy Scripture.* Louisville: Westminster John Knox Press.

Maddock, Kenneth, 1972, *The Australian Aborigines*, The Penguin Press, London.

Maher, John, and Groves, Judy. 1997. *Introducing Chomsky.* New York: Totem Books.

Mander, Jerry. 1978. *Four Arguments for the Elimination of Television.* New York: Quill.

Mankiw, Gregory N. 1998. *Principles of Economics.* New York: The Dryden Press.

Manning, Jeane, and Begich, Nick. 1995. *Angels Don't Play This Haarp: Advances In Tesla Technology.* Anchorage: Earthpulse Press.

Marshall, Steven (director). 2003. *Aftermath: Unanswered Questions from 9/11.* DVD documentary. Studio: Disinformation (in collaboration with the Guerrilla News Network [GNN]).

Matsumoto, Gary. 2004. *Vaccine A: The Covert Government Experiment That's Killing our Soldiers and Why GI's Are Only the First Victims.* New York: Basic Books.

Maxwell, Jordan. 2000. *Matrix of Power: Secrets of World Control.* San Diego: The Book Tree.

McInerney, Lt. General Thomas, and Vallely, Maj. General Paul. 2004. *Endgame: The Blueprint for the Victory in the Wary on Terror.* New York: Regnery Publishing, Inc.

Milgram, Stanley. 2004. *Obedience and Authority: An Experimental View.* New York: Perennial Classics.

Miller, Judith, Engleberg, Stephen, and Broad, William. 2001. *Germs: Biological Weapons and America's Secret War.* New York: Simon and Schuster.

Miller, Marc Crispin. 2005. *Fooled Again.* New York: Basic Books

Miller, Marc Crispin. 2004. *Cruel and Unusual.* New York: W.W. Norton.

Miller, Marc Crispin. 1989. *Boxed In: The Culture of TV.* 3rd Edition. Evanston: Northwestern University Press.

Morris, Errol (director). 2004. *Fog of War.* DVD documentary. Studio: Sony Pictures.

Moravec, Hans, 1999, *Robot,* Oxford: New York

Mueller, Denis, and Ellis, Deb (directors). 2005. *Howard Zinn: You Can't Be Neutral on a Moving Train.* DVD documentary. Studio: First Run Features. ASIN: B0007TKOSC.

Murphy, Timothy. 2004. *Case Studies in Biomedical Ethics.* Cambridge; MIT Press.

Nace, Ted. 2003. *Gangs of America: The Rise of Corporate Power and the Disabling of Democracy.* San Francisco: Berrett-Koehler Publishing, Inc.

Nelson, Jane. 1996 (1981). *Positive Discipline.* New York: Ballantine Books

Olds, Ian, and Scott, Garrett (directors). 2005. *Occupation Dreamland.* DVD documentary. Studio: Rumur Releasing, ASIN: B000DZ7XYI.

Orwell, George. 1977 (1949) *1984.* New York: Signet Classic, Centennial Edition.

Ovason, David. 1999. *The Secret Architecture of our Nation's Capital: The Masons and the Building of Washington, D.C.* New York: Perennial (Harper Collins).

Owen, Stephen. 2003. "Absolute Power, Absolute Corruption." In Herival, Tara, and Wright, Paul. *Prison Nation.* New York: Routledge. Pages 23-29.

Palast, Greg. 2004. *The Best Democracy Money Can Buy.* New York: Plume.

Paglen, Trevor, and Thompson, A.C. 2006. *Torture Taxi: On the Trial of the CIA's Rendition Flights.* Hoboken, NJ: Melville House Publishing.

Pappas, Robert Kane (director). 2003. *Orwell Rolls in His Grave.* DVD documentary film. Studio: Go-Kart Records.

Pawlick, Thomas. 2006. *The End of Food: How the Food Industry is Destroying our Food Supply, and What You Can Do About It.* Fort Lee, NJ: Barricade Books.

Perloff, James. 1988. *Shadows of Power: The Council on Foreign Relations and the American Decline.* Boston, Los Angeles: Western Islands.

Pinto, Christian J. (director). 2006. *The Secret Mysteries of America's Beginnings. Volume One: The New Atlantis.* DVD documentary. Studio: Antiquities Research Films. ASN: B000FIGJ84. This documentary consists of two hours of interviews with the premier experts on freemasonry, and the secret societies at the origin of America.

PNAC (Project for the New American Century). 2000. *Rebuilding America's Defenses: Strategy, Forces, and Resources For a New Century.* A report from the Project for the New American Century. 1150 Seventeenth Street, N.W. Suite 510. Washington, D. C. 20036.

Post, John F, 1991. *Metaphysics: A Contemporary Introduction,* Paragon House: St. Paul.

Reiss, Edward. 1997. *Marx: A Clear Guide.* London: Pluto Press.

Rich, Andrew. 2004. *Think Tanks, Public Policy, and the Politics of Expertise.* New York: Cambridge University Press.

Rocker, Rudolf. 1989. *Anarcho-Syndicalism.* London: Pluto Press.

Rosemann, Nils. 2005. "The Privatization of Human Rights Violations—Business Impunity or Corporate Responsibility? The Case of Human Rights Abuses and Torture in Iraq." *Non-State Actors and International Law.* 5: 77-100.

Ruppert, Michael. 2004. *Crossing the Rubicon: The Decline of the American Empire at the End of the Age of Oil*. New Society Publishers.

Ruppert, Michael. 2004. *The Truth and Lies of 9-11*. DVD recording of Portland State University lecture that occurred on November 28, 2001. From the Wilderness Publications. Can be found at www.fromthewilderness.com.

Russell, Bertrand. 1985 (1952). *The Impact of Science on Society*. New York: Routledge.

Russon, John. 2003. *Human Experience: Philosophy Neurosis, and the Elements of Everyday Life*. Albany: State University of New York Press.

Schechter, Danny (director). 2004. *Weapons of Mass Deception*. DVD documentary film. Studio: Cinema Libre. ASIN: B00074DXFS.

Schechter, Danny. 2002. *Media Wars: News at a Time of Terror*. New York: Rowman and Littlefield.

Schor, Juliet B. 2004. *Born To Buy*. New York: Scribner.

Scott, Peter Dale. 2003. *Drugs, Oil, and War*. New York: Rowman and Littlefield.

Silverstein, Ken. 1998. *Washington on $10 Million A Day*. Monroe Maine: Common Courage Press.

Simmons, Matthew. 2005. *Twilight in the Desert*. Hoboken: Wiley.

Simontacchi, Carol. 2000. *The Crazy Makers: How the Food Industry is Destroying Our Brains and Harming our Children*. New York: Tarcher/Putnam.

Singer, P. W. 2003. *Corporate Warriors: The Rise of the Privatized Military Industry*. Ithaca: Cornell University Press.

Slaughter, Anne-Marie. 2005. *A New World Order*. Princeton: Princeton University Press.

Smith, James. 1991. *The Idea Brokers*. New York: The Free Press.

Smith, Jerry E. 2006. *Weather Warfare*. Kempton IL: Adventures Unlimited Press.

Standing, Brian (director). 2004. *War is Sell*. DVD documentary. Studio: Prolefeed Studios. ASIN: B000BWFSNQ.

Stein, David B. 2001. *Unraveling the ADD/ADHD Fiasco: Successful Parenting Without Drugs*. Kansas City: Andrews McMeel Publishing.

Stinnet, Robert, 2000, *Day of Deceit: The Truth About FDR and Pearl Harbor*. New York: Touchstone.

Stone, Robert (director). 1986. *Radio Bikini*. DVD documentary. Studio: New Video Group. ASIN: B0000TPAMO.

Sutton, Antony C. 1995. *The Federal Reserve Conspiracy*. Boring Oregon: CPA Book Publishers.

Swinburne, Richard. 2001. *Epistemic Justification*. Oxford: Oxford University Press.

Taicher, Robert (director). 2005. *Rush to War*. DVD documentary. Studio: RTW Productions, LLC. ASIN: B0007NA3ZC.

Tarpley, Webster Griffin. 2006. 9/11 *Synthetic Terror: Made in the USA*. 2nd Edition. Joshua Tree: Progressive Press.

Tarpley, Websert G., and Chaitkin, Anton. 2004 (1992). *George Bush: The Unauthorized* Bibliography. Joshua Tree: Progressive Press.

Taylor, Kathleen. 2004. *Brainwashing: The Science of Thought Control*. Oxford: Oxford University Press.

Taylor, Richard, 1992, *Metaphysics*, 4th Ed., Pretice-Hall, Englewood Cliffs.

Tennpenny, Sherri. 2005. *Vaccines: The Risks, the Benefits, the Choices*. DVD lecture. Studio: NMA Media Press. ISBN: 0-9743448-1-8.

Thorn, Victor. 2003. *The New World Order Exposed*. Happy Valley, PA: Sisyphus Press.

Thornton, Bridget; Walters, Brit; and Rouse, Lori. 2006. "Corporate Media is Corporate America." In. Project Censored. 2005. *Censored 2006: The Top 25 Censored Stories*. New York: Seven Stories Press.

Tooley, Michael. 2001. "Personhood." In Kuhse, Helga, and Singer, Peter, 2001, A *Companion to Bioethics*. Malden: Blackwell. Pages 117-126.

Tremblay, Rodregue. 2004. *The New American Empire*. West Conshohocken: Infinity Publishing.

Vidal, Gore. 2004, *Imperial American: Reflections on the United States of Amnesia*. New York: Nation Books.

Watson, Andrew. 2004. *The Quantum Quark*. New York: Cambridge University Press.

Winkler, Allan. 1999 (1993). *Life Under a Cloud: American Anxiety About the Atom*. Urbana: University of Illinois Press.

Winslow, George. 2003. "Capital Crimes: The Corporate Economy of Violence." In Herival, Tara, and Wright, Paul. *Prison Nation*. New York: Routledge. Pages 41-56.

Zepezauer, Mark. 2004. *Take the Rick off Welfare*. Cambridge: South End.

Zepezauer, Mark. 2003. *Boomerang!*. Monroe Maine: Common Courage.

Zinn, Howard. 2003 (1980). *A People's History of the United States*. New York: Harper Perennial.

Zinn, Howard. 2004. *The People Speak: American Voices, Some Famous, Some Little Known*. Audio Book. New York: Harper Audio (Harper Collins Publishers).

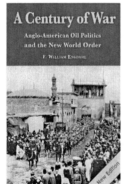

Terrorism and the Illuminati, A 3000-Year History. "Islamic" terrorists are tentacles of western imperialism—the Illuminati. 332 pp, $16.95.

Troublesome Country. A history of the USA in light of failure to live up to its guiding democratic creed. 146 pp, $12.95.

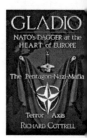

Psychology: Brainwashing

The Rape of the Mind: The Psychology of Thought Control, Menticide and Brainwashing. Conditioning in open and closed societies; tools for self-defense against torture or social pressure. 320 pp, $16.95. Classic study by Dr Joost Meerloo, who experienced both Nazism and McCarthyism first-hand.

The Telescreen: An Empirical Study of the Destruction of Consciousness, by Prof. Jeffrey Grupp. How mass media brainwash us with consumerism and war propaganda. Fake history, news, issues, and reality steal our souls. 199 pp, $14.95 Also by Grupp: ***Telementation: Cosmic Feeling and the Law of Attraction.*** Deep feeling rather than thought or faith is our secret nature and key to self-realization. 124 pp, $12.95.

Conspiracy, NWO

The Money Power: Empire of the City and Pawns in the Game. Two classic geopolitics books in one. The illuminist Three World Wars conspiracy, to divide humanity on ethnic and political lines to conquer us. 320 pp, $16.95

Corporatism: the Secret Government of the New World Order by Prof. Jeffrey Grupp. Corporations control all world resources. Their New World Order is the "prison planet" that Hitler aimed for. 408 pp, $16.95.

Descent into Slavery. How the banksters took over America and the world. The Founding Fathers, Rothschilds, the Crown and the City, world wars, and globalization 310 pp, $16. Also by Des Griffin: ***Fourth Reich of the Rich***, 316 pp, $16.

Dope Inc.: Britain's Opium War against the United States. "The Book that Drov Kissinger Crazy." Underground Classic, new edition. 320 pp, $12.95.

Final Warning: A History of the New World Order by D. A. Rivera. Classic, in-depth research into the Great Conspiracy: the Fed, the Trilateral Commission, the CFR, and the Illuminati. 360 pp, $14.95.

How the World Really Works by A.B. Jones. Crash course in conspiracy. Digests of 11 classics like *Tragedy and Hope, Creature from Jekyll Island*. 336 pp, $15.

The Triumph of Consciousness by Chris Clark. The real Global Warming and Greening agenda: more hegemony by the NWO. 347 pp, $14.95.

Conspiracy: False Flag Operations

9/11 on Trial: *The W T C Collapse.* 20 closely argued proofs that the World Trade Center was destroyed by controlled demolition. 192 pp, $12.95.

Gladio, NATO's Dagger at the Heart of Europe: *The Pentagon-Mafia-Nazi Terror Axis.* The blood-red thread of terror by NATO death squads in Europe, from WW2 up to 2012. 484 pp, $16.95.

Conspiracies, Conspiracy Theories and the Secrets of 9/11, German best-seller explores conspiracy in history, before tackling 9/11. 274 pp, $14.95.

In Search of the Truth: *An Exposure of the Conspiracy,* by Azar Mirza-Beg. A portrait of our times, society and religion, and the threat we face. 208 pp, $17

Subverting Syria*: How CIA Contra Gangs and NGO's Manufacture, Mislabel and Market Mass Murder.* Syrian "uprising" is a cynical US plot using faked news, provocateurs, opportunists, mercenaries, and Wahhabi fanatics. 116 pp, $10.00

Terror on the Tube: Behind the Veil of 7/7, an Investigation, by Nick Kollerstrom. The only book with the glaring evidence that all four Muslim scapegoats were completely innocent. 7/7 clinched the governmental assault on our rights. 3rd ed, 322 pp, $17.77.

The War on Freedom. The seminal exposé of 9/11. "Far and away the best and most balanced analysis of September 11th." – Gore Vidal. 400 pp, $16.95.

Truth Jihad*: My Epic Struggle Against the 9/11 Big Lie.* Kevin Barrett's outrageously humorous autobiographical testament. 224 pp, $9.95.

Coming Soon

Target China: *How Washington and Wall Street Plan to Cage the Asian Dragon,* by F. William Engdahl

Against Oligarchy Vol. III*: Essays and Speeches 1970-1996,* by Webster Tarpley

JFK-911: *50 Years of Deep State*, by Laurent Guyénot. *(available now as e-book)*

Iraq*: Truth, Lies and Consequences,* by Joseph Hoeffel.

Killing us Softly: *Causes and Consequences of the Global Depopulation Policy,* by Kevin Galalae

George Washington*: The Scoundrel and his Misdeeds.* George was a British spy who assassinated the French ambassador, starting the French & Indian War.

Twin Towers of Terror*: 9/11 and the Media Cover-Up,* by Geoffrey H. Smith.

The Real Pearl Harbor Conspiracy, by Webster Tarpley. Japanese aggression was part of a British empire scheme to conquer the US. Crypto-fascists, not FDR, let Pearl Harbor be attacked.

Subjugating the Middle East: *Integration into the New World Order through Fake Democratization and Engineered Insurrections,* by Takis Fotopoulos. The real story of the "Arab Spring," Syria and Libya.

Ukraine: The End of the New World Order? by Takis Fotopoulos.

E-Books

9/11 Synthetic Terror: Made in USA
Barack Obama, the Unauthorized Biography.
Gladio, NATO's Dagger at the Heart of Europe
The Nazi Hydra in America
Subverting Syria

THE "WAR ON TERROR" IS A HOAX
SUPPORT THE
TRUTH about 9/11 & 'NWO.'
Books & DVD's from
ProgressivePress.com
SEE HOW THE TOWERS FALL? THAT TELLS IT ALL!

CPSIA information can be obtained at www.ICGtesting.com
Printed in the USA
LVOW11s2147230615

443540LV00002B/416/P